Otto Mears

Paradoxical Pathfinder

OTTO MEARS

Otto Mears

Paradoxical Pathfinder

Michael Kaplan

SAN JUAN COUNTY
BOOK COMPANY

Silverton, Colorado
1982

The publishers wish to acknowledge with thanks
the special contributions and assistance of
Robertson Mears Pitcher, Duane A. Smith,
John B. Montville, Dell McCoy, Jerry Hoffer,
Steven J. Meyers, and George D. and Tom Zanoni

Edited by Allen Nossaman

Printed by The Silverton Standard and The Miner
Silverton, Colorado

Binding by Hawley Bookbinding Company
Denver, Colorado

Dedicated to Dr. Robert Athearn,
who selected this topic,
and to my parents, who encouraged me in every way
during the study's preparation

Foreward

Otto Mears! The name would have been much more readily recognized a century ago in Colorado than it is today. That is unfortunate, for a man who had such an impact on the state. Merchant, road builder, farmer, businessman, miner, politician, promoter, railroad owner, unofficial Indian agent—this small dynamo of a man was all these and more. The nineteenth century offers few better examples of a person seizing opportunity and riding it wherever it took him, sometimes up, sometimes down. Nothing daunted Mears. With perseverance, hard work, and a bit of luck he bounced back from several failures to recoup his fortune, restore his name, and enhance his fame.

Readers of this volume will find a great deal to interest them in the following pages. Some of Mears' enterprises will amaze them, others will seem appalling in motive and deed. Mears could not be other than a man of his own generation, a generation with its own business and ethical standards. That fact needs to be kept constantly in mind as this history unfolds.

Otto Mears—part sinner, part saint. He could be a hard-driving, practical man and a dreamer, an unscrupulous self-seeker and a helpful pioneer, a man possessed with confidence and driven by a fear of failure. Mears was contradiction personified. Yet throughout his vicissitudes of fortune, he contributed much to Colorado from the 1860s to well past the turn of the century, one of the last of the active pioneers. The story reaches beyond one state, however. Wherever Mears went, he generated action and more than his share of controversy.

He is usually associated with the San Juan region, where he built toll roads, operated mines, invested in real estate, and ran his own string of three railroads out of

Silverton and the much longer Rio Grande Southern from Durango to Ridgway. To him must be given the credit for developing a transportation network for this enormously beautiful mountainous district, assisting in developing its mining potential, supporting urbanization, and helping to promote it as a tourist mecca. A politician to the hilt, Mears also did much legislatively to help the San Juans, when he was not advancing his own interests. Sometimes the two coincided. Although Mears probably did not realize it at the time, his career paralleled that of the region with which he was so closely associated.

Overall, Mears' career duplicated the progress of Colorado, as it evolved from those frontier days of the sixties to the settled, tamed, and matured early nineteen hundreds. By then Mears had passed his peak of influence, outlived much of the animosity some of his actions generated, and become revered as one of the state's founding fathers. This is the story that is told in the pages which follow—the story of a man who had ambition, drive and intellect to match the problems and world he set out to conquer. Whatever else he was, Otto Mears was not dull; he is a fascinating individual to study.

Duane A. Smith

Contents

1

Pathfinder of the San Juan

"Denver is too dead to bury."
This assertion, attributed to a Cheyenne news-paper, seemed to many, applicable to all Colorado Territory in the years immediately following the end of the Civil War. Indian problems, the apparent depletion of gold bearing ores, lack of railroads and over-investment in mining gave the area such a bad reputation that instead of growing, as did most areas of the frontier, the region actually suffered a decrease in population after 1865. In spite of Colorado's domestic and economic problems, some persons saw the potential of the territory and settled there. One such individual was Otto Mears.

Mears, who was to play a large part in the future state's politics and transportation development, was small in stature. Only five feet five in height, dark complexioned, with black eyes and hair and sporting a beard, his dimunitive size belied his enormous gifts. He used his intellect with great facility in solving seemingly insoluble problems. He had the tenacity to see through to the end any project upon which he embarked.

Mears had two other important attributes besides sagacity and perseverance: He had engineering and mechanical genius, and an understanding of human nature. The most spectacular examples of his engineering ability are the toll roads and railroads he built in the San Juan Mountains over some of the most rugged terrain in

North America. While solving technical problems on the large scale, he was also able to apply his skill to everyday problems. In a never-ending quest for efficiency, he was always tinkering with machines, utensils and gadgets. In the 1880s, he invented and patented a pipe because he found the existing ones inadequate to the smokers' needs.

Mears' insight into human nature was, in the long run, even more important to his successful career than his technical and mechanical expertise. At an early age, he was thrown on his own resources and, realizing that he needed the assistance of others to survive, he learned to understand and get along with everyone. Subsequently, in virtually every group he came in contact with, he not only became an accepted member, but a leader. This was true whether he was dealing with blacks, Utes, Mexicans, Anglos or with politicians, railroad men, farmers or capitalists. To further his interests, he became a kind of human chameleon who reflected his surroundings.

One example of his adaptability was in the field of politics. To achieve his goals, he became a Republican in Colorado, a Democrat in Maryland and Louisiana, a Populist in 1896, a Fusionist after 1898 and a Republican again after 1902. He would go to any length to make himself agreeable if he thought the situation demanded it. He was charming, courtly in manners, erect in bearing, and fastidious in appearance. Since he spoke English with a heavy Russian accent, he often used gestures to make himself more easily understood. His intelligence and ability to please, and his genuine liking for people made him so persuasive that he was a super-salesman who could sell anything to anyone for any reason. When charm and logic were not enough, he would use bribery, manipulation and coercion practices in accord with the easy business morality of the post-Civil War era.

Mears' most striking characteristic, however, was his contradictoriness. The list of these contradictions is long. He spent his life looking for a home, yet he loved to travel so much that he was called the "ubiquitous Otto Mears." One newspaper account referred to Mears as having nine legal residences. He was happily married, but had many extra-marital affairs. David Frakes Day—controversial publisher of the *Solid Muldoon* at Ouray and Durango and the *Durango Democrat* and one of Mears' best friends—once described the latter's idea of a pleasure palace in the *Democrat* as follows: "If Otto Mears erects, or causes to be erected, a modern hotel in Silverton, there will be bars on every floor, sound-proof poker rooms, mutual consent connecting doors, a house-keeper that is deaf and dumb and a clerk who don't know straight up. Such a hostelry would draw the Sunday trade from Durango."

He was a hard worker, sleeping less than two hours a night when bent upon completing a project. But he did not care about money. He was a byword for shrewdness in business, but was notorious for his addiction to gambling, especially poker—his only hobby.

Jews and gentiles alike considered him Jewish, but in 1883 he was identified during Colorado legislative proceedings as a Quaker, in 1911 he was known to subscribe to the principles of Christian Science, and at his funeral, an Episcopal bishop presided. Evidently Mears considered Judaism more a way of life than a religion. Throughout his life, he was a heavy contributor to Jewish charities and was a member of various Jewish honorary associations.

To some he seemed outspoken; to others he was considered close-mouthed. To his admirers he was a self-made man who was an obvious success; to his critics he appeared as a self-seeking social-climbing snob who achieved his position by riding the coattails of the great. To intimates he was always at his best when under the most trying circumstances, and yet he was so basically insecure that he constantly undertook monumental projects to prove his worth. His extraordinary complexity must be kept in mind as his career is examined.

Otto Mears was born in Kurland, Russia, on May 3, 1840, the son of an Englishman and a Russian woman, both of whom were Jewish. His parents died when he was

3

very young, and he was raised by his mother's brother. His uncle had a large family—two girls and ten boys—and because the relationship between Mears and his cousins was not amiable, he ran away to or was sent to England between the ages of nine and eleven to live with a member of his father's family. He was rejected also by this relative, and was placed aboard a vessel bound for New York. During the six-week passage the boy was in the custody of an unidentified old woman.

Mears stayed with a relative in New York for a year. The hapless youngster was then sent to California to reside with one of his father's four brothers living there. He went to California by way of the Isthmus of Panama, traveling in the custody of another old woman.

When young Otto arrived in San Francisco, sometime between 1851 and 1853, every attempt was made to find his uncles,[1] but they could not be found, and the boy's custodian took him to a boarding house where her husband was staying. It was decided that Mears should support himself. He sold ice cream and newspapers in an effort to be independent. He pursued his new professions until he met an acquaintance of his European family who offered him a job in a store in Walkerville, California. The youngster worked in the store and then left to become a tinsmith, learning the trade from another family acquaintance. Mears soon became tired of tinsmithing and went to work for a small town merchant. His job involved milking the cows at dawn and then driving a team-drawn wagon ten miles, loading it with merchandise and returning to the farm. Discouraged with this job after a wagon-loading back injury, he quit and returned to San Francisco.

Mears was robbed of his savings in San Francisco, and in consequence, worked at a hotel to earn money for his passage to Sacramento. From there, he returned to Walkerville, where he met a young man who persuaded him to tour the mining regions of California. It was at this time that he began to speculate in mining stocks. His initial venture proved extremely lucrative, but when he reinvested his money, he lost everything. Undaunted, he made subsequent investments which had mixed results. Tired of this activity, he returned to San Francisco and applied for citizenship, remaining in that city until the outbreak of the Civil War. [2]

Mears answered Lincoln's first call for army volunteers by enrolling in Company H of the California Volunteers on August 14, 1861, in San Francisco. In Company H, a unit of 101 men, most of whom were miners, he was well-liked. Poker, the popular pastime of the men, was his great weakness, and on occasion, Mears played for high stakes.

But the soldiers soon had little time to gamble. Company H was ordered to Los Angeles and from there marched to New Mexico, arriving just in time to play a role in preventing the Confederate forces from wresting the Southwest from the Union. After the Confederate plans had been thwarted, Company H reinforced Kit Carson's forces, who were fighting the Navajos in New Mexico. Mears showed conspicuous bravery on several occasions and became a favorite with his fellow troops, and after spending three years and seventeen days of largely pleasant service, he was discharged at Las Cruces, New Mexico.

Mears then worked his way up the Rio Grande River doing odd jobs to get food and earn some extra money. Eventually he arrived in Santa Fe after walking nearly the entire distance from Las Cruces. He found employment with the Elsberg and Amberg Company, and then with Z. Staab & Brothers, both of which were Jewish firms. After five months, Z. Staab offered to put up enough capital so that Otto could start a store of his own. The enterprise was called Mears & Company. The ex-soldier ran the business and the Staab brothers, silent partners, furnished the funds. Deciding that prospects were better farther north, the proprietor moved the stock of Mears & Company to Conejos, Colorado, accompanied by Isaac Gotthelf, a business associate in Costilla, Taos and Santa Fe.

In 1865, Mears opened a store in Conejos, using as

stock the old merchandise of Mears & Company. At Fort Garland, an army post in the vicinity, the government bought lumber at the high price of $80 per 1,000 feet and paid an equally high $20 per hundred pounds for flour. Because of the prices the government paid for these products, the young entrepreneur built a gristmill and a sawmill in partnership with Major Lafayette Head, who would later be Colorado's first lieutenant governor.

Upon the completion of the gristmill, it was ascertained that more wheat would have to be obtained to keep the mill in operation. Consequently, Mears moved to the site of the future town of Saguache in 1866, where he bought government land in order to raise enough grain to keep his mill supplied. His total acquisition was 1,240 acres, worth $3,000, of which he put 80 acres under cultivation—40 in oats, 40 in potatoes. The following year, to hasten the wheat harvest, he introduced the first threshing machine to the area. His Mexican employees at first refused to use it, claiming it was stealing their wheat, but as they became more confident of Mears, they adopted this and other labor-saving devices.

Mears was also busy in town promotion and development. He moved his store from Conejos to Saguache, and with John Lawrence and others, incorporated the town—encouraging its growth at every opportunity. Mears later claimed the word "Saguache" [pronounced *Suh-watch*] meant nothing and that it resulted from a clerical error. It was his intention to name the area "Swatch" after the Ute term "sa-gua-gua-chipa" which meant "blue water" or "blue spring." Even after the spot was officially called Saguache, Mears referred to it as "Swatch."

A letter to the *Santa Fe Weekly Gazette,* March 9, 1867, is an example of the kind of advertising Mears gave the new community of Saguache:

Saguache occupies the southern portion of the San Luis Valley, and for fertility of soil, general productiveness, and salubrity of climate, it has no equal, and is universally recognized as "the garden spot'' in Colorado. Under such favorable circumstances, it is not to be wondered at that "squatters" are daily arriving from all parts, to inhabit, and permanently occupy, that rich and exciting locality.

In spite of Saguache's sparse settlement, local rancher Lawrence was successful in making the area around it — actually at the northern end of the San Luis Valley — a county. Governor Alexander Cummings appointed Lawrence judge and Mears was elected county treasurer. The latter served three successful terms in office. His main duty was tax collection. The first settlers in the area, being poor, usually could not pay taxes with money. The tax collector, therefore, took farm produce, buckskins, wagons and old plows from the delinquents and sold these items to cover taxes due. At the expiration of his third term, Mears turned over a balance of $1,500 to his successor.

The hard times of the early 1870s affected Mears adversely, as they did other pioneers in Saguache. His general store was in debt for $1,500 and an Englishman, H.R. Prior, financier of the enterprise, refused any more cash outlays until the debts were paid. Desperate, Mears induced William Laddingham, a visitor to the area, to invest $1,500 in a horse-raising venture. This was a spurious scheme, and Mears used the money to pay off his store's creditors. When the newcomer returned some months later, Mears managed to be out of town on business. Laddingham found out about the hoax and only when Isaac Gotthelf interceded and gave security for his investment was Mears saved from arrest.

Mears encountered other difficulties as well during this period. The price of flour dropped to $5 per hundred pounds and he found it unprofitable to continue sending his flour to Fort Garland. To save his agricultural interests in Saguache, he decided to send his wheat to the Arkansas Valley to the north, where in 1868, gold had been discovered in California Gulch and Granite Gulch in what would later become the Leadville district.

When he examined the route to his proposed outlets, he found only a primitive path over Poncha Pass. In order to improve the route so that wagon traffic would be able to negotiate it, Mears began the construction of a road from Saguache to Charles Nachtrieb's mill in the Arkansas Valley.

One day, during the construction of the road, ex-Governor William Gilpin rode by. Gilpin, owner of vast land holdings in the San Luis Valley, wanted that area accessible from the north and suggested the construction of a first-class road on a grade that would eventually be used for a railroad. He advised the young Mears, after building the road, to buy a charter for $5 and make the route a toll road.

Mears thought the older man was joking, as there were no railroads in Colorado Territory at the time and the roads of the future state were so bad that it was easier to travel to the East than to the interior. After he hauled the wheat into the Arkansas Valley and received $12 per 500 pounds for it, Mears decided that constructing a toll road between the San Luis and Arkansas Valleys was a good idea and would be as profitable as Gilpin had said.

As he was short of funds, Mears approached wealthy individuals in southwestern Colorado to raise money for his toll road scheme. The largest investor besides himself was Charles Nachtrieb. Nachtrieb, a German immigrant, owned a mill in the Arkansas Valley and, foreseeing possible profit if the grain raised in the San Luis Valley had easy access to his mill, agreed to invest in the project. He was to become a partner of Mears in subsequent business enterprises for the next decade, until he was murdered by a cowboy in a dispute over wages.

The Poncha Pass Wagon Road Company was incorporated on November 8, 1870, with a capital stock of $2,000 divided into 400 shares. The charter stated that the road would run from Poncha Pass in Lake County north, following Poncha Creek to its intersection with the South Arkansas River. The road was later extended from the proposed terminus north to Nathrop, the site of a majority

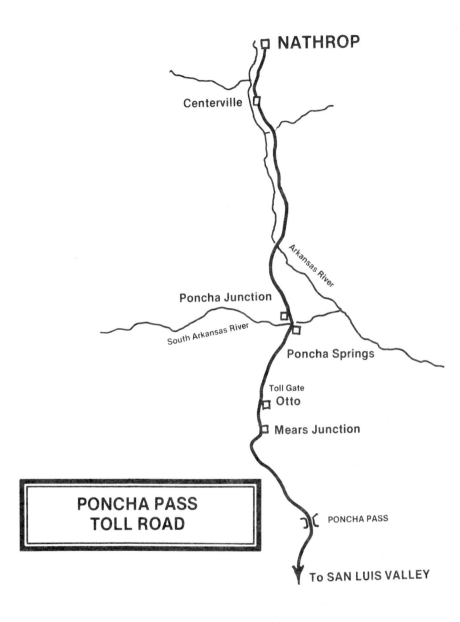

NATHROP

Centerville

Arkansas River

Poncha Junction

South Arkansas River

Poncha Springs

Toll Gate
Otto

Mears Junction

PONCHA PASS
TOLL ROAD

PONCHA PASS

To SAN LUIS VALLEY

9

of Nachtrieb's holdings. The trustees of the new corporation were Otto Mears and two Saguache merchants, Edward M. Wales and J.R. Foster.

Although the toll road was not profitable at first, it proved extremely lucrative later on. Alice Anderson, Nachtrieb's step-daughter, said that during some busy weeks, the toll road would earn over $1,500. The venture continued to be profitable until the road was sold to the Denver & Rio Grande Railroad in 1880.

The Poncha Pass Toll Road was important in the history of southwestern Colorado. It was the first well-constructed road between the San Luis and Arkansas Valleys. It was one of the first means of access into the entire area, and probably was the most well-built and profitable road in the region during this period. Mears' success in this enterprise encouraged him to invest in similar ventures, and the fifty-mile Poncha Pass road was eventually extended into a 400-mile toll road empire.

The Poncha Pass Toll Road became a model for Mears' subsequent toll roads. As on Poncha Pass, toll gates were established on later roads in canyons or at stream crossings so that those using the roads could not avoid payment. Toll charges at Poncha Pass — ranging from 1½ cents to 50 cents — were also used on future roads.

When preparations had been completed on the Poncha Pass Toll Road venture, and with lucrative returns in sight, Mears believed that he was financially secure enough to support a wife. He met his intended at Granite, in the mining region north of Nathrop. Mary Kampfshulte was a beautiful German brunette of 22 who accompanied her brother to Colorado when he came for health reasons.[3] Mary and Otto were married November 17, 1870, nine days after the incorporation of the Poncha Pass Toll Road. The Mearses had three daughters and one son. The girls were Laura May, who was born in 1872; Eva, who died on May 31, 1876, at the age of four and a half months; and Cora, born on November 25, 1879. The son, whose name is unknown, was born January 8, 1887, and died three days later.

During the early years of marriage, the newlyweds were close. Mary and the children accompanied Otto on his business trips, which sometimes involved traveling over one hundred miles a day on precipitous, rutted, bad roads. Mary's health became more delicate as the years passed, and she and her husband became more frequently separated as she spent an increasing amount of her time at health resorts. It was during the latter period of his marriage that Otto became a ladies' man, although he was a solicitous father who spent a great deal of time and money on his children.

Raising a family did not hinder the development of Mears' business enterprises. In fact, he was busier after he was married. In 1873, he and Gotthelf reorganized his mercantile business and purchased a large inventory of merchandise for the new firm. The general store did not enjoy immediate success, however. Shortly after the reorganization of the mercantile business, the depression that followed the financial panic of 1873 left many Coloradoans penniless. Mears was consequently forced to give his customers credit so that they could acquire the necessities they needed to survive the winter.

Another illustration of Mears' business acumen, besides his building of good will by the extension of credit, was his ability to profit from potentially unprofitable situations. Anne Ellis, a pioneer woman who lived in Saguache during its formative years, recounted the following story:

> Once all our husbands was out burying a man who had been killed in a drunken shooting scrape—some of them had been drinking a lot too—so us wives went up to Mears' Store . . . and we went in and smashed in the heads of the barrels and poured whiskey into the road. Mears never said a word, just looked on, but, lo and behold, when our husbands got their bills, they were charged with all that whiskey, between four and five hundred dollars worth. Money so scarce, too.[4]

In early 1874, about a year after Mears and Gotthelf founded their Saguache mercantile establishment, the former helped bring to light one of the most depraved crimes in the history of the West.

The events leading to the crime's exposure began one sub-zero March morning when a man named Alfred Packer emerged from the wilderness and made his way to the Los Pinos Indian Agency, a few miles from Saguache, and asked for aid. He stated that while guiding a party of miners from Salt Lake to the San Juan, he became very ill and was left to die, but recovering his strength somewhat, he managed to get to the agency.

Packer was allowed to recuperate at the agency, and a few days later he left for Saguache. A month later, a party of prospectors staggered out of the mountains more dead than alive. Upon learning of Packer's previous arrival they said they had been with him at Chief Ouray's winter camp. Packer, they claimed—anxious to be at the mines and against the advice of Ouray—induced others to accompany him despite the bad weather and treacherous country. Two groups were formed: One led by Packer would go to the agency by the shortest route possible, the other would follow the Gunnison River to the same destination. When the second group arrived and heard Packer's story, they became suspicious as they knew the members of the party would not abandon him. They asserted that he was a known robber, counterfeiter and probably a murderer as well. Nothing, however, could be proved and Packer was still allowed to come and go as he wished.

One day, Packer walked into Mears' store in Saguache and negotiated with the merchant over the price of a horse. The two agreed on a price of $70, but because the prospective buyer had a reputation as a counterfeiter, Mears refused to take his banknotes. Packer produced another wallet and presented him with different notes. The shop owner's suspicions were heightened when he saw a Wells Fargo Express Company draft in the second pocketbook, but he said nothing about it to the customer.

12

Later, Mears sought out Charles Adams. The latter, a German immigrant, was the Indian agent at the Los Pinos Agency and had an honorary title of general because he was the head of militia under Governor Edward McCook. Finding Adams, Mears described the incident, conveying to the Indian agent his impression that Packer was acting suspiciously. The two men then decided to induce Packer to go to the Los Pinos Agency, over which Adams had full jurisdiction, where he could either wring a confession out of the suspect or detain him while an investigation was made.

After much questioning, Packer broke down and told the following story: He claimed to have received the money from the five miners he was guiding from Salt Lake to the San Juan region. He said the party had run out of food several days after leaving Ouray's camp and that the prospectors had resorted to murder and cannibalism to survive. He said he killed no one except a man named Bell, who attacked him and whom he killed in self-defense. To keep from starving, he stated that he too had resorted to cannibalism, and after taking a few dollars from the corpses, he had made his way down to the agency.

Feeling ran high against Packer when his story was revealed, and the authorities incarcerated him until an investigation could be made. Two months later, when the snows melted in early June, the prospectors' remains were found. It was determined at an inquest that four had been murdered while asleep and a fifth had been killed with a blunt instrument after putting up a stout defense. The placement of the bodies at the camp site, where they were found, left no doubt that Packer was a murderer and a cannibal who had subsisted for perhaps a two-month period on the flesh of his former companions. After proving Packer's "confession" a lie, an order was sent to Saguache to put him on trial, but he had escaped a few days before.[5]

Ten years passed. One night in March, 1883, a miner from the Salt Lake party who was visiting Fort Fetterman,

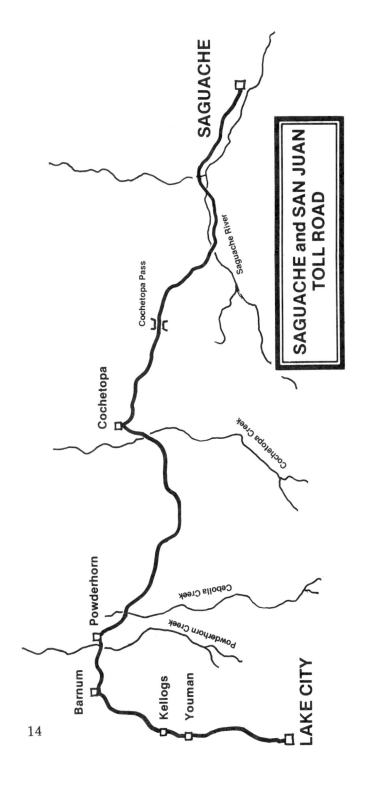

SAGUACHE and SAN JUAN
TOLL ROAD

SAGUACHE

Saguache River

Cochetopa Pass

Cochetopa

Cochetopa Creek

Powderhorn

Cebolla Creek

Powderhorn Creek

Barnum

Kellogs

Youman

LAKE CITY

14

Wyoming, heard Packer's voice in the next room. After General Adams was notified, the alleged cannibal was arrested and brought to trial the following month at Lake City, county seat of Hinsdale County, where the macabre campsite was located. Mears testified at the trial and offered firsthand evidence against the defendant. When Packer was found guilty and was sentenced to death, he swore vengeance on Mears, whom he considered to be the most damaging witness.

Mears' connection with this bizarre episode was to last nearly twenty more years. When Packer's lawyers appealed the case to the Colorado Supreme Court in October, 1885, Mears again was called upon to testify. The Supreme Court overturned the previous death sentence and Packer received, instead, a forty-year prison term. Fifteen years later the *Denver Post*, in a probable effort to increase circulation, depicted Packer as the martyr of the judicial system and the victim of Otto Mears' enmity. Polly Pry, one of the *Post's* writers, called Mears a craven coward for using his influence to keep Packer incarcerated. Polly claimed that Mears was afraid of Packer's vengeance. After a year's effort, the *Denver Post* succeeded in having Packer pardoned by Governor Charles S. Thomas. Leaving his violent intentions toward Mears unfulfilled, he died six years later.

Back in 1873, Mears had become interested in the mining and agricultural potential of Hinsdale County, an area which had been created by the Territorial Legislature from land vacated by the Utes. He invested in the Saguache and San Juan Toll Road Company, which was building a road from Saguache to the mining camp of Lake City by way of Cochetopa Pass and the Lake Fork of the Gunnison River. Isaac Gotthelf and Preston Hotchkiss, the Saguache merchants who were the majority stockholders of the toll road company, could not meet its financial obligations and in consequence Mears bought their shares of stock and took over the management of the company. By August, 1874, after the company had been under his control for only a few weeks, he had managed to raise enough money by recruiting additional investors to finish the road. The road was improved in June and August of the following year as the initial effort "received the excrations [*sic*] of nearly every teamster who drove over it," according to the Lake City *Silver World.*

Upon the completion of the Saguache and San Juan Toll Road, Mears began to consolidate his Saguache holdings. In October, 1874—to further his interests and to publicize the San Luis Valley—he founded the town's first newspaper, the *Saguache Chronicle.* He employed David Downer, an experienced newspaperman from Pennsylvania, as publisher. Beginning with the first issue on October 10, the paper printed editorials extolling the climate, mineral wealth and fertility of the land, thereby inducing many to settle in the Saguache region.

The following month, Mears, G.V. Gideon, S.W. Hodding, H.K. Prior, Isaac Gotthelf and others incorporated the Saguache Printing and Publishing Company in order to expedite the publishing of the *Chronicle* and to begin a business that would include job printing. According to its charter, this corporation was to have a twenty-year existence and would issue 100 shares of capital stock at $50 apiece.

During October, 1874, while he was organizing the Saguache Printing and Publishing Company, Mears found time to engage in politics and was responsible for establishing the county seat of Saguache County at Saguache instead of Milton. The rivalry between the two cities was settled at the polls and, as the following story shows, he used questionable methods to gain votes for his favorite in the contest:

> I [John C. Bell] would say I was at the town of Saguache in Saguache County in 1874 or 1875 when the first term of court was held there. Judge Moses Hallett and District Attorney Henry rode into the town and camped. Otto Mears and myself went over to welcome them to the camping ground. There had just been a warm contest between the town of Milton and Sa-

guache for the location of the county seat. Otto Mears was leading the fight for Saguache. He introduced himself to Judge Hallett. "Shuge, I 'spect you'll have to try me," he said. "Shon Lawrence tried to sell me votes for Siwach and I offered him five hundred dollars for the Mexican vote and he wanted seven hundred dollars and we don't trade. He is now going to have me indicted for trying to buy votes, and if he do, I'll pay my fine and then have him indicted for trying to sell votes. Don't you see?"[6]

While developing Saguache, the area made accessible by Mears' Saguache and San Juan Toll Road began to prosper. During the construction of this route, the contractor, Enos T. Hotchkiss, had found valuable ore deposits at Lake San Cristobal. This find caused the initial great interest in the Lake City region. Foreseeing a rapid growth for the region, Eugene Bartholfs, with the aid of associates, surveyed a townsite at Lake City—named after its proximity to Lake San Cristobal—and had it recorded at the Del Norte land office in the closing months of 1874. In September of the following year, William T. Ring, F. Newton Bogue and Harry Finely, using Mears' funds, founded the Lake City Town Company. With a capital stock of $11,000 divided into 220 shares, this organization was founded to buy surveyed land and hold it for sale to new settlers.

Remembering the value of publicity in the growth of Saguache, Mears subsidized Harry M. Woods and Clark L. Peyton to found a weekly newspaper called the *Silver World* at Lake City. The newspaper's first issue appeared on June 10, 1875. In addition to its primary function of advertising the wealth of the area, it included local news. Most of the editorials in the first years of the paper's existence extolled the attractions of the locale. Three months after its origin, the *Silver World* claimed 400 subscribers and two years later it boasted 1,000. The mushrooming growth of the paid subscribers to the publication was a reflection of the development of Lake

City. The newspaper described the amazing growth of the town in its first few months as follows:

> Little more than three months ago Lake City was but a cluster of crude log cabins. There was not a store, nor even that indispensible adjunct of a mining town, a rum shop. It had existence only in name . . . There are now five stores, two saloons, two blacksmith shops, two restaurants, two meat markets and a shoe shop.[7]

Three years later, the *Rocky Mountain News* reported that the town had 2,000 inhabitants. The astonishing influx of people justified Mears' interest and financial investment in the area and was exemplified by the report in the May 22, 1880, edition of the *Silver World,* stating that in the summer of 1876, between six and twelve vehicles a day paid the $3 toll for the use of the Saguache and San Juan Toll Road.

Within a few days of the *Silver World's* founding, another project of equal importance in the development of Lake City was begun. Taking note of the rapid growth of Lake City, the citizens of Del Norte decided to build a road to the new town and thereby give the area another outlet to the Eastern Slope. On June 23, 1875, a meeting was conducted at the Del Norte land office. It was decided that a new company, called the Antelope Park and Lake City Toll Road, be organized with a capital stock of $5,000.

Mears was not in favor of the new route at first because he believed Del Norte would attract much of the business away from Saguache. The intense rivalry between the towns for the trade of the hinterland is reflected in the following editorial:

> Evidently the *Silver World* does not want the road built from Antelope Springs to Lake City. We are assured, however, that it does not reflect the sentiments of the people in that vicinity so far as roads are concerned. The road will be built and when the travel comes by way of Del Norte, the *Silver World,* which has been set up to bark for Saguache, to sneeze when Mears takes snuff, will find that it has got wrong.[8]

Mears soon changed his mind. He decided that the new project would stimulate rather than hinder the growth of Lake City and Saguache. In late July, he bought a 10 per cent interest in the road and rushed its construction. He hired Enos T. Hotchkiss as supervisor and by late October the work was completed. This second route to Lake City formed part of the main transportation artery into the entire San Juan area for a number of years.

In the mid-1870s, while developing Saguache and Lake City, Mears—with characteristic energy and diversity— became a mail contractor. While in Washington in October, 1873, on a sight-seeing tour with the Ute delegation, he found time to bid on his contract. With W.J. Godfrey, he bid $2,179 for the route from Fairplay to Oro City, a distance of 95 miles, with mail delivery once a week. Mears never serviced it because the postmaster general decided there were not enough people along the route to warrant regular mail service. Beginning in 1874, Mears delivered mail from Los Pinos to Saguache, a distance of 40 miles, receiving $432 a year from the Post Office Department for the task. On June 11, 1875, the route was extended 100 miles, ending at Silverton, and service was increased to three times a week, for which the contractor was given an extra $4,018.50.

That fall, Mears contracted to deliver mail to Ouray and set up a route from the Los Pinos Agency to that mining region. Each of the mines in the area had separate service with all the routes converging at the agency, which served as the central station for the incoming and outgoing mail. The nearest road in the area was the Antelope Park and Lake City Toll Road, 75 miles away. He built three road stations 25 miles apart, setting up tall poles between the stations so a solid road would result from compaction of the snow from travel.

While the mail system was being constructed, a man by the name of Stewart Daniells stopped at the agency on his way to the mines. He was a prospector who had at one time delivered mail for the Hudson's Bay Company. He suggested to Mears the advantages of hauling the mail by dog sleds, and convinced him to inaugurate such a scheme. Daniells was hired to run the sleds and immediately he began training dogs for the purpose. After a few initial mishaps, when the dogs tried to take a short cut and leave the road, the plan proved to be successful.

To increase his profits, Mears began transporting supplies along with the mail. At every opportunity, the dogs would fight over the foodstuffs. Consequently, the Ouray women who had ordered clothing from eastern stores often found their apparel full of food upon arrival. The indignant ladies complained to the United States Post Office and the resulting publicity turned the entire episode into a national joke. Although Mears earned masculine sympathy for his efforts to increase his profits, the complaints from the mountain town reached the press and, as a result of government pressure, the Post Office forced the mail contractor to carry provisions and mail in separate toboggans.

At this time, Mears had other problems with his mail contracts. In January of the following year, the heavy winter snows made it impossible to use either dog sleds or mail carriers to deliver mail into the San Juan Mountains and he was forced to curtail service until the trails were passable. Indignant, the editor of Silverton's *La Plata Miner*, in an editorial January 8, 1876, complained about Mears' incompetence, and the *Denver Tribune* of February 3 carried the story. Eventually the authorities in Washington heard of the situation, and notified Mears in March that, unless he wanted to pay a heavy fine, mail had to be delivered into Silverton and Ouray.

Unable to get anyone to brave the elements to transport the mail, Mears was forced to make the trip himself. It took three days to make the journey, during which he experienced many difficulties and great fatigue. At one spot on the Lake Fork of the Gunnison River he had to hike through two feet of wet snow with swift, icy water running beneath him. Exhausted after the grueling trip to Ouray, he ordered the mail route re-opened and from that time the mail was delivered on schedule.

Notwithstanding mail contracts, city development, toll road building and other activities, Mears managed to find time to engage in politics. From the time of his arrival in Colorado, he had been involved in political activity. At first, he acted as county treasurer of Saguache County, and then as its representative to the Republican territorial conventions. Later, as his county's member on the Republican State Central Committee, he gradually widened his sphere of influence from Saguache and the San Luis Valley so that it encompassed the whole Colorado Territory. His agreeable manner, his efficiency, his political acumen, as well as his solid base in the San Luis Valley, made him a great power in the Republican party by the time Colorado achieved statehood in 1876.

Mears' political activities in that year indicate how eminent he was, and his successes in this area must have given him great satisfaction, since he was attracted to this field because of his lust for power. He also hoped his political connections would enhance his business career. His first political steps in 1876 were made at the local level. At the Republican County Convention for Saguache on August 17, 1876, he, W.D. Spencer and Edward M. Wales were appointed to serve on the credentials committee. Upon the completion of his committee duties, Mears, Herman Lueders and Edward Wales were elected delegates from Saguache County to the state convention at Pueblo.

On the first day of the Pueblo convention, August 23, 1876, Mears was appointed to serve on the convention's committee for permanent organization and order of business. He also participated in the selection of the party's slate for the state's first election. John L. Routt was an obvious choice as nominee for governor. He was the state's last territorial governor, and he had proven himself able in the office. It was anticipated he would be a good vote-getter.

The selection was much more difficult for lieutenant governor, although Lafayette Head, a former business associate of Otto's, was eventually chosen for the position. All available evidence suggests that Mears had much to do with Head's nomination, because the latter had many of the characteristics of a Mears candidate. The political boss, for example, only liked to sponsor men he was thoroughly familiar with. Some of his eventual business associates such as Fred Walsen, Frederick W. Pitkin, Alva Adams, Edward O. Wolcott and Simon Guggenheim, rose to high office in Colorado with his support.

Head in the same manner achieved a high government post. His mentor was never one to do something for nothing and consequently never campaigned for anyone unless he received a promise for a payoff after the individual gained office. Head, who was not known for his intelligence or intractability, probably gave in to Mears' demands and was in consequence put on the slate. Another factor which increased the protege's desirability as a candidate was that he was of Spanish American descent and, as he was married to a Spanish American, would command a large Mexican vote. Consequently, his sponsor probably convinced the other political bosses that it would be in everyone's interest to add Head to the slate. The Republican ticket, in any case, won a convincing victory at the polls.

The culmination of Mears' political activities for the year came in November when he was chosen to be one of three presidential electors for the state by a joint session of the legislature. This was a reward for his usefulness to the Republican party at the local and state level and a reward for his negotiating the Brunot Treaty with the Utes three years before. When he and the other electors—Herman Beckhurts and William L. Hadley—met, it was decided that Mears should be the messenger to carry Colorado's three electoral votes to Washington.

Upon his return to Colorado in January, 1877, Mears engaged in many activities. In the early spring, he opened a general store at Ouray. Ouray was a rapidly growing mining town where rich ore deposits had first been discovered in 1875. The growth of the area was so rapid that

Ouray County was created a few months later. By 1877, so many profitable mines were being worked and the influx of population was so great, that Otto decided to finance a well-equipped mercantile establishment, sorely needed in the frontier town. In April, he was making purchases for the new store, and the April 21, 1877, edition of the *Saguache Chronicle* described his activities:

> His purchases, if he made any, consisted of one of the two stocks of hardware of which the town of Del Norte boasts. Mr. Mears is now at Lake City, and we wouldn't be at all surprised to hear that he had bought the town and moved it to Ouray. That's his way of doing things.

In May, 1877, the *Saguache Chronicle* reported him to be involved in a farming experiment with 80 acres of land. He planted 50 acres with wheat and 30 with oats, taking care to keep an exact account of his expenditures so that he would know, when his crops were sold, precisely how much he had earned or lost.

Mears was energetic in other areas as well. He served as the agent for the Denver and Rio Grande Railroad at Saguache, a position which gave him an inside view of the operation of railroads, which he used later in running his own short lines. He was also busy as an entrepreneur in Saguache. He was half-owner of a now-thriving hardware store called Mears and Company, and was a partner to H.K. Prior in a dry goods store that sold such items as groceries, ready-made clothing and ladies' dresses.

This multifarious business activity, however, was subordinate to the building of toll roads. From 1877 on he built so many roads that within a few years he was known as the "Toll Road King of the San Juan." His take over of the Ouray and Lake Fork Wagon Road Company in May, 1877, marks the beginning of the period when road building began to be one of his chief interests.

The Ouray and Lake Fork Wagon Road Company had been incorporated on November 3, 1876, by Ira G. Munn, Thomas B. Munn and A.W. Begole, Ouray merchants. The proposed road was to be built from Ouray to the Lake

Fork of the Gunnison River and then to a point on the Saguache and San Juan Toll Road.

By spring of the following year, it was evident that the venture was under-financed and when Mears bought the company's stock at a premium, only a few miles of road had been built. He decided that the former owners' plan was too ambitious and built the road from Ouray to the site of the present town of Montrose. The distance and obstacles were so great between this point and his Saguache and San Juan Toll Road and the connecting link would cost so much that he decided a new toll road company would have to be formed and financed to finish the job.

Finishing the abbreviated road north from Ouray in August, 1877, Mears immediately began to organize and capitalize a toll road which would form the second stage of the route. A month later, he incorporated the Lake Fork and Uncompahgre Toll Road Company, with Frederick W. Pitkin and Robert F. Long as co-directors. With a capital stock of $25,000, this road was to run west from the Barnum post office on the Saguache and San Juan Toll Road crossing the Little Blue and the Big Blue Creeks to the Cimmaron River into what is now Montrose. This road was not finished until the following summer, being delayed by winter weather. Upon completion, however, Mears had a continuous road with fine grades from Ouray to Barnum—a distance of more than 100 miles.

The Lake Fork and Uncompahgre Toll Road was finished in time for the road builder to devote his considerable energy to the 1878 gubernatorial race. The party bosses decided that it would be necessary for party unity to select a candidate from southwest Colorado. Because he had so much influence in this area Mears was delegated to find the nominee. His choice was Frederick W. Pitkin, a business associate, who had come to Colorado for his health. Pitkin appeared more tractable than he actually was and Mears expected to reap a windfall if his candidate was elected.

In July, Mears induced the Republicans of Ouray,

Pitkin's home county, to back him for governor. Accordingly the members of the Ouray County Republican Convention voted that the delegates to the state convention should "stand unflinchingly by and vote for him [Pitkin] first, last, and all the time."

When the Republican State Convention was staged in Denver in the summer of 1878, William Story, one of the Ouray delegates, nominated Pitkin for governor as agreed. The nomination was ratified by the convention and later the candidate made a successful bid for office. Pitkin was governor for two terms and aspired to be senator. He made the mistake, however, of not paying his political debts. He ignored the people who had helped him attain his high office and he slighted Ouray, his home county, by failing to promote its interests whenever possible.[9] Because of this ingratitude, Mears and the other Republican party bosses thwarted the governor's ambitions after his second term and assured his political death.

A few months after Pitkin was elected to his first term as governor, Mears embarked on what was—up to that time—his most ambitious toll road construction scheme. In the spring of 1879, numerous settlers and miners swarmed to Gunnison County, where rich lodes of silver-lead carbonate ore had been discovered the previous year by Leadville prospectors. The roads into the area were in primitive condition, in most cases no more than wagon tracks. Mears decided it would be profitable to construct a good toll road into Gunnison. He determined that the proposed route would be most useful if it connected the mining camp with what was then the terminus of the Denver & Rio Grande Railroad at the South Arkansas River. To do this, he would have to build a road from his Poncha Pass Toll Road over 10,846-foot Marshall Pass into Gunnison.

Finding that a road over Marshall Pass would be feasible, Mears was quick to organize a company to build it. In March, 1879, he, Isaac Gotthelf and Charles Nachtrieb were the incorporators of the Poncha, Marshall and

Gunnison Toll Road Company. The venture was subsidized by 1,000 shares of stock worth $25 apiece, and was to have a 20-year life. A fortnight later, Mears began building the new road. By mid-May, the construction crew was averaging a half-mile of new road a day and to expedite matters, Mears purchased a large herd of cattle from Oregon so there would be meat on hand to feed his men. In September, the toll road was completed, and it was so well-built and convenient that it proved extremely profitable.

Of all business ventures in which Mears participated during his first four decades, the Poncha, Marshall and Gunnison Toll Road was by far the most lucrative. By May, 1880, there was so much traffic over the road that he was offered $175 a day if he would rent it. He found additional profit, besides toll receipts, in the coal deposits found on Poncha Pass during construction of the road. He became half owner of a coal vein five feet thick and he and his partners built a tunnel 250 feet into the claim so that the coal could be mined. He sold this road to the Denver & Rio Grande Railroad in 1881 for $13,000, the largest lump sum he had yet earned.[10]

About the time Mears was building the Poncha, Marshall and Gunnison Toll Road, he met David Frakes Day, who became one of his most intimate friends in the ensuing 35 years. Day, so close to him in business and social matters for so long, was born on March 7, 1847, in Hamilton County, Ohio. Day left home when his parents insisted he go to school and, after various adventures, joined Company D of the 57th Ohio Infantry before he was 15. In 1863, he earned a Congressional Medal of Honor for gallantry at Vicksburg. Subsequently, he was captured on three occasions and effected his escape each time. Because of his bravery and his initiative, he was promoted while only 16 years old to the position of chief of scouts for the 17th Army.

Upon cessation of hostilities, Day was discharged and went to Missouri, emulating his former commander Gen. Frank Blair. Day lived in Missouri for 13 years, where he

DAVID FRAKES DAY

*''God made Otto; the rest of us came into the country
from Missouri and other less civilized commonwealths.''* 27

contributed to local papers and ran a grocery store. He married in 1870 and raised five children and was on his way to achieving a modest prosperity when he was called to pay a defaulted note which he had endorsed for a friend. Having lost almost everything, he decided to go to Colorado and make a fresh start.

Day selected Ouray as his new Colorado home and chopped cord-wood for a year to support his family. In the summer of 1879, he was persuaded by fellow Missourian Gerald Letcher to buy a printing press for sale in Lake City and start a newspaper at Ouray. This new periodical made its first appearance on September 5, 1879, and was called the *Solid Muldoon*.[11] It became one of the most famous frontier newspapers because of its humor and because of Day's blistering attacks on frauds, charlatans and hypocrites.

Day's approach to journalism was as novel as his newspaper's name. He was a crusader for good. Intolerant of hypocrisy, absolutely incorruptible and faithfully conscientious, Day would assail in print or verbally what he considered to be against the best interests of Ouray and Colorado. He was probably born half a millenium too late, for his zeal was suited more to a medieval crusader than a 19th century newspaper editor.

Day's muckraking involved him in numerous confrontations. On one occasion, he had as many as 47 libel suits pending against him. However, he was never successfully prosecuted for libel, but was once jailed unlawfully for contempt. Besides legal battles, he was involved in at least one duel and in several fights over his offensive statements.

No matter how unfavorably Day wrote about others, he always had something good to say about Mears. The following quotation is typical of the comments he made about Mears throughout his newspaper career:

> The *Muldoon* has said very many naughty things about Otto Mears and is liable to say very many more, but the *Muldoon* has always con-

tended that Otto Mears has done more for the development of the San Juan Country than any ten men in Colorado. To his wealth and energy Ouray owes a large share of the boom she is now enjoying. Otto is a shrewd, far-seeing business-man, an adroit and cunning politician, and a speculator of more than ordinary nerve and judgement.[12]

Day's assessment of Mears is very important, as his newspapers, the *Solid Muldoon* and later, the *Durango Democrat*, are the best and most reliable sources of information about Mears. If Otto ever was likely to divulge his affairs to anyone, it would be Day. Day would, likely as not, print it. To other reporters, Mears would not be as frank as he would be to his Ouray friend and would generally tell them what they wanted to hear. This is why so many conflicting stories were printed about Mears during his lifetime and why, if Day is used as a touch-stone, his activities can be made comprehensible.[13]

At the time Day was preparing the first issue of the *Solid Muldoon* for publication, Mears incorporated the Uncompahgre, San Miguel and Dolores Toll Road Company. The new corporation—with Mears, Charles Adams and Leverett M. Kelly as directors—was to raise $25,000 to build a road from the Ouray and Lake Fork Toll Road to the mining town of Rico on the Dolores River, where rich carbonate deposits had been made and where a rush was going on. Despite the great need for a road to the Dolores River area, this corporation did not build one. While Mears was still examining the probable routes for the proposed road, the Meeker Massacre took place, and he was called upon to devote nearly all of his time for the next two years to Indian-white relations.

OTTO MEARS
*"You can call me bad names,
but you can't call me a damn fool!"*

2

A Permanent Funeral
Procession Gone to Seed

*F*or the fifteen years prior to 1879, when the Meeker Massacre took place, Otto Mears had close economic and social ties with the Utes. He had begun the association through Lafayette Head after coming to Colorado in 1865. Head, then agent of the Conejos Indian Agency, found it unprofitable and encouraged the younger man to become acquainted with the Utes and eventually to replace him as agent. Mears became familiar with the Ute customs. By learning their language, which was so difficult that only five or six white men could speak it, he won their respect. At the same time, he became a very good friend of Ouray, who later became the tribe's most powerful chief.

By the time he began his development of Saguache, Mears felt knowledgeable enough about the Utes to believe he could make the Southern Ute Agency profitable if it was moved to the new townsite. He received permission from the Department of Indian Affairs and effected the change. He became the tribe's official trader with Head's old clerk, William S. Godfoy, becoming the agent in charge.

Mears found his new position lucrative, but was disconcerted to find it threatened a few months later. By the terms of the 1868 treaty, negotiated while Mears was establishing the Southern Ute Agency at the new townsite, the location of the agency was to be moved to the Los

Pinos River. At the new spot, he would have difficulty supplying the Utes since the Los Pinos was nearly 200 miles from Saguache; he might, therefore, lose his government contracts to provide them with foodstuffs. As the treaty did not specify the exact location where the new agency was to be built Second Lieutenant Calvin T. Speer, the newly appointed agent, conferred with Mears about the best spot for construction. Speer then proceeded to fulfill his instructions in accordance with Mears' recommendations and the new agency was soon established on the Los Pinos River.

Mears, after some initial trepidation, found he could remain in his position as trader even though the Los Pinos Agency was approximately 175 miles from Saguache. By using the fairly good road that extended from Saguache to the Gunnison River and on to Salt Lake, freighting charges would be low enough to permit him to make a profit when transporting supplies to the Utes.

The merchant's money-making schemes extended occasionally to taking undue advantage of the Bureau of Indian Affairs. In a letter written by the new agent Calvin Speer to Governor Edward M. McCook, dated November 11, 1869, there is an example of this kind of questionable activity:

> Mr. Mears also advised Mr. Russell to leave out Fifty Cows and not brand them . . . he had some old hides that he would brand and then say the cows had died. Thereby making Fifty-Cows, and he would make it all right with Speer, he also advised *me* not to speak of the Cows at all. As it would fix me in Saguache. Insinuating that the Cows were very bad and that the Democrats would let you know it . . .
>
> This man Mears, has united himself to that party. That would stoop to any mean act to defeat the intentions of the government and he is assisted by every democrat in Saguache.
>
> I could mention others but do not deem it necessary. In regard to the Cows I have heard

> Messrs. Russell, Harris . . . and others say they
> consider them a remarkable good herd.[1]

Despite Speer's complaint, it is known that Mears continued to supply the Ute reservation with cattle in the early 1870s. Sidney Jocknick and Alonzo Hartman both state in their memoirs that they worked for him in fulfilling his contracts to provide the agency with cattle. Hartman recalls that by 1872 his employer was supplying Los Pinos with 100 head of cattle per month in addition to furnishing such items as flour, hay, potatoes, oats and beans.

Speaking their language, Mears respected Ute customs and always used great tact. By the early 70s, he became, in consequence, one of the most influential and trusted white men among the Indians. He was so well established with the tribe that he was often approached for advice concerning Indian-white relations. On the most important such occasion, he was able to counsel Felix Brunot how to best achieve the San Juan Cession.

Coloradoans had desired the San Juan area since 1869, when gold deposits had been found there. Prospecting near the site of present-day Silverton had taken place as early as 1860. As the San Juan Mountains were part of Indian territory stipulated in the 1868 treaty, Congress appointed a three-man commission to negotiate the cession. The chairman of the committee was Governor McCook of Colorado, and the other members were John D. Lang and Gen. John McDonald.

To facilitate the negotiations McCook invited Felix Brunot, a Pittsburgh steel magnate and an organizer of the American Church Missionary Society, to accompany the commissioners. Through past dealing, Chief Ouray did not trust McCook or his fellow appointees and consequently the commissioners found it impossible to bargain with the Indians. Observing the impasse and noticing the trust and affection growing between Brunot and Ouray, Mears suggested to the eastern capitalist he return alone the following summer if he wanted to induce the Utes to part with the rich mineral lands. Brunot remembered this advice when he returned east after the failure of the McCook commission to negotiate a new treaty.

By the following April, prospectors and settlers were clamoring for the San Juan Cession. They sent a memorial to Columbus Delano, Secretary of the Department of the Interior, in which they stated they had been in the southwestern part of Colorado for three years and had "developed a greater wealth of mineral than has ever been seen upon this country" and as no Indians had been seen in the area for the entire period of white occupation, it would behoove the government to secure this valuable region for which the Utes apparently had no use.

Accordingly, Felix Brunot was sent from Washington and arrived in Colorado in late August, 1873, to negotiate a new treaty with the Utes. Although taking Mears' advice and coming alone armed with broad general powers, he found the Indians very difficult to bargain with. An impasse was soon reached and, in desperation, Brunot went to Mears' home in Saguache and solicited his help. Mears returned to the reservation with him, talked with Ouray, and suggested to Brunot that the chief should annually receive a salary of $1,000 for ten years. He replied that the government would not extend a bribe, but Mears asserted that it was a salary, since the Indian was getting old and—being a chief—should have a more dignified means of support than hunting.

Fooled by this ruse, Brunot told Ouray he would receive $1,000 a year for ten years and that the Utes would receive the yearly interest on $500,000 which the government had set aside for them. In return, the Indians would give up four million acres in the San Juan area—retaining more than fourteen million where they could live undisturbed. The Utes agreed to these terms and gave their approval to what is now known as the Brunot Treaty. They surrendered the area which now comprises the counties of Dolores, La Plata, Hinsdale, Ouray, San Juan, Montezuma and San Miguel.

Brunot, exultant because the treaty had been signed,

recommended to his superiors that a one-month, expense-paid trip to the eastern part of the country should be arranged for Ouray and the nine important Ute chiefs, with Otto Mears, Gen. Charles Adams and his assistant Herman Lueders serving as their guides and guardians. This plan was approved and the government allocated $15,000 for the purpose.

On October 6, 1873, the members of the junket began gathering in Denver, and both the Indians and whites made final arrangements for the journey. The chiefs were provided with clothing and looked so distinctive that they inspired the following newspaper account:

> Said clothes are of the everlasting black, the coats being of a sack pattern, something like a parlor's pea jacket. They also have black soft hats to match, and each have a carpet bag in which to bring home his plunder. They have not yet become fully accustomed to first-class hotel life, and squat on the floor in their aboriginal manner. Their clothes fit them like a nightgown on a pair of tongs, yet doubtless they feel every inch like white men, though this attempt at dressing them up makes them look like a permanent funeral procession gone to seed.[2]

Despite all the preparations made, the excursion was almost cancelled. On the evening of October 7, disaster was narrowly averted at the Munger Hotel where the Utes were staying in Denver. Mears was about ready to go to bed when he thought he smelled gas. He went out into the hall and discovered that the odor came from one of the rooms occupied by the chiefs. He burst through the door and found that the wind had extinguished the lamp and the room was rapidly filling with gas. He woke the chiefs, just in time to save them from being asphixiated.

The party, without any further mishap, started east and its first destination was Washington. On October 15, the Coloradoans toured the capital until the Secretaries of Indian Affairs and of the Interior were available to discuss the settlement of the Brunot Treaty details. They were

MEARS POSES WITH COSTUMED UTES

given a tour of the naval yard, the Treasury Department and, after a ride on a warship, they saw other things calculated to impress them with the power of the white man.

The Cabinet officers were soon ready to negotiate and the principal issue was how the Utes could use their annuity. The Indians wanted to spend it their own way while the high government officials contended that it would be best for the Indians if their agent's recommendations took precedence over their own. The dispute was settled amicably, though not in the Utes' favor, when Brunot said that the money would be expended as the government saw fit but that the Indians would be able to buy anything they wanted as long as the authorities thought it reasonable.

To impress the Utes with the inviolability of the treaty which they had just ratified, they were taken on a visit to the White House. The supposed solemnity of the occasion was broken by Ouray. When President Grant, with his wife and daughter, stood in line to receive the Indians, Ouray spoke to Mrs. Grant, saying, "As the President is my father, you must be my mother, and as the President is my father and you are my mother, your daughter must be my sister."[3] Mears translated this to the other chiefs, and Indians and whites alike appreciated the joke and laughed. Upon completion of their visit to Washington, the Indians were anxious to return home and, as a result, the itinerary which included most of the larger eastern cities was cut down to include only Boston, Philadelphia, New York, Chicago and St. Louis.

While in New York, the Indians were taken to see a circus, where they were impressed by the feats of horsemanship. While visiting the city, Mears also took them to see *The Black Crook*, a drama presented nightly at Niblo's Garden. The presentation was characterized by elaborate sets and large numbers of nimble ballet dancers. The chiefs were not impressed by the sets, believing perhaps that the scenery in their country was more picturesque. They were not appreciative of the dancing either, thinking that their own dancers were much better. Not wishing them to be completely disappointed, Mears took them to the zoo in Central Park. The Indians thought the camel the most interesting of all the animals there, particularly because it could move quickly in the desert while carrying heavy loads. They debunked the deer, buffalo, antelope and bears which were smaller than those they had seen on their reservation.

The Indians could not recall the English names of the more unusual animals which Mears and Ouray had pointed out to them; several chiefs used long Indian names to describe the animals they had seen once they returned home. The elephant was called "the big high animal with a tail at each end." The camel was labeled as "the new kind of horse that the Indians wanted to have to ride fast in their country." The baboons and monkeys were designated as "the long armed creatures trying to look like men."

Mears took the Indian tourists to the exhibition of stuffed animals, where the visitors immediately detected that the animals were dead and congratulated themselves for not being fooled by a trick perpetrated by cheats. It was impossible for Ouray or for Mears to convey to them that these exhibits served a useful purpose and that they were not intended to deceive anyone.

The next day Mears took them to see art galleries, and then the party visited stores where books, prints and pictures were sold. At one establishment where the Indians expressed unusual interest in some photographs, the proprietor inquired whether they might not like to take a portfolio with them. Ouray replied that they would rather collect souvenirs in a jewelry store.

The Ute delegation returned to Denver November 10, 1873, where the party broke up so its members could return to their homes. The Indians had enjoyed the trip and it was to be a subject of interest and discussion with them for years to come. A disquieting note, however, was sounded in an editorial appearing in the October 17, 1873, issue of the *Chicago Tribune* describing some of the Indians' feelings of disgust upon their return west because of their cession of four million acres of some of the best land in the San Juan for a paltry sum of $25,000 a year. Sidney Jocknick, in close contact with the Utes during this period, stated that another less positive aspect about the trip east for the Indians was that they were given permanent feelings of inferiority in their discovery that they were no match for the white man in either knowledge or power.

From the end of the eastern junket to the close of the decade, when the next important Indian-white confrontation occurred at the Meeker Massacre, Mears retained his close ties with the Utes. As interpreter, he served as a kind of ex-officio advisor on Indian affairs. His friendship with Ouray and other important Ute leaders and his influence in the white community placed him in a unique position to act as a go-between for the two races. He was accorded much prestige and did what he could to earn this esteem by relieving, when possible, the tension caused by the everyday contact of two mutually incompatible races and cultures. It is quite possible that a major Ute-white confrontation would have occurred before 1879 had not he and other intelligent leaders of both sides acted with sagacity in defusing a potentially explosive situation.

Mears, of course, used his position with the Utes to his own advantage. Never one to act in a completely disinterested way, he saw that, as tribal life broke down from the increasing contact with white culture, the Indians would become more and more dependent upon the government for items which they had formerly supplied themselves. Decreasing Ute self-sufficiency meant the Bureau of Indian Affairs would have to provide more and more items for the Indians' survival. Mears seized this opportunity to increase his profit from government contracts. Before the Brunot Treaty, he supplied the Indians with cattle and foodstuffs, but after 1873 the Utes began to acquire a taste for the luxuries of their white neighbors. In addition to beef and cereals, Mears now contracted to furnish the Indians with soda, soap, salt, dry goods and hardware. By virtue of the toll road system he was building, he could afford to outbid his competitors on the hauling of these supplies to the reservation.

The road builder's relationship with the Uncompahgre Utes changed after September 29, 1879, when the Northern Utes ambushed a battalion of troopers under Major Thomas T. Thornburgh at Milk Creek and a few hours later massacred the males at the White River Agency and took the females into captivity. The massacre's immediate cause was the result of efforts of Nathan C. Meeker, the agent at White River, to enforce an agrarian way of life on a nomadic people. The Utes considered agriculture as women's work, and when Meeker persisted in attempting to change this, the tragedy ensued.

At this juncture, Mears was asked by Gen. Charles Adams—commissioned by Governor Pitkin to rescue Mrs. Meeker, Mrs. Price and Miss Josephine Meeker—to act as interpreter on the mission. Mears, Adams and M.W. Cline went to the Uncompahgre Valley, to the camp of Chief Douglas, who was holding the captives. Upon conclusion of the difficult negotiations, the women were released and were taken to Greeley.

The news of the Battle of Milk Creek and the Meeker Massacre had evoked in Coloradoans feelings ranging from hysteria to rage. Volunteer companies were organized to protect the towns near the White River and Los Pinos Agencies. Action was also taken in the political sphere with great pressure put on the Interior Department and the Bureau of Indian Affairs to move the Utes out of the state.

The fever pitch of public opinion might have eventually cooled down except for the circulation of rumors after the captives' release that they had been raped by their captors. The settlers were so incensed by this that Ute removal became necessary to avoid a further confrontation between the two races. The situation required extremely delicate handling. On one side were the whites who, through fear, rage and land hunger, wanted the expulsion of the Indians, and on the other were the White

River and Uncompahgre Utes who refused to leave their centuries-old home. It was Otto Mears who supplied the diplomacy which saved the situation. It required the expenditure of a great amount of his time for the next two and a half years and the loss of many friends among the Indians, but he averted another Sand Creek.[4]

Before any action could be taken, Secretary of the Interior Carl Schurz deemed a preliminary investigation of the outbreak necessary. The inquiry was headed by Adams, Colonel Edward Hatch and Ouray. Twelve Utes were implicated by the testimony of the women taken captive and Ouray insisted that the accused should be tried in Washington as he believed a fair hearing could not be had in Colorado.

That fall, Mears, Adams, Ouray and the twelve Utes were ordered to go to Washington for trial. But before the trip could be made, most of the accused Utes disappeared. At this juncture, it was decided to take a delegation of chiefs to the capital to avert, if possible, the Indian-white war which seemed imminent.

The trip was made in January, 1880. Upon arrival, the delegation conferred with Interior Secretary Schurz. He believed Ute removal from northern Colorado necessary and, in addition, believed that it was obligatory to bring the accused murderers to justice to satisfy public opinion.

The precarious peace was further threatened when it became generally known about this time that the female captives—Arvilla and Josephine Meeker and Flora Price—had been raped by their abductors. The murder of Nathan Meeker and the other white men at White River was bad enough, but according to Victorian morality the mistreatment of the women captives was barbarous. The Indians, always viewed with distrust by white men, now seemed to most Coloradoans to be devils whose liquidation would be a Christian duty.

The Interior Secretary thought that the potentially explosive situation could be kept under control if the implicated parties could be brought to Washington. As Mears and Adams believed that the miscreants could be induced to come to Washington for trial, they were ordered to go to Colorado and return with the allegedly guilty Indians.

Once back in Colorado, Mears and Adams sought out Chief Douglas and others incriminated in the White River tragedy, and after making many promises, induced the parties, who were now found, to go to Washington. At Kansas City, Chief Douglas was taken prisoner by the general and incarcerated at Fort Leavenworth for his part in the Meeker Massacre, while Mears and the remainder of the Indians continued on to Washington.

By the time Mears arrived in February of 1880, Schurz had persuaded Ouray and the other members of the delegation that Ute removal was required to avoid another major Indian-white confrontation. Constant pressure was applied to leaders of both races by Coloradoans professing to be terrified of an Indian attack, but in reality supporting removal so that they could acquire reservation land. The whites wanted all Utes removed from their state but many officials in Washington thought this would be too harsh a punishment since only a small number of the red men were responsible for the Meeker Massacre and the Milk Creek battle.

Earlier in the month, Mears expressed his opinion about this issue. He suggested in a letter to Judge James B. Belford, then in Washington as one of Colorado's Congressmen, that if the Utes were to be kept in Colorado, a spot on the Grand River would be the most suitable. Rep. Belford conferred with Secretary Schurz about Mears' recommendation and persuaded him that it would be a workable solution to the Ute problem.

During the conferences with the Ute chiefs, Schurz, adopting Mears' plan, convinced the Indians that their tribe had to be moved to land at, or adjacent to, the future site of Grand Junction—the confluence of the Gunnison and Grand [Colorado] Rivers. In June, Congress approved a treaty to this effect which required the ratification of the majority of the members of the tribe. To insure that the treaty would be properly ratified and its terms carried out,

Schurz appointed a special commission whose members were Mears, George W. Manypenny, John B. Bowman, John J. Russell and Alfred B. Meacham.

Upon the confirmation of their appointments by the Senate, the commissioners went to the Uncompahgre. Congress had set the deadline of October 15, 1880, as the date by which the commission had to secure enough Indian signatures to ratify the treaty made by their representatives or the agreement would become void. In order to insure the fastest possible confirmation of the treaty, a meeting of the most influential Utes was convened.

At the gathering, the commissioners explained the provisions of the treaty to the Indians. The Indians were told they had to move to a new reservation, and the junction of the Grand and Gunnison Rivers, or territory adjacent to it, had been designated as the new reservation location. The Utes were willing to move to the identified site, but refused to approve the treaty because of the ambiguity of the phrase ''adjacent territory.'' The Indians believed ''adjacent territory'' meant Utah and they were unwilling to leave Colorado.

The exact meaning of the phrase ''adjacent territory'' was as puzzling to the members of the commission as it was to the chiefs. Meacham and Manypenny maintained, in debates on this subject, that ''adjacent'' referred to either the major rivers' confluence or its immediate vicinity, while Mears, Bowman and Russell argued the term could mean territory as far away from the confluence as Utah.

This controversy was settled in a somewhat unusual manner. Alfred B. Meacham—arrogant, overbearing and sometimes obnoxious—was knocked down by Bowman, who was tired of being told what he should think. As a result, Bowman was forced to tender his resignation, and in consequence, the commission was deadlocked on the choice of a course of action and was therefore adjourned.

The situation was further complicated by the fact that Chief Ouray died on August 25. The chief had been favorably disposed to the treaty and wielded great influence over the Indians. His death, therefore, seemed to make the ratification of the treaty impossible. Mears realized that, if Ute removal was not effected, a war would result which would prove costly in money and lives. He took it upon himself to secure the approval of the tribe. He traveled on the reservation and offered each Indian $2 for his signature. He obtained the necessary number for ratification, and was thus able to get the treaty approved before the October deadline. Manypenny, disapproving of the manner in which Mears procured the confirmation of the treaty, reported to Schurz that he was guilty of bribery. Schurz, indignant, ordered an investigation of Mear's behavior.

Mears was ordered to make a report of his actions and went to Washington in late January, 1881, to interview the other commissioners so that his account would be complete. He received a cool reception in the capital city. Dave Day summed up the relationship between Mears and Schurz after Manypenny's accusation as follows:

> Otto Mears and Granny Schurz are not as love-
> ly as was Jonathan and David. They are pouting,
> so to speak. Guess Otto must have got away with
> the Ute swag.[5]

Mears' unenthusiastic reception was not only caused by bribery charges brought against him, but was also attributable to Meacham's repetition to everyone he knew of his colleague's observation, made in a moment of frustration, that "the Utes were deserving of a good thrashing."

Mears submitted his report to Schurz and returned to Colorado. But before Schurz could evaluate and act upon it, President Garfield assumed office and replaced Schurz with Samuel Jordan Kirkwood, the former governor of Iowa. The new Secretary of the Interior, however, being informed of Mears' conduct, ordered him back to Washington at once to face charges of misconduct.

The hearing was presided over by Secretary Kirkwood with Nathaniel P. Hill and Henry M. Teller, Colorado's senators, in attendance. Mears was asked why he had, on his own accord, secured the ratification of the treaty by allegedly disreputable methods. He replied by describing the explosive situation in Colorado, the ineffectiveness of the Schurz commission and the complication of the situation by Ouray's death. He asserted that in order to convince the Northern and Uncompahgre Utes to move, thus preventing another Indian war, he had given the Indians $2 apiece so the treaty would be ratified and disaster averted. He added that his money given to the Utes was worth more to them than the government's empty promises.

Mears' defense greatly impressed Kirkwood, and resulted in his exoneration. The former's $2,800 in payments to the Utes had been his own money, and Kirkwood assured him a reimbursement if a voucher was made. It was evident that Congress was going to ratify the treaty and Kirkwood asked Mears about the possibility of Ute relocation on a new reservation. The latter said this would be possible, but that the task would be easier if Manypenny was kept in Ohio and Meacham in Washington. The secretary granted this request and promised to supply government troops to effect the removal, along with every assistance possible.

Mears, accompanied by Judge Thomas McMorris of Colorado Springs, who had been appointed by Kirkwood to replace Bowman on the commission, returned to the Uncompahgre. Mears was now in a precarious position with the Utes, who thought he was going to betray them. Dave Day announced Otto's homecoming in the March 27, 1881, *Solid Muldoon* as follows:

> Otto Mears will arrive at Los Pinos simultaneous with the arrival of the cavalry. The undying love the red brother had for Otto is now in keeping with Shavenaux's [*Shovwāno*] exalted regard for the Muldoon—won't do to travel out.

Notwithstanding this danger, Mears continued to fulfill his duties as commissioner. On June 4, 1881, he, McMorris and Russell—the remaining members of the commission—met with Indian Agent W.H. Berry, Chief Sapinero and Subchief Shovwāno. The commissioners told

45

the chiefs that there must be compliance with the terms of the treaty, and that a selection of five Ute representatives was needed to help find a new home for the tribe. The chiefs refused to comply with this request, whereupon Berry was forced to choose the five Indians. Berry ordered Shovwāno and four other influential Utes to accompany the commission members when they searched for the site for the new reservation.

On June 10, the commissioners, Berry and the five chiefs, escorted by 100 cavalrymen, began the search for a new home. The party went first to the Grand Junction site, where surveyors were already laying out forty-acre farms for the Indians. According to the treaty, the new reservation had to contain fertile land, and because the area visited was reported to have great agricultural potential, the authorities in Washington had decided to move the Utes there if the location was approved by the Ute leaders.

Mears and McMorris, however, determined that it would be in Colorado's best interest to get the Indians out of the state. Apparently, they manipulated, bribed or coerced the chiefs to say that the Grand Junction area was unsuitable for farming and that they wished to be located elsewhere.[6]

By forcing the Utes out of the state, Mears reasoned that not only would the Indian menace be gone but that new territory would be available for settlers. Commenting on this last point, the *Saguache Chronicle* of July 15, 1881, stated that in an interview Mears had predicted that the land in the Grand River region would someday be valuable and that he expected great numbers of settlers to come into that area.

Mears, remembering his profits in the area opened up by the Brunot Treaty, decided it would be greatly in his interest to move the Utes from western and northern Colorado so he could service the needs of future new settlers by toll roads and mercantile establishments. Whatever degree of self-interest he may have had in seeing the Utes removed, he and others knew it was both

MEARS WITH SOME OF THE INDIAN-WHITE PRINCIPALS
The Commissioner Met a Challenging Commitment

necessary and inevitable that the Indians be moved. In a letter written almost a half-century later, shortly before his death, Mears attempted to explain once and for all why he participated in moving the tribe from its centuries-old home:

> It was in my blood to want to see new furrows writhing from the plow ripping through the warm earth that had lain undisturbed since creation. This has always, to me, represented freedom to individual opportunity, for all wealth, as Adam Smith said, comes from the soil. A new land depends on its farmers. Had the Utes been an agricultural people, they would still be occupying Western Colorado. Ouray, my friend, saw this and on his farm on the Uncompahgre raised extensive crops to demonstrate to his people their security and salvation. But they would have none of it. And, like the useless tribes since the dawn of time, they had to move on.[7]

After the Grand River area was judged unacceptable for the reservation by the chiefs, the party went west into Utah and found a site agreeable to all at a spot 175 miles southeast of Salt Lake where the Green, the White and the Duchesne Rivers intersect. Mears claimed that the new area was "superior" to the old and that the Indians would enjoy the more plentiful supply of game and fish at the new spot. The new location, he asserted, would be adequate to the needs of Colorado residents also. It was separated from Colorado by a fifty-mile stretch of desert. And if this would not deter the Utes from returning to their old home, the troops stationed in Utah would.

When the news of the reservation's relocation reached Washington, Meacham and Manypenny were quite vociferous in their denunciation of Mears, stating that his movement of Utes to Utah had violated the treaty. Secretary Kirkwood, however, supported the Coloradoan. Kirkwood stated that the phrase "adjacent territory" did not necessarily mean the area in the vicinity of the Grand Junction site. Approving of the proposed location in Utah, he appointed Mears to construct the necessary buildings and to haul in a supply of food. The contractor then built a warehouse, a hospital, a carpenter's shop and a residence for the Indian agent near Green River. After preparing the new reservation site for occupation, he returned to the Los Pinos Agency to see how the removal of the Utes was progressing.

Upon his return to Colorado, Mears found that Col. Ranald Slidell MacKenzie, in charge of the Ute removal, was having difficulty in persuading the Indians to move to their new reservation. The Utes, playing for time, had given excuses for weeks, and claimed they were not yet prepared to go. MacKenzie, after allowing them more than enough time to pack their belongings and prepare food for their long journey, realized the Indians would have to be forcibly moved.

Accordingly, at two o'clock one morning, he awakened Mears and McMorris, asking them to sign the order for the removal of the Indians, and he would effect it with his troops. After approval was obtained, he surrounded the Utes with his soldiers and gave them two hours to prepare for their journey. About five a.m., the Unitah, White River and Uncompahgre Utes began their trip, and the last band left the state on September 1, 1881. On September 13, the Indians arrived at their new home, which they named Ouray in honor of their deceased chief. Several days later Mears came to the agency to inspect the provisions and to pay Ouray's widow, Chipeta, $700 owed by the government to her late husband. Upon seeing Mears, Cojoe, a chief, tried to murder him, maintaining that he was responsible for the removal of the Indians from Colorado. After this assassination attempt Mears decided to leave. The *Ouray Times* of October 8, 1881, carried this note about his departure:

> Otto Mears came near getting his hair raised by the White River Utes, thirsting for blood. He narrowly escaped by traveling in the night across the mountains and through canons. The Indians are spoiling for a fight, and should be accommodated.[8]

The attempts on his life by the Indians did not prevent Mears from serving another year and a half as an Indian commissioner. He devoted a great deal of his time to it until his resignation from the commission in April, 1882, only too glad to concentrate his attention on the four things he loved most—transportation, politics, poker and women.

Mears was successful in removing the Indians from Colorado because he used bribery, coercion and manipulation. It is easy to condemn him for using such methods to dispossess a helpless people. The facts of the case, however, demand a more sophisticated evaluation of his conduct. He foresaw, after the Meeker Massacre, that an Indian-white war was almost inevitable. With the Utes hopelessly outnumbered and outgunned, they would have been wiped out in such a confrontation. Mears recognized the need for the Indians' relocation for their own protection.

He thought the Grand Junction area unsuitable for a reservation because its rich farmlands would induce the whites to eventually encroach upon Indian domain once again. He moved the red men to a site in Utah so remote from settled areas that they would be safe, he thought, for all time to come.

The Indians had to be both tricked and forced to leave Colorado, but they were not aware of their great danger in the situation and consequently failed to appreciate what Mears had done for them. Most Coloradoans also did not recognize the magnitude of his achievement. By using his considerable diplomatic skills he not only kept a lid on an explosive situation, but he virtually solved Colorado's Indian problem for all time. What enabled him to attain these results was the rare capacity to easily see a problem's solution and to effect it regardless of the cost.

His actions as Indian commissioner not only contributed to Colorado's growth but proved personally profitable as well. In his official capacity, he was given front-page exposure in every newspaper in the state. This coverage was not always flattering, but the publicity was invaluable. Instead of being merely one of the Republican party's several political bosses, he was now a household name and within one year after the removal, he had a large enough following to be elected a state legislator. Within two and a half years, he was the undisputed leader of the state's Republican party.

Mears, while complaining in newspapers that he had lost money by devoting his attention to public affairs for three and a half years, actually made a huge profit from the crisis after the Meeker Massacre. He was paid well as a commissioner, and in addition, he augmented his salary by fulfilling contracts to build and supply the new reservation at Green River. Nor was this all. He earned $100,000 from toll fees paid by the soldiers in the two-year period after the massacre.[9] This money was quite useful to him in subsequent elections. Politics is an expensive game, and he could not be a full-fledged participant without a large source of personal funds. Being well-funded, he could utilize to the maximum the publicity he received as an Indian commissioner. After 1881, he participated in politics more than ever before. He was to acquire such an iron-fisted control of the Republican party that he was able to claim that no governor or senator could be elected without his support.

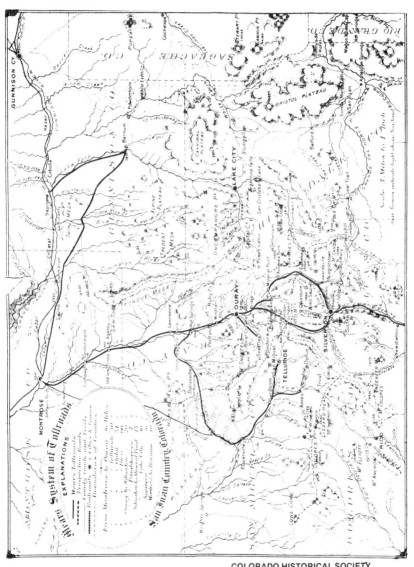

1886 MAP OF MEARS' TOLL ROAD SYSTEM

3

The Golden Stair Route

*J*n late spring of 1881, when it became apparent that the Ute removal would be accomplished, Otto Mears decided it was time to begin devoting some attention to his own affairs. He found time in the months preceding the explusion of the Indians to organize and finance two new toll road companies. Both of these companies were incorporated on May 31, 1881. The first was called the Dallas and San Miguel Toll Road Company. It was capitalized at $25,000, had a twenty-year life, and its directors, besides Mears, were Ouray merchants Ira and Charles Munn. The object of the company was to build a road from the town of Dallas in Ouray County to Telluride, a distance of about 27 miles. Dallas was at this time an important town because it was the junction of the route south to Ouray and west to the mines on the San Miguel River and its tributaries. The San Miguel area was characterized by rich ore deposits, and Telluride came to be a typical Rocky Mountain mining camp, as the following quotation from the August 17, 1883, issue of Ouray's *Solid Muldoon* suggests: "Telluride has seven lawyers and two dance halls; 0 church[es] and 000 school houses. Mercy, what a wicked village!" The toll road, completed in mid-September, was well constructed with grades of only 10 percent, a reflection of Mears' increasing expertise in mountain engineering. Its two toll gates were established at Haskell and at Keystone Hill.

The San Miguel and Rico Toll Road Company was the second organization incorporated on May 31, 1881, by Mears. This corporation, like the Dallas and San Miguel Toll Road Company, was capitalized by the Munn brothers and Mears with $25,000 in capital stock. The corporation was organized to build a road from Telluride to Rico. Rico was a thriving mining town with rich ore deposits which Mears had originally hoped to reach in 1879 when he incorporated the Uncompahgre, San Miguel and Dolores Toll Road Company. The Meeker Massacre had prevented any road building that summer and the project was deferred. The new company, like the former one, did not succeed in building a road to Rico, perhaps because the people of Rico did not offer enough inducements. Only a six-mile stretch of road was built from Vance Junction, a new townsite near Telluride named after Capt. J.W. Vance who owned an adjoining farm, to Ames at the mouth of the San Miguel River's Howard Fork. It was completed in the summer of 1882.

Although the San Miguel and Rico Toll Road scheme was unsuccessful, Mears was not deterred from investing in yet another toll road venture. On October 26, 1881, he incorporated the Durango, Parrott City and Fort Lewis Toll Road Company. A sum of $15,000 was to be raised by the directors—who included Otto Mears and the San Juan merchants Charles Munn and A.M. Camp—to build a road from Durango to Parrott City by way of Fort Lewis. Mears had purchased an old roadbed in September, 1880, which he now used for this project. He thought the acquisition would be a good investment because of Durango's seemingly great potential in 1880. The Denver and Rio Grande Railroad management planned to build to Durango—a community of the railroad's own creation— and give the fertile Animas Valley area an outlet to the east and north. Besides the railroad, another potential stimulus to Durango's growth was the stationing of 600 troops at the new location of Fort Lewis, a few miles west of Durango, after the Meeker Massacre. Desiring to capitalize upon Durango's growth, Mears decided in the fall of 1881 that the old road he had purchased was inadequate for the needs of the burgeoning city. He began improving it at once and construction was finished in the following spring. Upon completion, it was sold for a very high price to Col. Peter Tyler Swaine, an army officer. It was sold to La Plata County in 1890 for $2,500.

In the winter of 1881-1882, when the construction crew was finishing the Durango, Parrott City and Fort Lewis Toll Road, Mears became involved in still another toll road venture. In January, 1882, he visited Gunnison to determine if the spectacularly growing mining town presented any chance for profitable investment. Gunnison had "grown from a sage brush patch" to a city of 5,000, and its most optimistic boomers predicted it would become the second largest city in Colorado after Denver. After inspecting the metropolis, the road builder went to Cebolla, a tributary camp 26 miles west of Gunnison, which had the richest iron deposits in the state. Mears had first become interested in the area in 1879 and as a result incorporated the Saguache and San Juan Toll Road Company. At that time, he had planned to build the road from Cebolla to a point on the Tomichi River where it intersected his Poncha, Marshall and Gunnison Toll Road. He was not, however, able to build this road. The Meeker Massacre occurred less than a month after the company was incorporated, and Mears was forced to devote nearly his full time to Ute-white relations for the next two years.

Miners in Cebolla were in great need of a road to transport the millions of tons of iron ore being mined. In consequence, a flamboyant character named Sylvester Richardson constructed a road along the route of Mears' proposed toll road. Richardson, a colony planner, prospector and road builder, found that this road was such a prosperous venture he did not have time to manage it properly, and sold it to Mears in 1882. Although total construction costs amounted to $2,000, the buyer purchased it for half this price, "a business deal" asserted one historian, "altogether too typical of Richardson."[1]

The purchase of the Gunnison-Cebolla toll road was Mears' only new toll road venture for the ensuing year and a half. He spent most of his time between January, 1882, and the summer of 1883 immersed in political activities. During this period, he served as a representative from Saguache to the Fourth General Assembly convened in Denver in January, 1883.

Completion of the legislative session brought time for new additions to Mears' toll road system. He incorporated the Ouray and Canyon Creek Toll Road Company on August 20, 1883. Capitalized at $30,000, this corporation was organized to build a road approximately ten miles long from Ouray to the Mount Sneffels district. Mount Sneffels was an area extremely rich in valuable ore, and many unsuccessful attempts had been made to connect it by road to Ouray. The rough terrain necessitated road beds too precipitous for ordinary travel. Between 1876 and 1880 there had been four successive companies incorporated to build toll roads from Ouray to Mount Sneffels, but the task was so difficult that no construction was completed. A fifth toll road company—called the Mount Sneffels and Ouray Toll Road Company—was organized in February, 1880. It was more successful and built a road between the towns of Ouray and Sneffels. This road was so poorly constructed, however, that it soon became evident to residents of the two towns that a better road was necessary. It was at this juncture that Mears decided to build his road, as it seemed an obviously profitable venture.

In mid-August, 1883, the proposed Ouray and Canyon Creek Toll Road was surveyed. It was decided, because of the difficulty of the project, to divide the work into two parts. Bad weather beginning in early fall did not permit completion of the road until the following summer. The first part was finished about mid-September, 1883, and the remaining portion completed a year later.

The Ouray and Canyon Creek Toll Road, when finished, was an engineering triumph. Having average grades of 3 to 11 percent and, at the steepest places only 13 percent, it was one of the best-built roads in the Rocky Mountains.

Although Mears had done both Ouray and the Mount Sneffels district a service in building the road, there were soon many complaints about the high toll rates charged. He decided to sell the road to Ouray County in return for county bonds. The transaction was made in 1885 or 1886. When the matter became known to the taxpayers of Ouray County, they complained that Mears had been given too much for the road and that the transaction had been made without their knowledge or consent. The citizens of the mountain town demanded a judicial inquiry into the affair and received one.

What happened next is unclear. Mears, in his memoirs, gives a very muddled account of this episode. Evidently, the judge ruled that the sale was illegal and Mears was forced to appeal the case the following year. Using his influence with a state legislator, Mears was able to obtain a non-jury trial, and the new judge ruled in his favor and declared the Mears-Ouray County transaction legal. The Ouray and Canyon Creek Toll Road was accordingly sold to Ouray County in return for bonds.

Back in the early months of 1882 while Mears had been planning the Ouray and Canyon Creek Toll Road venture, he became interested in constructing another Ouray toll road. This new scheme involved the building of a road from Ouray to the Red Mountain mining district, a distance of 12 miles. Red Mountain was an area more than 11,000 feet in elevation, almost inaccessible from Ouray. In the decade prior to 1882, before the fabulously rich Yankee Girl Mine was discovered, the area had been prospected with mixed success. The discovery of the Yankee Girl marked a new era for the district. A great influx of people poured into the area and the rush became the largest in Colorado since Leadville. Reporting on the rapid growth of Red Mountain, Dave Day stated that:

> Never in the history of the San Juan country
> has a camp made such wonderful strides in the
> direction of permanent prosperity as Red Moun-

tain. Three weeks ago there was not a building to be seen on the spot where Ironton now stands. Over one hundred buildings of various dimensions under headway, and the inevitable dance house in full blast.[2]

The rapid growth of the Red Mountain region made the construction of better roads to the area imperative. Situated midway between the towns of Silverton and Ouray, Red Mountain was virtually isolated in winter because of the rugged terrain and the frequent avalanches on all sides. During the remainder of the year, the prohibitive freight rates caused only the richest ore to be transported out. It was obvious, therefore, to the residents of Ouray and Silverton that it would be extremely profitable to build a toll road to Red Mountain because the revenue accruing from the freight charges would more than defray the costs of the venture.

Silverton, it appeared, had easier access to Red Mountain; the terrain south of Red Mountain made building a toll road in that direction more feasible. The townspeople did not take advantage of their geographical edge, however. Ouray—with greater natural obstacles to overcome—was more enterprising and began building first, and was thus the first to reap the benefits of a toll road to Red Mountain. This task, however, was only accomplished after the expenditure of enormous sums of money and effort had been coupled with the engineering genius of Otto Mears.

Before Mears became interested in the project, two abortive attempts had been made to build a Ouray-Red Mountain road. The first corporative effort was launched in 1877, but lack of capitalization resulted in bankruptcy a year later. In 1880, the Ouray and San Juan Wagon Road Company was incorporated for the purpose of building a road to Red Mountain Park by way of Mineral City and Poughkeepsie Gulch. The terrain was so difficult that the company attracted few investors. The probable returns did not seem to justify the necessary heavy cash outlay, and the corporation was finally taken over by the Ouray

58

County Commissioners. The discovery of the rich deposits of ore at the Yankee Girl mine in August, 1882, and the resulting Red Mountain rush made Ouray County even more desirous of completing the Ouray and Red Mountain toll road, but the commissioners could not raise enough money to complete the task.

At this juncture, the commissioners invited Mears to examine the work already done on the project. They asked him to look at the financial records of the Ouray and San Juan Wagon Road Company to determine whether it would be profitable for him to complete the project. After doing the necessary research, he decided that not only would it be possible to build the road, despite the rugged country, but that it would be extremely profitable for him to do so. On June 14, 1883, he agreed to build the road, in return for controlling interest in the Ouray and San Juan Wagon Road Company.

Upon the completion of negotiations with the county commissioners, Mears was ready to embark upon what was to be the most difficult toll road construction he ever attempted. The principal problem, besides financing, was building a road bed in Uncompahgre Canyon. In the canyon there were two possible road bed sites—at the canyon floor near the Uncompahgre River, or in the cliffs high above the river. If the road bed were constructed on the canyon floor, the turbulent Uncompahgre River would wash it away. It seemed equally impractical to blast through the quartzite cliffs 800 feet above the canyon floor because of the expense and the great danger to the laborers, who could be killed or injured by dynamite charges necessary in the construction.

Mears finally solved the construction problems posed by Uncompahgre Canyon. He decided to blast a road bed into the quartzite cliffs by lowering men on ropes from the rim of the canyon, thereby constructing hundreds of feet above the canyon floor a longer-lasting road than could be built at the canyon bottom. The dynamite charges were to be equipped with fuses long enough to allow men to be pulled to safety before the explosives were ignited. This was to be a workable but expensive solution. A quarter-mile stretch, for example, blasted just south of Bear Creek Falls at an average height of 580 feet above the canyon floor cost more than $1,000 a foot.

The road was finished in mid-September, 1883. At a cost of nearly $10,000 per mile, it was probably the finest achievement in toll road engineering in the United States. The road's easy grades—less than 11 percent—made it economically feasible to haul the ore hitherto relegated to dumps. To facilitate the hauling of ore by team-drawn wagons, Mears planned an ingenious system whereby ore cars would be put on an iron railway built on the side of the toll road, filled, and then be rolled downhill from Red Mountain to Ouray. There, the cars would be emptied and then pulled by horses back up to Red Mountain. The iron railway scheme proved impractical, however, and it was never built.

Despite the abortive iron railway scheme, Otto earned much money from the Ouray and San Juan Toll Road. He added to his profits by operating a hotel at Bear Creek Falls. During the summer and early fall, the hotel was filled with tourists attracted to the area by the beautiful mountain scenery. A description of the scenery was written by the rugged frontier editor David F. Day who, in the following quotation, more nearly reached poetry than in any other writing in a journalistic career that lasted nearly 40 years:

> In point of scenic grandeur the road is un-equaled on the continent. Leaving the mountain-clad village of Ouray, it ascends by serpentine and easy grade to a level with bluffs above town, where it winds in a southerly direction around cliffs, through wooded parks and over bridges spanning wild and romantic gulches to Bear Creek Falls: here the route passes over the head of the roaring cataract, 253 feet above the boiling cataract below, and entering the quartzite bluffs coils round them upon a bed of solid rock from 600 to 800 feet above the river, for a distance of

60

TOLL GATE AT BEAR CREEK FALLS
A Picturesque—and Effective—Collection Point

61

two miles, when the Uncompahgre river is crossed. At this point is afforded one of the grandest views in all the land. A few hundred yards below the waters of the Uncompahgre and Red Mountain creek join and go roaring down a box canyon on either side of which is margined with precipitous bluffs of red sandstone, dark slate and bright quartzite capped with mountains, crags and peaks of gray trachyte, reaching from their quartzite base into the land of perpetual snow.[3]

Mears operated the Ouray and San Juan Toll Road for a little more than eight years when he was forced, due to the complaints about his way of running the enterprise, to sell it to Ouray County. The principal point of contention were the exhorbitant toll rates charged on the road. Most people who used the road believed that it was outrageous to be assessed $5 for a team and wagon, $2.50 for a trail wagon and $1 apiece for saddle animals. One irate customer expressed his displeasure by throwing a chain over the toll gate and hauling it away. In 1891, after years of haggling, Mears sold the Ouray and San Juan Toll Road to Ouray County at a price less than the cost of building. He exercised his influence on the Twelfth Assembly to have a bill passed that would reimburse him for construction costs on the road, but the governor, Charles S. Thomas, vetoed the measure for political reasons.

The construction of the Ouray and San Juan Toll Road caused great consternation among the people of Silverton. With all the rich Red Mountain ore being shipped through Ouray, Silverton faced economic disaster unless it, too, could build a road to Red Mountain. The Silverton newspapers reflected the mood of the townspeople and editorials alternated between boasts about the town's potential and despair about its bleak future. Dave Day thoroughly enjoyed seeing the people of Silverton suffer because he felt that they were not as enterprising as the residents of Ouray. After reading one particular misleading article in the *La Plata Miner*, he commented that "Silverton has a boom. We saw it going by, a few days since— three gamblers, two women and a 'yaller dog.' "

The city fathers of Silverton finally realized that to compete with Ouray they would have to build a road to Red Mountain. They knew that only one man in the Rocky Mountains, Otto Mears, had the capital and the expertise to build the road. But most, at first, did not want him to do the job. Mears' detractors, led by editor of the *La Plata Miner* George Raymond, believed that Silverton could not afford the road as the town was already in debt. If Mears built the road, it would just increase his toll road monopoly and he would charge the same high rates on the proposed road as he did on his others. Raymond also believed that what was really needed was a railroad between Silverton and Red Mountain. If the Denver and Rio Grande Railroad would not build one, he thought someone who would charge less exhorbitant rates than Mears should be found to build a road between the two points. [4]

The Denver and Rio Grande Railroad officials refused to build a connection between Silverton and Red Mountain because it seemed financially unsound. Since no one could be found to build a toll road between the two points, Silverton's leaders were forced to ask Mears to consider the job. He went to the scene in early fall 1883 and examined the terrain the proposed route would cross. After a conference with the local officials, he agreed to build the road.

"The hatchet is buried," announced the *Solid Muldoon* after Day learned of the verbal contract between Mears and the town of Silverton. The editor then listed the terms of the agreement. In return for building a toll road between Silverton and Red Mountain, Mears would receive $25,000 in municipal and county bonds. It was also understood that he would have complete control over the operation of the toll road. The arrangement, Day asserted, would be beneficial to both parties, as the outlet to the Red Mountain mines would help make Silverton prosperous and the road builder would earn a good return upon his investment.

Although Mears and the county commissioners had

made a verbal contract it was still necessary to put it in writing to make it binding. Before both parties signed the written agreement on June 28, 1884, there was much maneuvering to make the agreement more favorable to each side.

Mears wanted a contract that would give him as much latitude as possible. An editorial in the *Silverton Democrat* commented on his efforts to avoid a binding contract:

> Mr. Mears' forte is in having contracts that will shrink or swell as the weather is wet or dry, and that seem one way by the sun and another way by the moon.[5]

This same editorial charged that Mears, in order to gain favorable toll road contracts, had seen to it that county commissioners of both Ouray and San Juan counties would be elected only if he could easily manipulate them.

When the contract, after hard bargaining, was signed in late June, 1884, the terms of the verbal contract made the preceding fall were kept, but the following stipulations were added:

1. There should be a continuous down grade from the summit [of Red Mountain Pass] to Silverton.
2. The maximum grade should be no more than 350 feet to the mile.
3. There should be no curves so sharp as to prevent six animals from exerting their whole force upon the load at every point.
4. The width of the road should be such as to allow teams to pass each other at all points.
5. Ample provision should be made for drainage and for protection to winter traffic.[6]

Mears began building the Silverton-Red Mountain Toll Road on July 8, 1884, a little more than a week after signing the contract. He hired 350 men to work on the road and the construction went rapidly, despite the rugged terrain. It was completed in late November.

The opening of the road was the occasion of a large celebration. A group of distinguished Ouray residents interested in booming the San Juan region arrived in Silverton on December 5. A banquet followed, during which speeches of congratulations were given by some of the guests; after the banquet, a dance was conducted, open to everyone.

The people of Silverton had good reason for the merry-making. The new toll road, besides making travel between Ouray and Silverton easier, also lessened freight rates on products hauled between the towns. It also was less expensive to haul ore down into the towns from the mines on Red Mountain. As a result it became profitable to move lower grade ore off dumps and send it to smelters.

With the freight charge decrease, mine owners were encouraged to transport already mined low grade ore. This encouraged the discovery of new ore deposits. The Red Mountain area boomed and continued to do so for more than a decade.

The roads between Ouray and Silverton became famous not only because of their impact on the economy of the region's mountain towns but because of the beauty of the country they traversed and because they were extremely well-engineered. They were the best designed, most carefully constructed and most expensive roads ever built in the Rocky Mountains. As the roads became more well-known, they acquired picturesque nicknames that gradually replaced the names originally given by Mears. Within a few years after construction both roads were called the "Rainbow Route," a name given by Dave Day to describe their rainbow-like shape. Later, the roads became popularly known as the "Million Dollar Highway." This nickname was acquired because of the popular belief that the roads cost a million dollars to build, and has also been attributed to the rich mineral resources of the area through which the roads pass.

During the summer of 1884, while he was overseeing the construction of the Silverton and Red Mountain Toll Road, Mears was approached by the commissioners of San Juan County, who had another toll road proposition.

This new scheme involved the building of a road from Silverton to Mineral Point by way of Howardsville, Eureka and Animas Forks.

A road owned by the county already existed between Silverton and Mineral Point, but it was in very poor condition. It cost the county $3,000 to $4,000 yearly to repair the road, and the annual spring flood of the Animas River dumped tons of debris over the road which could not be cleared. Consequently, travel on this road was difficult, particularly for wagons. Several wagons had been abandoned in the mire between Silverton and Animas Forks, and the occasional successful teamster who managed to get his wagon into Silverton from points higher up on the Animas River would become so encased in mud as to be unrecognizable. The mean elevation of this challenging road was in the neighborhood of 10,000 feet above sea level.

Bad roads, the county commissioners realized, prevented full development of the mining towns along the upper Animas River since low grade ore from these places could not be transported profitably into Silverton. A better road would encourage more investment in the area and make the entire county more prosperous, they reasoned. In consequence, they were willing to make financial sacrifices as inducement to have the road built. They offered Mears the old road plus $15,000 in county warrants, plus complete control over the new road if he would build one.

The proposition of the county commissioners was so attractive that Mears agreed to the terms of the plan and signed a preliminary contract in August, 1884, and a final contract in October. He could not start work on the new toll road until the following spring, as he was in the process of completing the Silverton and Red Mountain Toll Road.

After completion of the toll road on November 21, 1884, Mears had time to devote to other toll road ventures. While waiting for good weather so he could begin construction of the Silverton and Animas Forks Toll Road, he decided his profits would be increased on his Saguache and San Juan Toll Road if an extension were built. The extension would stretch the road to the Denver and Rio Grande Railroad on the Gunnison River. Accordingly, he incorporated the Sapinero and Barnum Toll Road Company on December 2, 1884. This road was completed in the summer of the following year at a cost of $10,000 and proved to be an extremely lucrative investment.

There was simultaneous construction on the Sapinero and Barnum Toll road and the Silverton and Animas Forks Toll Road in the summer of 1885. Mears, Fred Walsen and H.E. Wheeler, the underwriters of the Sapinero and Barnum Toll Road Company, incorporated the Silverton and Animas Forks Toll Road Company on July 31, 1885.

While the Silverton and Animas Forks Toll Road Company was being organized, the route of the toll road was surveyed and road work begun. The building began at Silverton and went rapidly, and by mid-July, 1885, the road was completed as far as Eureka. The stretch from Eureka to Mineral Point, however, presented many more construction problems than the Silverton-Eureka part of the road. The main objective was to build the road in such a way that snow slides would not injure the road during the spring run-off. While building the road up on the slopes partially solved the problem of snow slides, many engineering problems were presented and construction was protracted until early October, 1886, when the Animas Forks-Mineral Point section of the road was finished. This road was operated profitably by Mears until 1896 when it was sold to his Silverton Northern Railroad Company for use as a track bed.

The Silverton and Animas Forks Toll Road was the last toll road ever built by Mears and its completion marks a watershed in his life. For the decade and a half previous to 1886, his principal achievements in transportation had been in the construction of these toll roads; in the future he would be primarily interested in the construction and operation of railroads.

His toll road achievements were considerable. Since

1870, he had built a network of roads almost 450 miles long at a cost of approximately $400,000. This toll road system had enormous impact upon southwestern Colorado. Settlers and freight could be moved into the area cheaply and a lower grade of ore could be profitably shipped out. It was no accident that the San Juan region experienced a period of dramatic growth during the operation of his toll roads.

As important as Mears' achievements in toll road construction were, they were always exaggerated by him as he enjoyed playing the role of San Juan's benefactor. He claimed, for example, except to close business associates, that he built the roads at a loss and that he never made a profit from them.[7]

This assertion was not even remotely true. He never explained why a man of his known business acumen would continue to build toll roads if they were unprofitable. A detailed cost accounting of Mears' financial affairs was done by Robert Weitbrec in 1887. Weitbrec was a railroad man and speculator from southern Colorado who wanted to invest in the Silverton Railroad, which Mears was then building. Weitbrec examined Mears' business records to determine the degree of his managerial ability. During the course of his investigation he uncovered revealing information about Otto's toll road operation. Weitbrec found that in 1887 Mears still operated six toll roads, of which he owned 55.12 percent, worth $113,000. Fred Walsen, the other major stockholder, had invested $86,000 and owned 41.94 percent of the stock. In order to calculate the net return upon investment, Weitbrec listed the earnings and expenses to determine the net profit. This list, reproduced here, discloses much about the operation of Mears' toll road system.

In addition to the good financial return of the toll roads, Mears derived other benefits from them. In building these roads he earned the gratitude of the people in the San Juan area, which was repaid politically in the support of Mears' election candidates. In 1926, the *Rocky Mountain News* described Mears' hold over the San Juan:

In political affairs in this state for a number of years, Mr. Mears was the balance of power in Republican state conventions, and without his consent neither governor nor senator could be chosen because he held in the hollow of his hand a tier of southwestern counties which, cast solidly, turned the convention one way or the other.[8]

Associated with the building of toll roads was packing and freighting in which Mears had been involved since the late 1860s. The bulk of this packing and freighting was done to fulfill Indian contracts, but by 1885 he decided it would be profitable to freight ore down from Red Mountain into Silverton, which the Denver and Rio Grande Railroad had reached in the summer of 1882. Accordingly, on October 2, 1884, Mears—together with Fred Walsen and Silverton entrepreneur J.L. Pennington—incorporated the Mears Transportation Company. This firm, capitalized with only $6,000, soon became the largest freighting company in Colorado.

In 1885, the company hauled 12,550 tons of ore from Red Mountain, still leaving large amounts of ore in dumps waiting for removal. In 1886, the capital stock was raised from $6,000 to $50,000 so that more teams and wagons

WEITBREC ANALYSIS OF MEARS' TOLL ROAD FINANCES[9]		
Toll Road	Earnings	Expenses
Ouray and Lake Fork	$12,471.57	$ 3,110.00
Dallas and San Miguel	9,394.35	5,232.72
Ouray and San Juan	6,073.35	1,983.36
Ouray and Canyon Creek	3,660.28	2,310.33
Silverton-Red Mountain	1,581.08	462.10
Silverton-Animas Forks	684.82	1,028.20
	$33,865.45	$14,126.71
Net:	$19,738.74	
Miscellaneous earnings:	7,569.80	
Total Net:	$27,308.54	
Approximate return of cash invested: 13 percent		

could be purchased. The new equipment enabled the company to ship 18,150 tons of Red Mountain ore in 1886; in the following year, even more was shipped. Though his company was hauling immense amounts of freight, Mears found that animal power was too slow to service Red Mountain and decided to build a railroad from Silverton to the mining district. When the railroad was completed in 1889, the Mears Transportation Company merged with it and Mears from then on had little or nothing to do with wagon freighting.

The diversity of Mears' interests is illustrated by his involvement about this time with experimental modifications in the smoking pipe, discussed by his friend Dave Day in the January 28, 1887, issue of the *Solid Muldoon:*

Otto Mears is the patentee of a smoking pipe that will revolutionize things in Smokeville. The stem, which can be cleaned in a second's time, is the main feature. The laboratory where the Pathfinder does his experimenting is elaborate in its belongings and convenient by reason of its accessibility. It is situated on the roof of his five-story mansion in Denver.

In 1886-87—the Silverton Railroad still in the future—Mears engaged in mining and town-planning schemes using the revenue from the Mears Transportation Company and his toll roads to subsidize the ventures. In October, 1886, he decided to lease the Buckeye Mine in Silver Lake Basin, a few miles from Silverton, at a small annual rent. The mine owners had gone into debt and, not realizing the huge amount of ore in the mines, let Mears assume control. A year and a half later, finding deposits overlooked by the previous operators, he was in possession of one of the most productive mines in the San Juan.

Mears' next business deal was much less successful than the Buckeye Mine investment. This new scheme involved the Ramona Town Company, incorporated December 15, 1886, for the purpose of laying out a townsite and selling the lots to settlers. Ramona was located only four miles north of Ouray, but it was at a spot easily reached from Montrose. The residents of Ouray had been trying to persuade the officials of the Denver and Rio Grande Railroad to build an extension from Montrose to their town since 1883. In 1886, before the incorporation of the Ramona Town Company, the railroad's officers promised to build the extension. It became apparent, however, to Dave Day and Otto Mears, that the Ouray extension would not be built because of the cost.

Mears and Day believed that unless Ouray could obtain a railroad it would be doomed. They decided to start a new town—Ramona—that would be more accessible from Montrose. The site they chose was 6,800 feet in elevation with good water, hot springs and magnificent scenery. After incorporation, the townsite company of Ramona (later called Chipeta) sold many lots and seemed assured success when William S. Jackson, president of the Denver and Rio Grande Railroad, promised to build an extension of the railroad to the townsite from Montrose.

Subsequent developments, however, proved fatal to the townsite scheme. Jackson was replaced as president of the Denver and Rio Grande by David Moffat. Moffat, a Denver mining magnate, was one of the original stockholders of the Ramona Town Company, and seemingly should have done everything possible to further its interests when he became president of the Denver and Rio Grande. This did not prove to be the case. Six months later he decided, following an old Denver and Rio Grande management practice, that if the citizens of Ouray would raise the necessary funds, the railroad would be extended to that point. When the residents of the existing mountain hamlet concurred with Moffat's proposal, the Ramona townsite company was doomed; prospective settlers saw no reason to move to an undeveloped spot when Ouray was just four miles away. The directors of the Ramona Town Company dissolved the company and returned the money to those who had already purchased lots. These investors still lost the interest on their money, however, and those who had constructed buildings were not reimbursed. The only director or investor in the company to salvage anything from the abortive townsite idea was Dave Day. Ramona became the site of Day's farm and ranch where he vacationed to get a respite from the pressures of his newspaper business.

Undaunted by the failure of his Ramona townsite venture, Mears embarked on what was until 1889 his most difficult project—The Silverton Railroad. When completed in 1889, it connected Silverton and Albany, on Red Mountain, by following the roadbed of his Silverton and Red Mountain Toll Road.

Mears had become interested in building a railroad to Red Mountain when he discovered that the Mears Transportation Company was unable to carry all the ore mined at that place. He had long known that team-drawn vehicles were too slow and troublesome to be efficient in hauling ore and freight over the precipitious roads in the San Juan Mountains.

In the early months of 1887, Mears made a careful survey of the Red Mountain mines to determine the profitability of operating a railroad there. He estimated if a railroad were built, Red Mountain would ship 170,975 tons of ore annually, and would carry as many as 12,000 passengers a year. In addition, he calculated that the railroad would haul 1,700 tons of freight and mail a year. After careful consideration, he estimated his gross earnings on the proposed twelve-mile railroad to be $10.86 per mile. After expenses the railroad would net approximately $2.12 per mile.

Such calculations excited Otto. At the time, one dollar net per railroad mile was considered a good return upon investment, but two was unusually lucrative, and if the railroad was built it would be one of the most profitable in the world. As a result, he began the organization of a company to build the railroad. Although he tried to keep his activities concerning the proposed railroad secret, rumors circulated about a big project in the planning stages. Dave Day, in his usual tongue-in-cheek manner, suggested that something was afoot:

It is rumored that Otto Mears will carry freight from Marshall Basin to Silverton by balloons. While we don't believe in all the rumors floating about, still this seems to be reasonable and practicable that we are satisfied that Otto has told some one of his scheme and they have let the cat out of the bag, hence the green cheese in the moon. Otto certainly has a scheme of some kind brewing. [10]

Three weeks before the appearance of Day's story, Mears had completed the final arrangements for the organization of the railroad. On July 8, 1887, in association with J.H. Ernest Waters, manager of the Sheridan Mine, John A. Porter of the Durango Mining and Smelting Company and George Crawford, part owner of the Yankee Girl Mine, Mears incorporated the Silverton Railroad Company. According to the articles of incorporation, the company was to have a capital stock of $150,000 (later to be increased to $350,000). The money was to be used to build a railroad from Silverton to Ouray following the roadbeds of the Silverton and Red Mountain and the Ouray and San Juan Toll Roads. The first officers, according to the charter, were Otto Mears, president; George Crawford, vice president; John W. Wingate, secretary; and Fred Walsen, treasurer.

When word of the incorporation finally reached the San Juan mining towns, Mears' friends ridiculed the idea of building a railroad to Red Mountain. They asked him if he remembered that, despite an 1883 survey to Red Mountain, the Denver and Rio Grande Railroad had not built there because of high costs and difficult engineering problems. Weather was another problem which made the project foolish according to Dave Day, who claimed that:

Mears will wake up some storming morning and find that his Silverton-Chatanooga [sic] summer route has bumped up against one of the Polar region's semi-daily slides and gone over to Ophir on a vacation. Railroading around Silverton is about as profitable as engaging in some townsite schemes [*Day is referring to Ramona*] that we have heard of.[11]

Such criticism only made Mears more adamant in his desire to build the railroad. Undaunted, he began the process of building the railroad. A fortnight after the new corporation was formed, grading began, was quickly finished, and tracklaying was started. An unusually rainy summer prevented more than 5.3 miles of track—from Silverton to Burro Bridge—from being laid and work was discontinued until the following summer.

Building was renewed in late May, 1888, at Burro Bridge. By the time the construction season ended in mid-November, the track was finished as far as Ironton. The remaining one and a half miles were completed to Albany in 1889. Mears planned to extend the railroad to Ouray after raising more money and making a survey of the route. He found that the necessary funds would be forthcoming, but that it was impossible to lay track any farther because of the precipitious grades, although he went so far as to buy a site for a depot and warehouse in Ouray in 1887.

Though Mears was frustrated in his attempt to extend the Silverton Railroad, he felt justifiably proud of the railroad building. Because of the ingenious way difficulties of mountain railroading were overcome, the road represented an engineering triumph. Grades of five percent and track laid in almost serpentine fashion on the jagged surface were features of the construction. Even more spectacular were the two loops and the four switchbacks. One switchback was built at Red Mountain as there was no room for a loop, and the second was constructed at Corkscrew Gulch. The third and fourth switchbacks were built at the Yankee Girl Mine. The switchback at Corkscrew Gulch attracted much attention from engineers because a turntable, to save space, was located on the main track.

Although many tourists traveled on the Silverton Railroad to see the novel solutions to problems of mountain railroad construction and to observe the magnificent

FIRST PASSENGER TRAIN AT RED MOUNTAIN TOWN

Noteable Turnout for an Inaugural Run

75

scenery, the Silverton Railroad was built primarily to service the Red Mountain mines. The building of the line spurred investment in the mining district since it was now possible to ship low grade ores profitably. Real estate prices in the area were affected as well. In Ironton, for example, after the railroad reached there in November, 1888, prices on lots jumped 25 percent. The railroad had even more impact on the towns of Silverton and Durango. Silverton prospered because it became the supply center for the Red Mountain area and Durango thrived because its coal fields became a source of fuel for the mining region. Conversely, ore and concentrates passed to both communities for refinement.

Because of the daring and imagination which inspired the Silverton Railroad and the financial success which attended its completion, the railroad captured the attention of many of the residents of the San Juan. Dave Day, who in 1887 believed that building a railroad to Red Mountain was a foolish undertaking, became in 1889 its greatest booster. He became fascinated with the railroad and devoted much space in the *Solid Muldoon* to accounts of the activities of its officials. In these stories, he coined some of the most picturesque names ever given to an American railroad. At one time or another he called the railroad "the Golden Stair Route," "the Isaac Short Line," "the Serpentine Whizzer" and "the Muldoon Short Line." Day also nicknamed the railroad the "Rainbow Route" because the tracks made a bow on Red Mountain. This nickname was the most popular of the many given to the line, and was incorporated in the railroad's official herald for advertising purposes.

Day's enthusiasm for the railroad was shared by almost everyone in the San Juan. Silverton ladies, who lived along the route, did not feel the nearly universal enthusiasm for the railroad, however. They complained that their equestrian sports were disturbed whenever a train appeared.

Mears seemed oblivious to the reaction of the San Juan residents to his railroad. He was too busy operating his

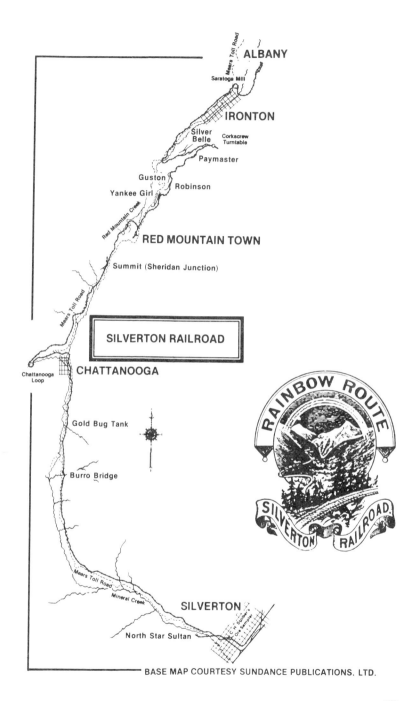

ALBANY

Mears Toll Road

Saratoga Mill

IRONTON

Silver
Belle

Corkscrew
Turntable

Paymaster

Guston

Robinson

Yankee Girl

Red Mountain Creek

RED MOUNTAIN TOWN

Summit (Sheridan Junction)

Mears Toll Road

SILVERTON RAILROAD

CHATTANOOGA

Chattanooga
Loop

Gold Bug Tank

Burro Bridge

Mears Toll Road

Mineral Creek

SILVERTON

North Star Sultan

RAINBOW ROUTE

SILVERTON RAILROAD.

BASE MAP COURTESY SUNDANCE PUBLICATIONS. LTD.

77

short line to be distracted by the publicity. Dave Day humorously exaggerated the extent of Mears' activities at this time as follows:

> The Midland Railroad folks should imitate the economic example and precedent followed and established by Otto Mears. Otto is president, general manager, the traffic manager, general passenger agent, auditor, station agent and section boss on the Silverton and Red Mountain railroad.[12]

While Mears was not as busy as Day claimed, he still undertook the bulk of the railroad business himself. In particular, he attended to the paper work, because of the difficulty in finding trustworthy personnel.

Mears operated the Silverton Railroad as efficiently as he had his previous business enterprises. The Silverton Railroad had about 25 miles of track including the main line and the branches to the mines. The line began at Silverton, the terminus of the Denver and Rio Grande Railroad. At Silverton, cars from the Denver and Rio Grande, loaded with supplies and coal at Durango, were transferred to the Silverton Railroad and hauled to Red Mountain. At Red Mountain, the cars were unloaded and loaded with ore and sent to Silverton, Durango or Denver—depending upon the marketing arrangements made by the owner of the ore. The Silverton Railroad as the originating carrier on outgoing traffic was able to net more than $2 a mile on freight charges.

Another factor in Mears' high net earnings pertained to his time tables. Those for 1889, and probably those for other years, deliberately misrepresented the actual mileage of the Silverton Railroad. This meant that shippers had to pay a much larger freight rate than they would have had to pay on the actual distance.

Besides the profitability, another distinctive feature of the Silverton Railroad was the novel railroad passes Mears issued for use on the line. In 1888, he issued buckskin passes two and a half by four inches in size. The following year he issued silver passes with a scene depicting a mountain railroad and mining operation. In 1890, he issued watch fob or medallion passes. Made out of silver and oval-shaped, these passes were approximately one and a half by one inch in size. Three years later, he celebrated the completion of his Rio Grande Southern Railroad with a new kind of pass. Fashioned out of either silver or gold filigree, it was intended for the exclusive use of patrons of either the Rio Grande Southern or of the Silverton Railroad. The precious metals were notably appropriate for the regions served by the railroads, and the silver—at least in many cases—came from Mears' Buckeye Mine. The passes were probably unique in world railroad history and in consequence elicited much interest. They were highly prized and were given to Mears' friends, business associates and to politicians. Today these passes are valuable collector's items and only 54 of those issued to 1893 are known to exist.

Otto enjoyed operating the Silverton Railroad. During the June to November operation period, he devoted much of his time to it. He seemed fascinated with his railroad—so much so that he studied each one of the 36 freight cars, the two locomotives, and the mail, combination and coach cars to determine individual characteristics that resembled people he had known. Then, upon finding a resemblance, he nicknamed the piece of equipment after the individual in mind. For example, he called his private car "Hill" because it had trouble staying on the track. The allusion was to Nathaniel Hill, a Republican political boss, who jumped from one side to another in an election as it suited his interest. Mears also named one of his locomotives—No. 100—"Ouray" after his old friend.

Aside from money-making, the enjoyment Mears received in the operation of the railroad came from the feeling of importance it gave him. He had an inferiority complex and was particularly self-conscious about being an immigrant with a poverty-stricken childhood. He wanted to belong and desired to associate on an equal basis with the most important political, social and financial personages in Colorado and in the West.

Because a railroad presidency had so much status and prestige associated with it he was now able to do this.

Dave Day satirized Mears' social climbing as follows:

Otto Mears, who used to extract comfort from the hurricane deck of a mule, now rides in a private car. Next thing Otto will be wearing stripped silk underwear and eating pie with a fork. [13]

Mears liked to flaunt his new importance in other ways besides moving in high social circles and riding in his own railroad car. Upon occasion, he liked to give tours of his railroad to influential people in order to show off his

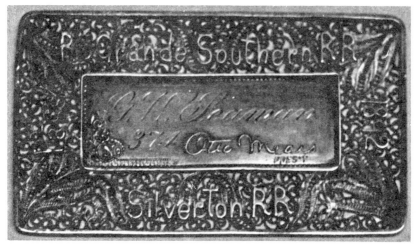

THE SILVERTON STANDARD AND THE MINER

A MEARS SILVER FILIGREE PASS
Novel Publicity from Precious Metals

ENGINE 100 HEADS A FULL TRAIN AT SHERIDAN JUNCTION
Steam Railroads at 11,018 Feet Above Sea Level

engineering skill which had built the railroad and his managerial talent which enabled it to show such a high profit after construction. Dave Day recounts what happened on one such occasion, and the story is so characteristic of his friend that the anecdote is quoted in full:

> Shortly after Otto Mears had completed the Silverton railway, and while taking a party of tenderfeet over the route, he was anxious to make them believe how handy he was in running an engine, and to be convincing, invited a quartet of St. Louis capitalists to get on the engine and watch him do the throttle act. The fireman, seeing his opportunity for some fun, was coaling liberally, and about the same time Otto thought he was impressing his guests the [safety] valve broke loose, and being unable to account for the roar and somewhat rattled over the way the show was terminating, simply yelled, "Shump, boys, tot tum boiler vos bustin." In less time than it requires to write, there were four children of Israel rolling down the mountain side, and Otto was in the baggage car hiding his San Juan County warrants in the coal box. The fireman stopped the engine and flow of surplus steam, and as the excited Hebrews came up, Otto (who had collected his wits) was down under the engine with a monkey wrench, and it required but a moment for him to convince all that he had tightened "up dem tam bolts shost in time." [14]

The completion of the Silverton Railroad marked the culmination of a decade which Mears devoted in large part to transportation development of the San Juan area. His feats in toll road and railroad building in the mountainous region were spectacular. His ingenious methods for solving the problems caused by the precipitous terrain are still admired. But his greatest achievement in mountain transportation development, in which he eclipsed his previous accomplishments, was still to come with the building of the Rio Grande Southern Railroad.

4

The Joker
in the Republican Deck

*O*tto Mears, busy in the decade between 1881 and 1889 with his various business enterprises, still allowed himself enough time to engage in politics. Political activity was a reflection of his increasing influence and was a personal venture in which money and power were his goals. Until 1882, Mears had been elected to only one office, that of Saguache County treasurer. He was an important political boss, perhaps the most important in the state, yet he seemed to have no ambition for higher office. Just why he decided to run for the state legislature in the summer of 1882 has been something of a mystery. In his later career, he was content to choose governors, senators and other officials without reserving offices for himself. He viewed politics as a kind of chess game with himself in control of the pieces. At some point after 1882 he recognized that influence and money, rather than position, formed the basis of power. In the latter part of his life he was content to let others fill the offices he controlled.

But in 1882, Mears still aspired to reach for high elective office. As Ute commissioner, he had been constantly in the public eye and, if a career in elective office was to be pursued, he decided 1882 would be an ideal year. People would vote for him, he believed, because of his role in the Indian removal.

He announced his candidacy for state legislator from Saguache in the summer of 1882. In early September, he arrived at Saguache to begin his campaign. However, the *Saguache Advance,* a Democratic weekly, immediately interjected a sour note:

> Otto Mears . . . come to take part in the county convention today. He is a resident of Denver, but that don't make any difference, as he is a privileged character, and can vote in or represent any county he chooses.[1]

The Republican pre-primary county convention conducted in September soon adjourned to permit its members to campaign for their own re-election in the following month's primaries. On October 7, enough pro-Mears delegates were returned at the primaries to guarantee Otto's nomination for the legislature at the Republican county convention a week later. From the day of his nomination until election day November 7, the candidate did everything he could to insure his victory. He spent most of his time stumping Saguache County and making speeches in which he asked for support on the basis of his record as Ute commissioner. Although the appointee had a good record, many local friends, and the endorsement of such newspapers as the *Denver Times,* the *Pueblo Chieftain* and the *Silver Cliff Herald,* he found the Democratic nominee, G.B. Carstarphen of Villa Grove, difficult to defeat. Carstarphen's strategy was to denounce his opponent for having dictatorial control over Saguache County politics. The contest, in consequence, was between Mears' supporters and his enemies, regardless of political affiliation. The bitterly contested campaign was decided November 7 when the Republican candidate received a majority of 60 votes.

The voting was so close that the early returns indicated Mears had lost. Not waiting for a complete tabulation a jubilant Democrat telegraphed Dave Day that Mears had failed in his bid for office. Day commiserated with his friend in print: "To defeat a man is bad enough, but to bleed financially [alluding to Mears' campaign expenses] and defeat both—well, it's horrid." [2]

When the final count had been made and it was evident that Carstarphen had lost the election, the Democrats were disgruntled. Their premature boasts of victory had made them seem foolish. Thoroughly piqued, they decided to contest the election, alleging that Mears was both an alien and a non-resident of Saguache. These charges were unfounded as the immigrant had been naturalized in 1877 and, while away from Saguache a great deal for business reasons, still considered it his home. Testimony was taken from both sides and sent to Denver for examination by Secretary of State Norman H. Meldrum. After proving the charges groundless, Mears was allowed to take his seat in the legislature.

The Fourth General Assembly began its first session on January 3, 1883, in the plush surroundings of a newly constructed building on Larimer Street. A few days later, the House organized its standing committees and Mears joined the corporations and railroads committe, the Indian affairs committee, the irrigation committee and the counties and county lines committee, of which he was later elected chairman.

Mears introduced his first bill on January 7. It provided for the foundation of experimental agricultural stations located in various parts of Colorado. The object of this proposal was to encourage new developments in farming. However, the committee on agriculture killed the bill— probably because the federal government already subsidized a system of agricultural experimental stations.

After the presentation of this bill, Mears devoted the next three weeks to his counties and county lines committee. The principal piece of business before this committee was the division of the land lately vacated by the Utes into counties. There was much competition between various parties to make their favored counties larger at the expense of adjacent counties. The bitterest rivalry was between the speculators of Grand Junction and those of the Montrose Townsite Company. Those individuals desirous of investing in the Grand Junction region wanted Montrose incorporated into their own proposed county while Montrose residents insisted upon autonomy. Both groups of contestants sent lobbyists to Denver and Dave Day advised both sides that Otto Mears "was painfully susceptible" to bribes and suggested that the lobbyists, therefore, "go with a wad."

After listening to the arguments of the lobbyists, Mears presented both sides of the controversy to his committee. The committee members then decided that a county with the name of "Mears" should be created with Montrose as the county seat and a county called "Palmer" should be formed with Grand Junction as the county seat. Upon consideration of the committee's recommendations the legislators decided to adopt the suggested boundaries. In accordance with the wishes of their inhabitants, however, the names of the proposed counties were changed from "Mears" to "Montrose" and "Palmer" to "Mesa."

The committee was also responsible for recommendations which led to the formation of other counties by the legislature. Additional counties carved out of what was former Indian territory were Delta, Garfield, Eagle and Dolores.

Although Mears was quite busy with the creation of new counties, he found time to become involved with other matters he believed important to the legislature. On January 28, 1883, he introduced two bills for House consideration. The first of these was a proposal to advertise Colorado by placing an exhibit at the National Mining and Industrial Exposition. The legislators were not willing to appropriate the necessary funds to put the measure into effect. The second piece of legislation provided for the establishment of a Colorado Invalid Mining Men Asylum to furnish aid to injured miners. This bill was not approved either. Mears had more luck with another bill he sponsored later. This measure, as enacted into law, forced landlords and innkeepers to take precautions on behalf of their guests to prevent robbery and other crimes.

In addition to normal legislative business, it was the duty of the Assembly member to help select Colorado's members of the United States Senate. In 1883, it was necessary to elect both a long-term and a short-term senator. A vacancy resulting from Senator Henry M. Teller's appointment as Secretary of the Interior by President Chester A. Arthur necessitated the election of a short-term senator to fill the remaining 30 days of Teller's term.

A senate seat was considered one of the highest honors, and contenders for the position would do almost anything to achieve it. There were several hopefuls but only three candidates commanded enough votes to stand any chance. These were Frederick Pitkin, the ex-governor, and mining magnates Horace Tabor and Thomas Bowen. During Mears' campaign for legislator, he stated that, if he were elected, he would vote for Pitkin. Pitkin was popular in Mears' district and this pledge undoubtedly gained the candidate votes he would not otherwise have had. However, it was never his intention to vote for Pitkin for senator. Pitkin was a political ingrate and by not repaying his debts he had violated one of the principal political rules. Mears never tolerated anyone who betrayed his trust, and he went to the January, 1883, session of the legislature expecting not only to vote against the senatorial aspirant, but to do everything else in his power to keep him from being elected.

In Denver, Mears became a Tabor supporter—being influenced by that candidate's arguments that he was the best man for the office. In the meantime, Bowen emerged as Tabor's chief competitor for the office with Pitkin being unable to muster more than minimal support. After 95 ballots—a record for a Colorado senatorial election—Bowen and Tabor remained deadlocked. Throughout the country the bitter contest was well-publicized and came to be known as the ''Battle of the Millions'' because of the wealth of the contestants. The tremendous interest shown in this election was indicated by a *Denver Republican* editorial that originally had appeared in the *St. Louis*

Globe-Democrat. Being the most important Republican newspaper in the Missouri Valley, it had great influence on Colorado politicians. The Missouri editor asserted that the Colorado senatorial battle was not only a disgrace but that it dishonored the Republican party, the United States Senate and the country as a whole because of the corrupt methods used by the contestants.

The Republican bosses in Colorado realized that the deadlock between Bowen and Tabor would have to be broken as fast as possible. Manipulation, bidding for votes, and coercion by the candidates had given the party too much adverse publicity, the Republican leaders decided. The only solution was for a principal supporter of one of the candidates to be induced to change sides and end the impasse. At this juncture, Mears took it upon himslef to resolve the crisis. He was approached by Bowen and asked to change his vote. In return for his support, Otto possibly demanded and may have been given a bribe. He recognized that by switching his vote he would not only profit personally but would save his party. On the next ballot, the ninety-sixth, Mears accordingly voted for Bowen and persuaded enough other legislators to do the same to end the deadlock. The result of this sensational election was that Bowen was selected to fill the long term and Tabor was chosen to finish Teller's term.

Most of the Colorado Republican party members believed that Mears had done them a service by breaking the deadlock. Venal political conduct of the kind that he had exhibited was condoned as long as this first rule of politics was observed: "self-preservation." Since party prestige had been saved by Mears, his betrayal of Tabor and his susceptibility to bribery were overlooked by the majority of the Republicans, who subscribed to the lax morality of the post-Civil War era. To them, his actions seemed something of a joke. He was nicknamed the "joker in the Republican deck" by the *Rocky Mountain News.*

Some of Tabor's supporters were so disgruntled by his election loss that, against the wishes of the majority of

Republicans, they vigorously denounced Mears, and thus risked renewing party discord. The *Denver Republican* caricatured Bowen and Mears as follows:

> Otto Mears clung to Bowen's coat-tails and looked as if he was particularly desirous of creating the impression that Bowen never would have gained the victory but for him. [5]

A more abusive attack appeared in the *Saguache Advance,* which printed a picture of Mears, portraying him with a gaping mouth and holding a banner which read: "This is Otto Mears, the traitor, howling for Tabor for United States Senator after pledging himself for Pitkin." Despite this revilement by Tabor's supporters, the object of derision was so esteemed by the rank and file of his party that less than four years later the *Rocky Mountain News* was calling him "The present Napoleon of the Republican party."

The legislative session ended in March, 1883. Mears had learned about the characteristics of legislative bodies, which he was to apply for the rest of his life. He found elective officials were easily influenced by skilled lobbyists who employed bribery, manipulation and coercion to gain their goals. Moral standards were so lax that legislators expected gratuities, and constituents gave their tacit approval. He realized that if he ever wanted to sponsor a measure, it was only necessary to induce the most pliable lawmakers to vote for it by bribing them. Consequently, he resolved never again to run for elective office; to him it was a waste of time. An effective lobbyist could exercise just as much control outside the legislature as an enterprising legislator could inside, Mears reasoned. He followed this practice and became such an effective lobbyist that whatever bills he favored were passed and those he thought inimical to his interests were killed by the Colorado legislature. His reputation as a lobbyist became so widespread that he was hired by others to use his influence in their behalf.

As a manipulator of elective bodies, Mears acted in accordance with the political maxim that the end justified the means. His political ideas departed in only one major way from nineteenth century political thought: after 1883, he did not want elective office. The great majority of the state's politicians built a power base to satisfy their ambition for high office. He thought differently. Politics was only a game to him. No matter how much time and cash he lavished upon it, he considered it subordinate to making money.

Mears, after completion of the March, 1883, legislative session, spent the remainder of the year building and operating toll roads. He did not participate in politics until the following spring. In May, 1884, he was selected by the Republicans of Ouray County to be one of Colorado's representatives at the Republican National Convention at Chicago. His ambivalence toward issues was satirized by Dave Day, who stated that:

> Otto, aside from being pledged to Blaine, Logan, Arthur, Lincoln Edmunds and David Davis, favors free trade, protection, tariff reform and possesses definite views on either sides of all questions of national importance. [6]

He attended the convention in early June and returned to complete contract negotiations for the Silverton and Red Mountain Toll Road. While constructing this road, Mears found time for another political venture. He now decided William Meyer was to be the state's next governor. Besides the obvious advantage of installing in office a high government official favorable to his interests, he wanted to participate in the gubernatorial race because politics fascinated him.

Meyer was selected because he was tractable and would be a big vote-getter. The candidate was a German-born immigrant, a former business associate of Mears and one who had invested heavily in his toll road ventures. Meyer had acquired much political experience from his association with Mears and had built up good will from his ready and generous support of the Republican party in previous campaigns. With good connections and the political debts that were owed him, he seemed to be a good bet to win the gubernatorial nomination in September's state Republican convention.

In August, the campaign manager came to Denver where he hoped to gather support for Meyer in the Republican state convention. The boss was not overly sanguine about his candidate's chances. To obtain enough votes, he was evidently willing to resort to his usual practice of bribery if he could not procure support any other way. The *Rocky Mountain News* reported:

> He came with a bundle, and is prepared to pay any reasonable price for Meyer delegates. Otto don't carry anything less than $50. Tap him for one and you may get two if you kick.[7]

Mears was not the only individual spending large sums to line up delegates. So much money was being spent that the *Rocky Mountain News* asserted the campaign to be the most corrupt in state history. Self-aggrandizement and not honor was the ruling consideration among the elected officials.

Despite the amounts of money and influence used to assure Meyer's nomination, his manager encountered difficulties from the outset. In late August, he suffered a major reverse, one so critical that it was a principal factor in the candidate's losing the nomination in September. Fred Walsen, a long-time business and political associate of Mears, was defeated in his bid to be elected as a Meyer delegate from Huerfano County. Politically speaking, Walsen was supposed to have Huerfano County bought and paid for, and when he could not deliver his own county for the gubernatorial aspirant, it indicated to many Republican bosses that another candidate would be more desirable.

When the Republican state convention began on September 10, the likelihood of Mears achieving his goal seemed small because of Walsen's failure. Three candidates were placed in nomination for governor— Meyer, Benjamin Eaton and Horace Tabor. In spite of the fierce competition for votes and Walsen's failure, Mears appeared to have amassed enough votes to gain Meyer the nomination when Thomas Bowen, supposedly an important and staunch Meyer supporter, defected to the Eaton ranks. Eaton, in consequence, won the Republican nomination for governor.

To the editor of the *Rocky Mountain News,* Bowen's defection was only the outward manifestation of dissatisfaction with Meyer. How, the editor asked, was it possible for anyone to vote for the German-born Meyer? If this was not enough, how could anyone accept a German immigrant who had married a Mexican?

What was even more objectionable to some was that a Jew had the effrontery to try to shove a foreigner down the throats of the delegates. The omnipresent editor of the *Rocky Mountain News* overheard the following statement from a Bowen supporter, which illustrates the strength of the xenophobia of the time: "The damn little Jew thinks he'll work his Dutchman through, but we'll show him a trick worth two of his in a few minutes." [8]

For two years, Mears smarted over Meyer's defeat. In 1886, he again supported his protege for the Republican gubernatorial nomination. At this time a Republican nomination was tantamount to election and Mears was convinced that Meyer would win at the polls if he won at the convention.

Mears worked very hard in the months preceding the 1886 convention to insure the nomination of his candidate. He had something to prove: He wanted to demonstrate once more his political acumen. His reaction to Meyer's 1884 defeat was similar to the manner in which he reacted to other reverses—a burning desire to overcome any obstacle even if it meant challenging impossible odds. He was so afraid of the stigma resulting from failure that he would do anything to succeed.

The manipulator was better prepared for the convention of 1886 than he was for that of 1884. The convention opened September 28 and proceeded as planned. Mears placated several important party leaders to insure their support for Meyer. He promised Horace Tabor, Edward

O. Wolcott, Nathaniel Hill and William Hamill each a term as senator if they would support his candidate's nomination and subsequent election. Mears also made a bargain with another party leader, Denny Meldrum, a Larimer County representative at the convention. The former agreed to add the latter to his ticket as lieutenant governor in return for Meldrum lining up support for Meyer from the other Larimer County delegates.

As a result of this maneuvering, Meyer was nominated as the Republican candidate for governor and Meldrum for lieutenant governor. Mears succeeded in having Meyer nominated because he was careful to line up loyal supporters for his candidate—something he had not done well enough in 1884. The *Rocky Mountain News* was impressed with his handling of the delegates. The editor expressed his admiration for the manner in which the political boss controlled the convention:

> Otto Mears was the autocrat of the Republican state convention. Bill Hamill, Ed Wolcott and Tabor only jumped when Otto pulled the string.[9]

Mears, it turned out, had more luck at the convention than his candidates had in November at the polls. Republicans evidently did not approve of a German-born candidate with a Mexican wife backed by a Russian Jew.[10] To counteract the complaints about the foreign birth of Meyer and his wife, the supporters of the gubernatorial candidate asked that people vote for him and ignore his heritage. Meyer's backers also asserted that Republicans should vote for the slate to avoid party discord. These arguments were ignored by the rank and file of the Republican party and the Democratic slate headed by Alva Adams was voted in by a wide margin.

In 1888, the Republican party regained the state offices it had lost in the disastrous 1886 campaign. Mears backed the Republican gubernatorial candidate Job Cooper of the German National Bank of Denver. Mears helped secure Cooper's victory by using his influence to restore unity and amity among the Republican political bosses who had been at odds since the bitter 1886 campaign.

After exercising all his power to insure the election of the Republican party slate headed by Job Cooper, Mears decided that it was time to gain revenge on Sen. Thomas Bowen, whose antipathy towards William Meyer had cost him the gubernatorial nomination in 1884. Mears had been instrumental in electing Bowen in 1883 to the United States Senate. If he did not anticipate lifelong gratitude, he certainly did not expect the treachery he felt Bowen had shown in September, 1884, by switching his vote from Meyer to Benjamin Eaton. Meyer's defeat in 1884 was particularly galling to Mears because a man he had once helped was responsible.

Mears determined that the thing which would harm Bowen most would be his defeat in his bid for re-election as senator, and began working in earnest in late summer and early fall of 1888 to effect this outcome. He chose Edward O. Wolcott, a business associate, professional lobbyist and corporation lawyer, as the individual he desired to succeed Bowen. Wolcott was a shrewd politician, a good vote-getter, a magniloquent speaker; he was the most formidable foe to oppose Bowen.

After selecting a suitable candidate, Mears next set about electing legislators who would vote for Wolcott the following January. An organization was formed with the objective of returning Wolcott men to the legislature. Mears concentrated on the primaries of the tier of southwestern counties in which he exercised a great deal of influence and control. At first Bowen seemed to be ahead in the race. He defeated Wolcott in San Juan, La Plata and Conejos counties—usually regarded as Mears' territory.

Bowen's stunning victories in three counties supposedly controlled by Mears made the latter more determined than ever. The boss redoubled his effort in the other southwestern counties in order to make sure that Wolcott legislators would be nominated and returned. He was particularly active in Ouray County, a Democratic stronghold for the previous decade. His achievements there illustrated the workings of the Mears-Wolcott machine in the other counties.

In Ouray County, Mears was successful in having Wolcott supporter A.G. Dunbar nominated as the Republican candidate for legislator. Dunbar was an individual who was evidently not intelligent, shrewd or competent, but he was obedient. He was backed by Mears because of his willing compliance. Otto was tired of men of ability after Bowen's 1884 defection.[11]

Dunbar's Democratic opponent was R.R. Rowan. The latter had much more ability than Dunbar, but he did not have supporters who were as politically powerful as Mears. Rowan's most influential supporter was Dave Day. Day was a Democrat who thought Dunbar incompetent and refused to endorse him. Day stated in one editorial that:

> Doc Rowan has more ability in an hour than Dunbar can muster in a week. But then Mears was more interested in obedience than intelligence, and he generally knows what he wants.[12]

Day's low opinion of Dunbar and his decision to support Rowan forced Mears to found two newspapers in Ouray County to counteract the *Muldoon,* by then one of the most influential newspapers in Colorado. The first of these newspapers founded in the 1888 campaign was called the *Pacific Slope,* a weekly published at Ironton in southern Ouray County, edited by Jo Winchester.[13] The *Ouray Plaindealer* was the second newspaper founded by Mears to support Dunbar. Edited by Harry Lee, this paper was also a weekly, and was attractively printed in an eight-column format. It was the seventh attempt to compete with Day's *Solid Muldoon* since its founding.

Mears wrote most of the editorials that appeared in the *Pacific Slope* and the *Ouray Plaindealer.* In spite of the journalistic rivalry between the *Muldoon* and Mears' newspapers, Day and he remained best friends, disagreeing only on politics. When Dunbar was victorious in the November election, Day was able to congratulate the political boss in print.

The election of Dunbar was the harbinger of Bowen's defeat. When the seventh legislative session convened in Denver in January, 1889, Mears was on hand to supervise the senatorial slection. He was able to line up enough votes to secure Wolcott's election and thus obtain revenge for Bowen's 1884 treachery. The senatorial election might have been fixed earlier than January, 1889. It is possible that Mears already had arranged for Wolcott's election the previous October, from references in the *Solid Muldoon* during that month.

The remaining months of 1889 were to be just as satisfying as January was for Mears. Defeating Bowen and finishing the Silverton Railroad were the major events of the year for him, but there were other highlights as well. In April, he was appointed by Governor Job Cooper to serve on the Board of Capitol Managers. The board had been organized in 1883 and consisted of seven members whose jobs were the planning and construction of a new capitol building. The appointment was intended to be honorary, rewarding him for his support of Cooper in the election of 1888. This was to be the only important governmental post Mears filled in the ensuing thirty years, as he had neither the inclination nor the time to serve in a public capacity in any other position.

After attending his first meeting as a capitol manager soon after his appointment, Mears discovered that the affairs of the board were in such a sorry state that he would have to devote a major portion of his time to the body or resign. By June, 1889, the capitol managers, through incompetence and dishonesty, had done very little but ask the legislature for larger appropriations for the project.

Mears had too much pride to be associated with such a moribund organization and he manipulated the other managers so the board's business would devolve upon him. He became its most active member, and remained so until the capitol building was completed a decade and a half later.

After assuming control of the board, Mears' first task was to cancel the purchase of a consignment of granite from Georgetown for use in the superstructure of the capitol building. He opposed the transaction because of the low grade granite involved and because there seemed to be a dishonest agreement between one of the capitol managers and the would-be seller. Mears was not usually so scrupulous in his execution of public business but he felt more responsibility as capitol manager than in any

THE COLORADO CAPITOL EARLY IN ITS CAREER
Patronage Under a Gilded Dome

public office he ever held. During his tenure in that office he gave no cause for complaint about his discharge of the duties.

The cornerstone was laid on July 4, 1890, just 14 months after Mears was appointed to the Capitol Board. After overseeing the construction of the superstructure and the landscaping of the grounds, Mears thought the building, though architecturally beautiful, still needed a distinctive feature. He supported a proposal to cover the dome with gold leaf to symbolize Colorado's rich mining industry. The members of the board thought this idea too costly and impractical to implement but he was able to exercise his considerable influence and the suggestion was approved. The gold leaf eventually was placed upon the dome at a cost of $4,500. The sum paid for the gold plating was a small price to pay for the distinctiveness it gave to the new capitol building.

Electing a senator, completing the Silverton Railroad and working on the new capitol building did not exhaust Mears' public activities for 1889. In mid-November, he was selected to represent San Juan County at the National Silver Convention conducted on November 25, 1889, at St. Louis. The convention was designed to discuss the problems and prospects of those who advocated the use of silver as a medium of exchange. Mears designed a medal which he presented to the other delegates of the convention. It was intended to represent the position of the Colorado delegation on the place of silver in the national economy. To symbolize bimetallism, the medal was manufactured out of gold and silver and was extremely popular with the delegates. It was quite a persuasive method of presenting the ideas of the people of Colorado about the United States monetary system.

Upon his return from St. Louis, Mears did not vacation as usual during the winter months when the weather in the San Juans made it impossible to operate roads or railroads. What the politician began to do upon his return was to organize a new railroad company—the Rio Grande Southern.

5

The San Juan Wizard

C⁀he Rio Grande Southern was the most ambitious
railroad project Mears ever attempted. Before
amassing the necessary capital to begin the construction
of the Rio Grande Southern, Otto Mears needed to be
fortunate in two mining ventures. In July, 1889, he had
become involved in the first of these. In association with
three Ouray mining men—D.C. Hartwell, E.J. Bent and
A.G. Herzinger—he incorporated the Calliope Mining
Company. The mining firm was organized with a million
dollar capital stock for the purpose of extracting silver ore
deposits at the Calliope Mine located in the Paquin
district of Ouray County.

The Calliope became one of the largest ore producers in
the San Juan. At its peak the mine averaged 92 tons of ore
per week. The diggings were so rich that after Mears had
operated the mine for six months, there was still enough
ore to occupy a full complement of miners for an additional 14 months, according to newspaper reports.

After Mears and his colleagues had put the Calliope
Mining Company into semi-independent operating condi-
tion, Otto engaged in another lucrative mining venture.
He leased the Comstock Mine on Brown Mountain in the
Red Mountain district. This mine had such rich deposits

that ore did not have to be sorted or sacked before shipping. How long he operated the Calliope and Comstock mines is not known; but it is certain that he utilized a considerable portion of the profits to help subsidize the Rio Grande Southern Railroad.

In the fall of 1889, Mears embarked on the Rio Grande Southern Railroad project. He had long dreamed of building a railroad along the route of his toll roads. The new line would connect the Ouray and Durango branches of the Denver and Rio Grande Railroad by a route located to the west of the termini of both branches. The mining camps along this route included Placerville, Ophir, Telluride and Rico. The last three of these towns were over 9,000 feet in elevation, and the severity of winter and spring storms kept the roads closed from six to seven months of the year. Not only was it difficult to freight goods into these high mountain towns, it was also difficult to ship ore out.

Mears probably conceived the idea to build the railroad in 1881 at a time when engineers employed by the Denver and Rio Grande Railroad were surveying a route between Durango and Rico. The railroad officials decided that to build a railroad between the two points was not feasible. Construction costs would outweigh profits, they believed.

Although the Denver and Rio Grande management thought the Durango-Rico road impractical, Mears knew better. Enormous profits were involved if the line were built. Huge returns could be expected from shipping of freight into and hauling ore out of the mining camps along the proposed route. After seven years of amassing capital he could now afford a survey of a possible route between Durango and Rico. In November, 1888, C.W. Gibbs, engineer of the Silverton Railroad, was ordered to survey a portion of the proposed route from Dallas on the Ouray branch of the Denver and Rio Grande to Telluride. Survey results showed that it would be possible to build a railroad between the towns.

On October 30 of the next year, Otto Mears' dream was born. In conjunction with Governor Job A. Cooper, John

100

L. McNeil, Fred Walsen and M.D. Thatcher, Mears incorporated the Rio Grande Southern Railroad. The incorporators agreed to raise $3,500,000 by selling 35,000 shares of capital stock for the purpose of building a railroad from Dallas to Durango—a distance of 160 miles. Capital stock was increased to $5,000,000 in June, 1890.

The new railroad was called the Rio Grande Southern because of the close working agreement Mears had arranged with the Denver and Rio Grande management. The Rio Grande Southern was to be of narrow gauge and was to serve as a feeder into the older railroad. The track bed was to be built to facilitate the eventual conversion of both railroads to standard gauge.

Because of the close working agreement between the two railroads, the officials of the Denver and Rio Grande decided to invest heavily in Rio Grande Southern bonds. So much money was invested by the management of the Denver and Rio Grande Railroad that, by the summer of 1893, it owned $2,000,000 worth of the sister railroad's stock and was the largest stockholder in the enterprise.

After its incorporation the first step taken to build the new railroad was the commissioning of a second survey of the proposed route. The first survey ordered by Mears was only between Dallas and Telluride. He now wanted the entire route surveyed. C.W. Gibbs began the second survey in mid-November, 1889, and had it completed by March of the next year.

While Gibbs was surveying the route, Mears traveled east to raise money for the new venture. His presentation in New York City was so successful in promoting investment interest that he was able to raise the necessary funds. The eastern financiers had heard of the tremendous profits which the Silverton Railroad returned and were convinced that Mears' proven ability justified their investment in this newest venture. Naturally, the westerner's salesmanship played an integral part; any objections of would-be investors were easily overcome.

After his successful stay in New York, Mears traveled to Washington, D.C., on behalf of the San Juan residents who wanted the Southern Utes removed from Colorado. He had been approached by a delegation of prominent Durango merchants when it had become known that he was going east to raise funds for his new railroad. He was requested to lobby for the passage of the bill, then under consideration, providing for Southern Ute removal. Mears agreed to the businessmen's proposal believing that the mission would gain him much favorable publicity.

Indian-white relations had been a problem for decades in Colorado. Confrontations had been occurring for years when in 1881, in an attempt to curb hostilities, the Northern Utes had been removed from the San Juans. The Southern (New Mexico) Ute reservation—including one forty-mile-wide strip into Colorado near the Four Corners area—had been left intact, partially because the Southern Utes had participated in neither the Meeker Massacre nor the battle at Milk Creek. By the mid-1880s, however, Coloradoans wanted the Utes removed entirely from the southwestern part of their state as they were desirous of Indian lands. Since red men were considered savages and because it was supposed to be impossible to civilize them, any tactic at that time was deemed justified in order to divest them of their holdings.[1]

The initial organized attempts to move the Southern Utes occurred in 1887 and 1888, but the Indian Rights Association was able to block the proposed move to Utah. In 1890, however, the residents of Colorado's Four Corners area were ready to renew their efforts to take over the Indian land. With the completion of construction on the Rio Grande Southern only months or a year away, they were anxious to have the Utes moved as soon as possible as the new railroad made the reservation land that much more valuable.

Representing the settlers of southwestern Colorado, Mears and attorney Adair Wilson arrived in Washington in early January, 1890. They found many Congressmen receptive to their pleas for Southern Ute removal. Mears felt his campaign was so successful that he returned to Colorado in mid-February to begin construction of the Rio

Grande Southern. Without Mears, however, Wilson found it difficult to keep the senators and representatives from changing their opinion about Ute removal. Lacking Otto's persuasiveness and political savvy, Wilson was unable to counter the Indian Rights Association, which argued that the proposed reservation in Utah was so infertile that it was unsuitable for Ute settlement. In consequence, the bill was defeated, and the Southern Ute Reservation exists in southwestern Colorado to this day.

Back in Colorado with the necessary construction funds, Mears was ready to begin building the new railroad. Initially he planned to start construction at Dallas, a village about 15 miles north of Ouray. When it became known that the new railroad would have its northern terminus at Dallas, land values soared. Real estate became so expensive that Mears decided he would save tens of thousands of dollars by choosing another spot to begin building. In early March, therefore, he and Fred Walsen selected and bought a new townsite two and a half miles south of Dallas at the junction of the Denver and Rio Grande Railroad's Ouray branch and the proposed Rio Grande Southern route. The new townsite was first called Magentie, later was named Dallas Junction, and finally Ridgway after R.M. Ridgway, superintendent of the Rio Grande Southern.

To facilitate the development of Ridgway, it was decided at this time to incorporate a townsite company to sell lots and otherwise improve the would-be town. May 22, 1890, found the Ridgway Townsite Company incorporated by Fred Walsen, Charles H. Nix and D.C. Hartwell. Capitalized with 500 shares of stock, worth $100 apiece, the company was to have a twenty-year life.

The town planners were gratified by the rapid sale of lots. Purchasers of real estate realized that not only would Ridgway be a railroad center—serving as a junction between the Denver and Rio Grande Railroad and the Rio Grande Southern—but that it would be a major supply center for the mining towns in the area. There were other attractions as well to would-be residents. Coal was easily obtainable from mines just outside the city limits and building materials of all kinds could be found within a short distance of the town. For those interested in civic improvements the town planners advertised a water works, electric lights, street lights, a hotel, a depot, fine roads and every other city convenience.

As time passed, Ridgway's growth accelerated. By mid-October, the newspaper editor of Dallas' *Western Slope* could report that "houses and stores are both going up like magic at Ridgway." A month later the editor claimed that the attractions of Ridgway were so alluring that people were deserting Dallas. In one of his reports on the growth of Ridgway, the editor included the following humorous account of the rise and fall of frontier towns:

> Three houses were torn down and moved to Ridgway the past fortnight, and a skunk made its appearance inside the business portion of town in broad daylight. Mayor Stegner seized the animal, put it in a box, wrapped the box with wire and sent it down the river towards Montrose. When the town is declared open for owls, bats and varmits [sic] due notice will be given[2].

In December, 1890, the Dallas editor moved his paper to Ridgway. The *Western Slope* was renamed the *Ridgway Herald* after a few issues. The coming of the paper to Ridgway symbolized the decline of Dallas and the growing prosperity of its sister city. It must have given Mears a large amount of satisfaction when he contemplated the decline, which was the direct result of the cupidity of its residents in refusing to make him a reasonable offer on land. Ridgway was to be prosperous until the summer of 1893, when a depression and a fall in the price of silver forced the closing of many of the region's mines.

While the new town was being developed, Mears was busy with the construction of the Rio Grande Southern. With the completion of the second survey in March, 1890, grading was begun at Ridgway on April 9. A total of 2,400 men were employed by early summer. In mid-July enough grading had been done to permit tracklaying to begin.

Throughout the summer of 1890, Mears was busy over-seeing the Rio Grande Southern construction. During this period he had three problems which occupied him constantly: construction difficulties on the rugged terrain, the scarcity of good workers, and the unusually wet summer and early autumn weather. Engineering and weather problems were easiest to solve. He had an aptitude for engineering and had been building toll roads in the Rocky Mountains for two decades. He had learned from building the Silverton Railroad that engineering problems were soluble by hard work and initiative. Although the problems posed by the steep grades on the proposed route of the new line were difficult, he was notably confident that because of his experience in road building he could master any terrain in the Rockies. He had coped with adverse weather in his previous projects and his solution then, as it was during the construction of the Rio Grande Southern, was to await good weather, and, if necessary, raise additional funds to cover the additional expenses caused by the delay.

The railroad builder, however, had more difficulty in solving the labor problem than he had in coping with the terrain or bad weather. Initially, a great majority of the workers had been recruited from outside the San Juan area. As soon as Mears had transported these men into the mountains, they abandoned the railroad and left for the mines. He then decided to recruit Mexican-Americans. Hundreds were hired and during warm weather were found to be good workers. But with the onset of fall the workers went home, not being accustomed to or equipped for cold weather. By mid-September, the need for workers was so great that it was necessary to search Kansas and Missouri for laborers. Eventually, an adequate number of men was secured, but there were never enough as far as Mears was concerned. Throughout the construction of the Rio Grande Southern, one of his primary concerns was raising and maintaining a construction crew.

Mears worked hard keeping the construction of the

railroad moving during the summer and fall of 1890. Dave Day humorously described his frenetic activity:

Otto Mears returned Tuesday from a ride over the Rio Grande Southern and the caresses of the sun and deposits of sediment having given him the appearance of an Apache. Otto now works 22 hours per day, leaving two hours for sleep and scheming; he never eats.[3]

Mears' hard work paid off. Despite weather and labor problems, the Rio Grande Southern Railroad was completed to Telluride in late November, 1890. On the weekend of November 22 and 23, the residents of the city staged a large celebration to commemorate the completion of the railroad to that point.

The Telluride celebration marked the end of construction on the northern part of the route for 1890. The bad winter weather made it expedient to transfer men and machines to the Durango end, where 5.5 miles of track were laid before January, 1891.

While work was progressing at the Durango end of the Rio Grande Southern, the promoter again was in the East raising funds to be used for the completion of the railroad. In mid-May the spring snow began melting and he was able to begin tracklaying at Telluride, where construction on the north end had stopped the previous November.

Outside of Telluride Mears encountered some of the greatest natural obstacles ever to confront a North American railroad builder. Approximately ten miles south of Telluride, an area later known as the Ophir Loop presented a very rugged terrain. At this point the San Miguel River meandered around canyons whose walls rose precipitously from the river below. The only feasible route for the railroad to Rico stretched from the San Miguel River Valley floor to the high divide between the drainages of the Dolores and San Miguel rivers.

Nearly the entire summer of 1891 was spent finding solutions to the problems caused by trying to build a railroad over almost vertical cliffs and deep canyons. Finally a route through the mountainous region was

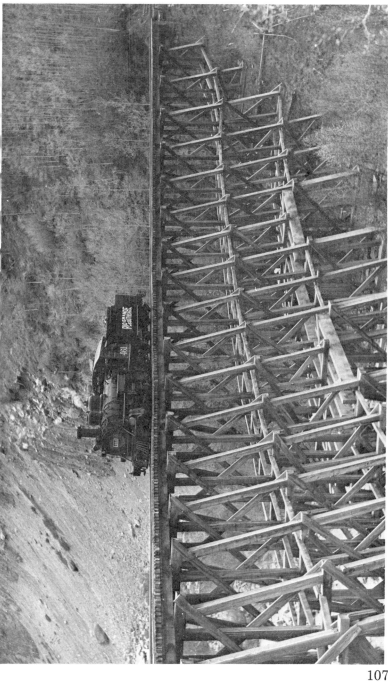

BUTTERFLY TRESTLE ON THE OPHIR LOOP
Climbing a Wall with Wooden Crutches

decided upon and grading and tracklaying through the Ophir district followed. The biggest problem to the builders, once a route had been selected, was the construction of the bridges necessary to span the yawning gulfs between the river valley floor and the canyon walls. The Ophir Loop was divided into two parts. Two lofty bridges and one smaller one were constructed on the lower segment. On the upper part, five more bridges were built to carry the track in its ascent. So difficult were the problems presented by the terrain that the bridges had to be assembled beforehand and then lowered into place.

With the completion of the Ophir Loop in mid-September, 1891, the construction crew worked rapidly so that the railroad would reach Rico before the onset of winter. Three weeks later, in early October, the first train steamed into Rico and the event was celebrated by spontaneous rejoicing. To further commemorate the occasion a gigantic banquet took place October 15, and Mears ran a special train to Denver so that many distinguished people could attend the festivities. After the banquet, speeches of congratulation were given and Mears was presented with two silver spikes, one from the citizens of Rico and the other by the Enterprise Mining Company of Dolores County. The after-dinner speeches were followed by a dance and a western style "blowout."

As soon as the merrymaking was over at Rico, the railroad builder was back on the grade. Bad weather and insufficient workers had already been responsible for a several month delay in the completion of the Southern. To avoid having to raise more money, a task increasingly more difficult because of the country's worsening economic condition, he worked 18 hours daily to complete the railroad to Durango by December, 1891.

Mears was so successful in his effort to hasten construction work that the grade between Rico and Durango was completed by the end of November. In the meantime, tracklaying was proceeding at the rapid rate of two miles a day. So swiftly did the tracklaying proceed that by December 1, only 21 miles of rail remained to be laid.

Crews were working day and night to take advantage of the good weather.

On December 20, 1891, the Rio Grande Southern Railroad was completed to Durango. The occasion was festive in spite of bad weather. The driving of the last spike signalled the start of a celebration among the employees of the railroad. Durango residents joined the festivities, with Mears donating fifty turkeys and three barrels of beer for the occasion. An even larger good-weather celebration was scheduled for July 4, 1892, with everyone in the San Juans invited.

Newspapers hailed the completion of the Rio Grande Southern as a significant event in Colorado's history. The *Rocky Mountain News,* for example, described it as "the most important railroad event of the year" and one of the most important advances in transportation development in Colorado history. The *Jewish Voice* of St. Louis, on February 21, 1892, added an anecdote about Mears to the coverage of the Southern's completion. At a celebration of the accomplishment in a San Juan mining town, Mears said, "I vas de Moses vad leads you out of de wilderness." An elderly prospector immediately spoke up and exclaimed, "You bet your life, Otto, and you are charging us ten cents a mile to get out of it, too."

The journalistic assessments of the new railroad's significance were proven by the immediate and profound affect of the Rio Grande Southern on San Juan mining. The advent of the railroad made it profitable to ship ore that had heretofore been thrown on the dumps. J.H. Ernest Waters, manager of the Sheridan-Mendota Mine at Telluride, reported for example that upon completion of the railroad he was able to save $7.50 a ton on transportation costs. The lower freight rate enabled Waters to salvage 100,000 tons of ore that had been thrown on the dump.

When it became evident that mining in the area traversed by the Rio Grande Southern would be more profitable because of lower transportation costs, capitalists were encouraged to venture more money into the region. New ore deposits were discovered and new mines were opened. Money was also invested in the mining camps of the area, with those located on the new line experiencing the largest growth.

Durango benefited the most from the railroad connection. Its geographic position and its connection with the Denver and Rio Grande Railroad allowed it to monopolize the trade with mining camps further north. A brisk exchange grew between Durango and the surrounding towns: merchandise and machinery were procured from Durango in return for unrefined ore. Durango gained in another way from the Rio Grande Southern connection. Mears' railroad stimulated the already rapidly growing coal mining industry in the Durango area. Not only was more coal than ever mined and shipped to the San Juan towns, but it was anticipated that coal could be cheaply shipped to Denver. Anthracite coal, used in Denver before the building of the Rio Grande Southern, was purchased from dealers at Crested Butte at the very high price of $9.25 per ton. Despite the hopes of Denverites for cheaper fuel, however, no coal was shipped from Durango. The officials of the Denver and Rio Grande Railroad made an agreement with the management of Colorado Fuel and Iron Corporation that no coal would be shipped east of Alamosa. This division of the coal market stabilized the coal mining industry and helped to prevent cutthroat competition between mine owners in the various parts of the state.

The impact of the Rio Grande Southern on agricultural development of the San Juan region was almost as important as that on mining and town growth. There were limited areas in the southwestern part of Colorado where farming was profitable. The Dolores and Montezuma valleys were the most fertile in the area and the railroad made it possible for farmers living there to make lucrative returns by enabling them to send their produce to distant markets. In addition to lessened transportation costs and more accessible markets, agricultural development was encouraged by the luring of immigrants to the San Juan.

Mears believed that more people in the area would bring more business to his railroad. He offered special rates to those who would settle in the area.

The stimulation given to San Juan mining, commerce and agriculture by the Rio Grande Southern was reflected in the railroad's profits. In October, 1892, Mears, in a stockholders' meeting, presented an accounting of the railroad's income and expenses. This financial statement was described by the *Rocky Mountain News* as "one of the most unique documents of the kind ever presented at a meeting of a board of railway owners." It showed that the net earnings for the first five months were almost $130,000. The tremendous net profit was contrary to what experts had predicted ten months previously. It was forecast, soon after the Rio Grande Southern was completed to Durango, that the railroad would not earn enough to pay expenses. So impressed was the financial editor of the *Rocky Mountain News* with the returns of the enterprise that he declared that Mears was one of the few men in the United States who could both build and operate a railroad profitably.

There were three reasons why Mears' outstanding managerial skill helped make the Rio Grande Southern Railroad such a financial success. First, as on the Silverton Railroad, he did much of the work himself. He loved to work, and the novelty of owning a railroad reinforced a love of detail. He at first was reluctant to delegate authority as his experience in the Rocky Mountain mining camps had shown him that most people could not be trusted. He was so efficient and capable a manager that he could deal with most aspects of the operation himself.

The second reason for Mears' financial success on the Southern was that when traffic increased he was finally able to find competent subordinates to aid him in operating the railroad. Careful in choosing his employees, he supplemented the recommendations of others with his own thorough knowledge of human nature. As a result, he seldom hired the wrong person for a job.

Mears' careful employee selection was not his only way of insuring competent help. Once hired, his men were well treated. His subordinates were his equals as well as his assistants. He realized that individuals would work harder and more efficiently if they had a share in the decision making process. He pursued a cooperative course with his employees and negotiated such things as wages, hours, vacations, and company policies with them.[4]

Occasionally a dishonest or incompetent employee would be hired, but almost never would one fill a position of importance. In the early period of the Rio Grande Southern operation the president had bad luck with only two of his underlings. Dave Day presented a humorous account of one:

> Since Otto Mears' express messenger on the Rio Grande Southern got tangled up with a woman and a six shooter, Otto has decided to send to Turkey for a full line of express messengers, conductors, and station agents. The moral standing of the Rio Grande Southern will be maintained if the harems have to go unguarded.[5]

The third aspect of the Rio Grande Southern operation which contributed to its large profits was Mears' promotional skill. He had learned the value of publicity in previous ventures. From his Silverton Railroad experience he discovered that more novel advertising would bring better publicity. He had so much success with the use of specially made silver and gold passes on the Silverton Railroad that he decided to have some made for the Rio Grande Southern. This brought about the silver and gold filigree passes and the joint passes to be used on both of Mears' lines. These passes provided the Southern with enough free publicity to pay for their manufacture.

The operation of the Rio Grande Southern was so efficient that the president had time to engage in other activities. In January, 1892, he and O.P. Posey, a rich Ouray mining magnate and former Silverton merchant, purchased the C.H.C. and Black Hawk mines located at

Rico for $325,000. The Black Hawk Mine had been discovered the year before and the partners were able to take it over because the original owners did not have enough money to develop the property. By March, 1892, it was evident that the new operators had made a very good deal. Mears, usually conservative in mine appraisal, stated that "the Black Hawk has struck one of the largest bodies of high grade ore ever discovered in Colorado." By early May it was estimated that the Black Hawk had over a million dollars worth of ore. So much ore was found that Mears decided that a reorganization of the mine was necessary to operate it more efficiently. He thus incorporated the Black Hawk Mining Company with shares selling for $1.50 each. By the end of the decade, however, the mine was a poor producer, and was no longer profitable.

After the Black Hawk Mining Company had been more efficiently organized, Mears engaged in other mining ventures. By June of 1892 he had purchased stock in the Golconda Mine and had also invested in the San Juan Consolidated Gold Mining Company. Three months later he bought an interest in the Last Chance Mine, and by April of the following year, he owned one-third of the Harvey lode, one-third of the Black Lemon lode, and one-third of the Little Maggie lode, all located near Rico.

Mears found these mining speculations so profitable that he decided he had money to invest in a project he had found interesting in the winter of 1890. He had realized at that time that the Rio Grande Southern Railroad would have a tremendous impact on southwestern Colorado mining operations. Mine owners who had their ore smelted in Leadville and Denver would, with the coming of the railroad, find it cheaper to send their ore to Durango. Accordingly, he and Denver financier David Moffat examined the possibility of building another smelter in Durango to help service the Rio Grande Southern customers. Mears was over-extended financially at this time, however, and did not embark in this new scheme.

A year and a half later, however, his lucrative mining speculations encouraged him to invest in the smelter project. He accordingly traveled to New York in March, 1892, to discuss the scheme with George Crawford and other eastern capitalists who had invested in the Rio Grande Southern. He had no difficulty in persuading these men that a smelter's investment would show good returns. In consequence, they advanced the necessary funds. Upon his return to Colorado, he began the construction of the smelter. He stayed in Durango during the spring of 1892 to superintend construction. By the end of April the buildings began to take shape and the smelting machinery was in operating order by mid-summer. This smelter, to be known as the Standard Smelter, was designed primarily to treat copper ore.

While the Standard Smelter was being built, Mears engaged in other projects. He invested heavily in the Rico area, particularly in real estate. In partnership with O.P. Posey and others he bought the First National Bank of Rico, one of several banks in which he was to invest. About the same time he was developing Rico, he became a large stockholder in the Globe Express Company. The Globe Express Company was an outgrowth of the Rio Grande Express Company. The younger company was organized when the parent company was found inadequate to serve the public needs. The new company was incorporated with a capital stock of $5,000,000. In order to make a good return on the invested funds, its objective was to serve a larger clientele and a larger area than the Rio Grande Express Company.

In spite of his involvement in many business ventures, Mears was primarily interested in railroad building. He loved being out on the grade more than he did anything else. Even before the completion of the Rio Grande Southern to Durango he cast about for new railroad projects. He finally chose two schemes which seemed the most feasible—an electric railroad between Ouray and Ironton, and extension of the Rio Grande Southern.

Mears had been interested in building a railroad between Ouray and Ironton since the mid-1880s. He had connected the towns in the summer of 1883 by the construction of the Ouray and San Juan Toll Road. Six years later he considered building the Silverton Railroad over the same route. He did not do so because of the engineering problems and the high costs. He had been obsessed since 1889 with the idea of supplanting the Ouray and San Juan Toll road with a faster mode of transportation. He was motivated by economic consideration and egomania. The San Juan mines and mining camps were never more prosperous than in the years just preceding the Panic of 1893. Railway connections were built to most of the heaviest producing mines when construction was possible and profits accrued to the operators of these lines.

The Red Mountain mines were among the richest of the San Juans, but ore could only be shipped by way of the Silverton Railroad, whose practical terminus was at Ironton. There were also many mines between Ironton and Ouray. The production of these mines was shipped by team-drawn wagons over Mears' toll road. Animal-powered transportation was costly and slow and he calculated that a fortune could be made if a way was found to speed up the cumbersome existing mode of transportation. He was also aware that tourists would swarm into the area if transportation facilities were made more convenient. He noted the brisk tourist trade on the Silverton Railroad and the scenery was, if anything, even more spectacular between Ouray and Ironton. He believed, therefore, that the new area could be developed as a tourist attraction.

Besides being motivated by the profits that would accrue from freight and passengers, Mears was actuated by a fear of failure. He hated to be defeated at any undertaking and would avoid by every possible means even the most trifling failure. When he found that it was impossible to build a conventional railroad between Ouray and Ironton, it made him more determined than ever to bridge the gap between those towns by rail.

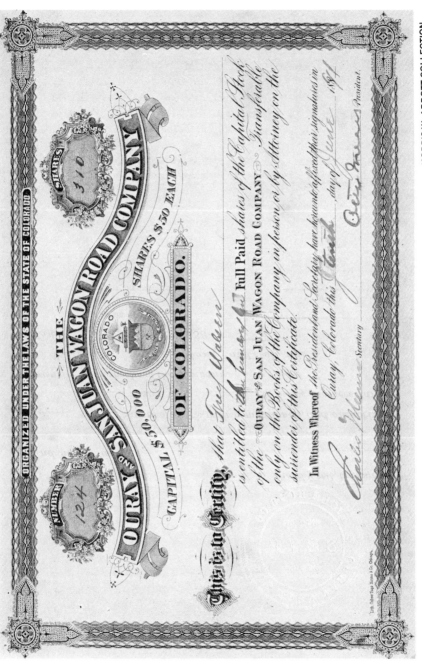

OURAY AND SAN JUAN WAGON ROAD STOCK CERTIFICATE

Finally he found a solution to his problem. In his numerous trips to the East to raise money for the Rio Grande Southern and other projects, he had visited the largest cities to keep abreast of the latest developments in transportation technology. In Chicago and New York experiments had been made with the use of electric railroads. He studied the experimental railroads and decided that the results of these pioneering efforts indicated that electric railroads would negotiate steep grades better than steam-powered railroads. This determination and innovation prompted the *Denver Times* to dub Mears "the San Juan Wizard."

Once he had decided upon the feasibility of an electric railroad connection between Ouray and Ironton, he lost no time in making arrangements to begin construction. In late November, 1891, he, Fred Walsen, Charles Munn, a Ouray merchant, and Joseph N. Cassanova, a Philadelphia financier, incorporated the Ouray-Ironton Electric Railroad, Light and Power Company. With a capital stock of $800,000, the company was organized to build and operate an electric railroad between Ouray and Poughkeepsie Gulch and between Ouray and Ironton, following the route of Mears' old toll roads. The corporation, to increase its profits, would use the power station it built to supply power and light to Ouray area mines.

The next step in this well-conceived project was to order the chief engineer of the Rio Grande Southern Railroad, C.W. Gibbs, to prepare an expedition to make a preliminary survey of the proposed route. This survey was delayed by inclement weather and, in the meantime, the promoter went to New York and Chicago to sell stock in the enterprise.

Successful in raising the money he needed, he returned from New York on March 9, 1892, eager to rush the construction of the electric road. In June, as soon as weather permitted, he ordered Gibbs to make the long-planned preliminary survey of the route. With the completion of the survey and with the construction funds in hand, Mears was ready to begin building the electric railroad in the summer of 1892. But mining in the area decreased to such an extent that the project was deferred until the next year.

With an increase in mine production in 1893, Mears was again ready to build the electric railroad. But the dramatic repeal of the Sherman Silver Purchase Act that summer caused silver prices to fall to such a low level that most San Juan mines were closed. Construction on the new line was again postponed. Mears was never again in the financial position to build the electric railroad. The mine owners were his most important customers on his railroads and with the closure of the mines he could meet neither the operating expenses nor the interest payments on these lines. Even though Mears' finances were in a chaotic state the electric railroad scheme was not dead. He tried unsuccessfully to get the railroad built in 1894, in 1899 and in 1900, but the depressed state of Colorado's mining economy discouraged eastern capitalists from investing in the project.

Back in 1892, when Mears had put forth so much effort in behalf of the abortive electric railroad idea, he was also quite interested in a project which, if completed, would have made him one of the principal railroad figures in the United States. He intended to extend the Rio Grande Southern to the Pacific coast. He had always dreamed of grand endeavors which would make him nationally famous. The idea of the extension of the Rio Grande Southern therefore appealed to him, not only for the tremendous profit potential, but for egotistical reasons.

Mears had decided to extend the Rio Grande Southern some time in 1891, when it became apparent that the railroad would be profitable. In early fall the gross receipts of the line were more than $40,000 a month and were expected to increase to $70,000 when construction was completed to Durango. The high returns on the Southern would be a strong incentive for further investment in the railroad, he believed. He was so convinced that financiers would be willing to underwrite an extension that he began making plans to build to Phoenix and Los Angeles.

In anticipation of railroad building beyond Durango, Mears began to consolidate his assets and put his affairs in a more orderly fashion. In June, 1892, he purchased a beautiful house in Denver which he thought would be appropriate for a president of a major railroad. This mansion, located on the corner of Washington and Colfax, is no longer standing. In July, he sold his remaining interests in Saguache with the goal of centralizing his assets in Durango.

He had been interested in the Durango area since 1881, when he built the Durango, Parrot City and Fort Lewis Toll Road. For the next decade he had little to do with the city except for buying and selling lots upon occasion. In 1891, however, he decided to make Durango the headquarters of a personal business and railroad empire. The new site, he reasoned, would make an excellent control center for the Rio Grande Southern as it was being built southward and westward. The city had a salutary climate, good rail connections, a ready access to large coal fields and cheap real estate. It also had the advantage of proximity to Silverton, the southern terminus of the Silverton Railroad.

Throughout the fall and winter of 1891 he developed Durango to suit his idea of an efficient railroad center. He was so busy that in late September, when he was being considered for the presidency of the Denver and Rio Grande Railroad, he refused because he could not spare the time from his own enterprises. As a result, E.T. Jeffery was selected instead.

One of Mears' schemes at this time was to move a good newspaper to Durango. He realized that newspaper promotion was a necessary factor in Durango's development. In 1890, Durango comprised 2,726 residents, most of whom supported the *Daily Herald,* the town's principal newspaper. Founded in 1881, the *Daily Herald* was edited at the end of its first decade by George N. Raymond, an early Silverton newspaperman and one of the few individuals with whom Mears could not get along.

Knowing the strength of Raymond's antipathy, Mears

induced Dave Day to move the *Solid Muldoon* from Ouray to Durango. Mears and Day had been close friends for nearly 15 years and had close financial ties as well. During the period of their friendship, Day had not profited from his friend's success. Although by this time Day was one of the most famous frontier journalists, he had fallen on bad times financially. The *Solid Muldoon* by 1891 had a circulation of more than 3,000 a week and was one of the most popular and widely quoted newspapers in Colorado. Day had used the profits from his newspaper to invest in mining schemes with varying success, but he lost all that he had invested on the Ramona townsite plan. To make matters worse, the *Muldoon* had been boycotted by Ouray merchants since the abortive Ramona [Chipeta] townsite venture. The merchants resented the fact that the editor had attempted to aggrandize himself at the expense of his old friends and acquaintances in Ouray. Day, looking for greener journalistic pastures, agreed in December, 1891, to move to Durango.

Day moved to Durango in early March, 1892. He had so little money that Mears had to purchase a tan suit for him so that he would look presentable in the new town. The editor enjoyed his new surroundings and soon became as enthusiastic as Mears about Durango's future. Day's optimism about Durango's prospects and his humor so appealed to the city's inhabitants that the *Daily Herald,* which had successfully been able to withstand six previous competitors, was forced to come to terms with the seventh. Accordingly, in late June, 1892, the *Daily Herald* and *Solid Muldoon* were consolidated with the *Muldoon* appearing weekly and the *Herald* daily. After the merger, the *Herald-Muldoon* continued with the promotion of the Durango area begun by the *Solid Muldoon* and thus promoted Mears' interests. Day served as one of the editors of the *Herald-Muldoon* until the following year when—tired of working in a partnership— he founded the *Durango Democrat,* of which he had the sole control.[6]

While Day was engaging in various journalistic enterprises in Durango, Mears had Rio Grande Southern extension plans under consideration. The residents of Phoenix were anxious for a Colorado railroad connection through the Salt River Valley. The proposed extension was expected to reap a windfall for the railroad builder. The principal customers of the new line would be Arizona fruit growers who had heretofore been unable to realize the potential of their orchards because of the loss of fruit due to spoilage on the long trip to markets. The railroad, by providing the fruit growers with easily accessible transportation, was expected to minimize fruit spoilage and thereby turn the Arizona fruit industry into one of the nation's most profitable enterprises. The financial returns appeared to be so great on the scheme that in January, 1892, Mears ordered preliminary surveys of the route.

The next step was to raise funds for the extension. Mears accordingly left Denver the evening of January 21, 1892, for conferences with financiers in Chicago and New York City. He skillfully presented his reasons to the prospective investors for wanting to extend his railroad. He needed, he said, $5,000,000 to tap the fertile Salt River Valley in southern Arizona because oranges grown there ripened six weeks to two months earlier than those grown in California, and would, therefore, be more readily marketed. He stated that profits on the proposed extension would be increased by running the rails through the Navajo Reservation in northern Arizona. The railroad would carry freight to the Indians and ship out the wool grown on the reservation. He added the statement that any area between Durango and Phoenix with prospective customers would be on the line of the Rio Grande Southern extension.

Even with the United States in a recession, moneyed men approached by Mears readily invested in his new idea. He had no problem raising the necessary funds for the lengthening of the Rio Grande Southern. Upon his return to Colorado, he decided that another, more comprehensive, survey of the proposed route was necessary in order to finalize construction plans. Two preliminary surveys had already been taken the previous winter.

These surveys had followed the La Plata and Animas Rivers respectively—heading south from the existing Southern system and winding up in Phoenix. A new route was selected for the third survey, however. The third survey crew, with H.P. Carpenter in charge, was ordered to begin on the Mancos River and from there go south to the San Juan River. At the San Juan River, the party was ordered to travel southwesterly by the most direct route to Lee's Ferry and Phoenix.

Carpenter's survey took most of the summer of 1892. Mears, in the meantime, was besieged by newspaper reporters who wanted to discover his plans. He would not satisfy their curiosity, however, because a premature disclosure of his intentions would be fatal. There were reportedly two other competitors who were believed to be planning construction of railroads south out of the San Juan Basin. Jay Gould, the first of Mears' competitors according to Denver newspapers, was ready to build a railroad between Pueblo and Albuquerque by way of Durango. The other potential rival was B.L. Cook, who had a Durango-Albuquerque railroad under consideration and was having a probable route surveyed at the same time as Mears.

Because of Mears' silence about the contemplated extension of the Rio Grande Southern, speculation was rife in Colorado newspapers about his possible plans. According to various theories he was building to Albuquerque, to Phoenix, to Flagstaff, to Texas, to Grand Junction, and to San Diego. It was even reported that the Southern would be built into Bluff, Utah, to take advantage of the gold rush there.

For nearly ten months, Mears refused to divulge any information about future railroad construction, his preoccupation characterized by the chain-smoking of cigars. During this period he evaluated the results from the three surveys of the Durango to Phoenix extension. Only after meticulously examining all relevant material was he ready to reveal his program.

In January of 1893, the railroad president finally

disclosed, through subordinates, what his latest plan involved. His new project concerned more than an extension of the Rio Grande Southern to Phoenix. On the basis of data collected in 1892, he believed that it would be profitable to build the line southwest through the Salt River Valley into Phoenix and from there to San Diego. At some point on the way from Phoenix to San Diego, he intended that the railroad intersect with the Sonora Railroad, which was constructed between Guaymas, Mexico, and the border.

When Mears had made his long-awaited announcement about the Rio Grande Southern extension, he was almost 53 years old. He had spent the preceding 28 years in hard work in Colorado and it was now apparent that this backbreaking labor was about to return huge dividends. If the proposed extension was built, he would be catapulted into national prominence as the owner and operator of a multistate railroad. His earnings from this venture would make him one of the richest and most powerful railroad magnates in the country, a magnificent achievement for a man who had been a poor, homeless immigrant.

This classic rags to riches story did not, however, take place. While Mears was making the final arrangements for the southwestern extension óf his railroad a series of economic disasters engulfed Colorado and precluded the building of the line.

Colorado's economy was to a large extent dependent upon silver mining. So close was its economy tied in with silver mining that every major fluctuation in the market value of silver had an immediate effect on the state's economic life. The United States government, under the provisions of the Sherman Silver Purchase Act of 1890, was obliged to buy 54,000,000 ounces of the metal at market value annually from the states. During the period immediately after the passage of the act, the silver purchase by the federal government absorbed nearly all of the market and the price of the metal was well over $1 an ounce. Colorado experienced her greatest prosperity to that point as a result.

The wealth proved ephemeral, however. Mine owners, encouraged by the initial results of the Sherman Silver Purchase Act, were induced to invest more in their holdings to increase production. The resulting glut of silver upon the market caused the price of the metal to drop. In the early summer of 1893 silver was worth only 83 cents per ounce.

The silver industry suffered a further setback in June, 1893. At that time the British government in control of India announced that the country would not mint any more silver coins and consequently would not purchase any more American silver. Within four days after this announcement, the value of American silver dropped to 62 cents per ounce. This was such a low price that many Colorado mine owners did not find it profitable to continue mining silver and decided to close their mines.

With July, more adversity was to come to Colorado. While the state's economy was reeling from the blow of the silver mine closures came the first effects of the panic and depression from the East. The panic developed in the East when it became apparent that the nation's gold reserves were sinking below the hundred million dollar level. The nation's economy was sound as ever but a hundred million dollar gold reserve was incorrectly deemed necessary by the general public. As the gold reserves sank, businessmen became frightened. In an effort to protect their investments, they cut expenses by firing employees and tried to have a supply of gold and silver money on hand by withdrawing savings from banks. Unemployment and bank failure resulted from this precipitate action. A depression followed the panic and spread westward, finally reaching Denver. By September 1, 1893, half of the producing mines in Colorado were closed, 377 businesses had failed, and 45,000 individuals were unemployed.

President Grover Cleveland, who had just taken office, decided to combat the depression by repealing the Sherman Silver Purchase Act. Cleveland reasoned that the panic was caused by the gold reserves falling below the hundred million dollar level and that a principal reason for this decline was the government purchase of silver. Hoping to end the drain on government funds, Congress, at Cleveland's insistence, repealed the Sherman Silver Purchase Act in August, 1893. The repeal of this act meant the end of the subsidization of the silver industry by the federal government, and was followed by the closure of the remainder of the silver mines. The administration's solution to the country's financial problems only worsened the depression in Colorado.

During the period in which Cleveland was attempting to ameliorate the crisis, Mears worked at a furious pace to save his holdings. Most of his considerable fortune was invested in businesses whose prosperity depended upon high silver production. His immediate concern was with the financial condition of his railroads where the bulk of his capital was invested. He soon found that the fall in silver prices would not adversely affect his Silverton Railroad. The line was, in fact, as prosperous as ever, because mine owners were shipping copper-bearing ore which had good market value. Conditions were so bad, however, that he had to wait between two and three months for payment by his customers; they could not raise money to pay the freight charges.

The Rio Grande Southern did not continue to share the prosperity enjoyed by the Silverton Railroad. As early as April, 1893, three months before Colorado experienced the full impact of the 1893 depression, Mears was having difficulty operating this railroad. With the price of silver declining because of the glut of the metal on the market, some Colorado mines had already started to close. With the loss of some of his best customers he was forced to reduce expenses. To cut labor costs, he decided to pay engineers and firemen on the basis of a mileage scale instead of a daily wage. When his employees objected to this new arrangement, he assured them that the mileage-scale base for payments was only temporary and would only be used until business improved.[7]

Conditions became much worse instead of better,

however. In June, when India announced that it would purchase no more United States silver, the price of the metal—already low—dropped precipitously. Most of the Colorado silver mines closed and, in an effort to induce those mine owners still operating to ship their product, Mears reduced freight rates. Finding it necessary to further reduce expenses, he fired his passenger agent.

In late June as the depression spread westward conditions in Colorado deteriorated rapidly. In early July the State National Bank of Denver, of which Mears was a stockholder and where he kept large sums on deposit, closed. He lost nearly all available funds with the closure of the bank. To raise money to pay the expenses of the Rio Grande Southern, he was forced to liquidate much of his real estate and to sell the stock he owned in various enterprises. Never before had he been so financially hard pressed. He described his predicament to Charles H. Graham, a Chicago financier, to whom he owed a large debt:

> We have had a terrible panic and it is imposs-
> ible to get any money at any rate, and I am abso-
> lutely unable to pay it. No man can get any
> money, no matter what security he has, even at
> 10% per month. You cannot possible [sic] have
> any idea of the condition of affairs here . . . .
> Never in all my experience have I seen such hard
> times financially. [8]

While Mears was trying to raise money to pay his debts the amount of freight carried by the Rio Grande Southern declined drastically. More and more mine owners, affected by the fall of silver prices and by the depression, had found it unprofitable to continue operations. In mid-July, Mears ordered his station agents to interview the mine owners in their vicinity to determine if a reduction of freight rates would induce a resumption of ore shipments. He found, however, that nothing would persuade the mine owners to reopen their mines.

Not only was Mears unsuccessful in his attempt to revitalize the moribund mining industry, but he was also unsuccessful in his own attempt at financial retrenchment. He was not able to reduce railroad expenses enough to pay the creditors with its income. He had lost most of his customers due to the low price of silver. His remaining clientele could not afford to pay cash because of the depression and the Rio Grande Southern management was forced to extend credit or do no business at all.

After trying every expedient in an effort to make the Rio Grande Southern profitable, the president was forced, because of the line's increasing indebtedness, to take a drastic step to save his railroad from bankruptcy. In order to build the railroad, he had issued 25 $1,000 five percent bonds per track mile. An equal amount of capital stock was also issued. Although the Denver and Rio Grande Railroad was the largest single bond and stockholder in the Rio Grande Southern, eastern investors were the main source for the construction funds used to build the line. He feared that the eastern investors would attempt to take over the railroad once it became known that the railroad management could not meet the interest payments due. To protect his and other investors' holdings, Mears filed an application for receivership in District Court on August 1, 1893. Upon consideration of the petition, the court appointed the Denver and Rio Grande Railroad as receiver because of its large investment in the Southern.

For the twelve months following the Rio Grande Southern receivership, Mears was powerless to do anything but wait. He hoped the depression would end and that the market for silver would improve and allow the mines to reopen. During this period, he spent most of his time managing the Silverton Railroad. This railroad was doing a good business and required much attention. To supplement the income earned from the Silverton Railroad, Otto became the general manager of the Standard Smelter in January, 1894. He had been the organizer of the Durango concern in 1892 and still owned a large amount of stock in it. The position of general manager required very little time as the smelter had lost most of its customers because of the depression. He was, in fact, in Durango only twice during 1894 to supervise and inspect smelter operations.

The entrepreneur was more interested at this time in the Rio Grande Southern. His hopes for a general mining recovery for the San Juan region did not materialize. The railroad, in consequence, was sinking further into debt. During the late spring and fall of 1895, Mears worked with E.T. Jeffery, receiver of the Rio Grande Southern and president of the Denver and Rio Grande Railroad, to solve the financial problems of the Southern. The railroad, at this point, was millions of dollars in debt. As Mears did not have even enough money to pay his living expenses, he realized he would have to sell the railroad or risk the total loss of the millions of dollars he and his friends had invested in it.

The Denver and Rio Grande Railroad management believed that the Southern would be a good long term investment. Business conditions were improving slightly in Colorado and promised to get much better at an accelerating rate. Jeffery consequently offered Mears and the other stockholders a very good price for the railroad. Finding the terms acceptable, Mears sold the line on November 30, 1895. He still retained enough stock, however, to remain on the board of directors. In 1905, he lost the remainder of this stock due to a stock reorganization. His shares evidently were taken over by George Gould. The loss of the Rio Grande Southern was the biggest reverse ever suffered by Mears. He never regained the financial position he had enjoyed before the Panic of 1893.

6

The Present Napoleon
of the Republican Party

*D*uring the early phases of the Rio Grande Southern's organization and construction, Mears had
little time to devote to politics. Given a respite, however,
when bad weather forced a construction slowdown in early
January, 1891, he used the opportunity to attend the
Eighth General Assembly in Denver. He wanted to be on
hand to work against the passage of adverse railroad
legislation. During a February 27, 1891, interview, he
elucidated his position:

> I don't say that a law would hurt the railroads
> if it was rightly administered, but it prevents us
> from getting money, for the capitalists of the
> East have had all the experience they wish with
> railroad legislation, and they are afraid of any
> kind of law. [1]

Mears believed the laws in existence were restrictive
enough and that the current rates charged to shippers
were fair. According to him, any tactic was justified to
keep an incompetent legislator from meddling with a
situation already satisfactory to businessmen. About this
time he developed a *modus operandi* he used in lobbying
against railroad legislation for the succeeding two
decades. He would ascertain the opinion of each repre-

sentative and senator about railroad regulation. Those found to be in favor of the *status quo* would be recommended for membership on the railroad committee of the appropriate house.[2]

Packing the railroad committee of both houses apparently did not achieve the desired result. Reform sentiment was so strong among the legislators that allegedly Otto was forced to resort to bribery to obtain what he wanted. Though most assemblymen were corrupt, not all the legislators were willing to be suborned. One such member, C.B. Bowman—a representative from Huerfano County—was offended by Mears' supposed attempt to bribe him and he pressed charges before the legislature. On February 3, 1891, a committee of the whole in the House heard a report from the investigating committee and decided that Bowman's charges had enough substance to warrant a grand jury investigation.

Accordingly, when the Arapahoe County grand jury met for its April session, it investigated Bowman's accusation. The grand jurors found, during the course of the hearings, significant evidence to bring indictment. On April 12, 1891, Otto Mears, Fred Walsen, Jerome B. Frank, Edwin Mitchell and A.M. Stevenson were indicted for bribery and attempted bribery of members of the Eighth General Assembly. The charges contained in the indictments were as follows:

1. On January 9, 1891, that Otto Mears offered C.B. Bowman $500 to support Speaker of the House Eddy's motion to have James W. Hanna succeed him in office.

2. On January 17, that C.B. Bowman was offered a chairmanship of a committee if he would support James W. Hanna.

3. On January 20, 1891, C.B. Bowman was threatened by James W. Hanna with exposure in a trumped up scandal.

4. On January 16, 1891, that C.B. Bowman reported to James W. Hanna that there were ''corrupt ele-

ments" in the lobby of the legislature and that Hanna did nothing about it.

5. Prior to January 17, 1891, Edwin Mitchell was an agent for a bribery attempt of another member of the legislature.

6. On January 16, 1891, Edwin Mitchell was offered a bribe to change his vote and Mitchell although refusing the bribe did not divulge who proffered it.

7. On January 6, 1891, C.J. Chapman was offered a $500 bribe to vote for James W. Hanna and Chapman, although not accepting the offer, refused to reveal who made it.

8. On January 6, 1891, representative Thomas Thornton was offered a series of bribes if he would vote for Eddy for speaker and, although refusing, Thornton refused to reveal the individual who made the offers. [3]

When the charges were made public it was the most sensational state political scandal since the bitter senatorial election of 1883. The indictment of Mears, who was by now a household name in the state, and several prominent business associates caused the public to follow the proceedings of the grand jury with great interest. Although widespread bribery in previous assemblies was common knowledge, this was the first time that such a widespread conspiracy had seemed to have been exposed.

The newspaper editors of the various Colorado journals all had comments about this episode and, almost without exception, stated that Bowman was mistaken or lying. The San Juan newspapers carried particularly violent denunciations of Bowman. These editors wondered why Mears, whose liberality was well known, would offer only $500 when a larger sum would be more in character.

Dave Day, who knew Otto better than any other editor, believed that Mears was capable of extending a bribe. However, the circumstances related by Bowman and the sum he was supposedly offered by Mears did not comply with Day's assessment of his friend. Day reasoned, therefore, that Bowman was lying. Said Day in the *Solid Muldoon* (still at Ouray) January 30, 1891: "Otto might have tendered a plug hat, meal ticket or a lot in Ridgway, but that $500 story don't go in this shop." Believing Bowman's charges without foundation, Day suggested in the same edition that "if Otto Mears will fumigate himself and come home all will be forgotten."

More was needed than fumigation to clear Otto of the charges. Apparently he was doing all he could to clear himself of Bowman's accusations. Rumor had it that he even resorted to more bribery. On April 15, 1891, the day after the public announcement of the indictments in the newspapers, an even more sensational story came to light. It was now charged that Mears was tampering with the grand jurors. He had been indicted by a 10-2 majority, and to present an indictment, it was necessary to have at least nine votes in favor. It was clear to all that the changing of two votes would cause the charges to be dropped. At this point, it was charged that Mears had succeeded in persuading an unnamed juror to change his vote. It was also alleged that Mears had decided to approach juror F.H. Baker to convince that individual, by whatever means, to change his vote.

Baker was a carpenter, disabled by rheumatism, and therefore he appeared to be an easy bribery target. Supposedly Mears sent an unidentified intermediary to Baker and the latter was sounded out about his preference in return for a vote for reconsideration of the indictment. Baker, an honest man, was indignant about this offer and attempted to force the go-between to make a specific offer so that he could file charges. The middleman refused to commit himself and only told Baker that a sedentary job would not be too difficult for him to find after the grand jury's business was transacted.

Because of the vagueness of Baker's accusations, Mears could not be prosecuted on these new charges. When asked by a *Rocky Mountain News* reporter about his knowledge of Baker's complaints, Otto replied peevishly: "I don't know anything about it, and I don't care, either."[4]

Despite Mears' attempts to exude confidence, he was

132

obviously very nervous when he posted $1,500 bail on April 15, 1891. He lacked his usual sangfroid and it was apparent to reporters that he was in desperate straits.

Mears was seemingly using every tactic he knew to extricate himself from the situation. After allegedly trying unsuccessfully to suborn the grand jurors, he now attempted to discredit the entire investigation by stating that the jurors were actuated by motives of personal vengeance for political reasons. These unelaborated countercharges, however, affected neither public opinion nor the grand jury investigation. For a week afterward, the grand jurors heard testimony from witnesses. It appeared to observers that enough evidence was found against Mears and the other accused to make an acquital doubtful.

It was the astuteness of his lawyers that saved Otto from the consequences of the indictment. The principal charge against Mears had been his alleged January 9, 1891, offer to Bowman of a $500 bribe to vote for Hanna for speaker. One of Otto's friends pointed out an obvious fact that the grand jury had, for some reason, ignored: Hanna had been elected speaker on January 7 and therefore Mears could not have offered a bribe on Hanna's behalf two days later. When the indictment was proven to be defective it was thrown out.

Bowman still pressed charges against Mears for attempted bribery, however. He stated that he was offered money to vote in favor of Eddy's motions; he said he had never testified that the bribe was proffered for his support of Hanna's candidacy for the speakership.

District Attorney Issac N. Stevens consequently impaneled a new grand jury on April 12, 1891, and an indictment was returned against Mears the same day. The second indictment did not include the defect of the first and Mears was now charged with the attempted bribery of Bowman in return for the latter's support of the motions of H.H. Eddy.

It was evident to all by this time that the second indictment was just a formality.[5] With only one witness against him, Mears was able to convince the second grand jury of his innocence. Apparently, as judged by later events, Mears learned nothing from the lengthy legal proceedings except to be more careful about his lobbying in the future.

After his exoneration by the second grand jury, the boss' fortunes took a dramatic turn for the better. Until the charges listed in the indictments against Mears were refuted, it was extremely difficult to sell Rio Grande Southern bonds. Capitalists were reluctant to invest money in a venture managed by a man with an uncertain future. When the grand jury failed to prove him guilty, Mears was able to raise the necessary construction funds to resume work on the new railroad. Work had been curtailed during the first four months of 1891 because of insufficient funds.

Busied by the resumption of construction work on the Rio Grande Southern Railroad, Mears did not engage in politics until January, 1893, when the Ninth General Assembly was convened. As in 1891, he lobbied against proposed railroad legislation. He again decided that his best chance to prevent railroad regulation was personally to supervise the organization of the railroad committees of both houses. He described his activities in a January 13, 1893, letter to George Coppell, an eastern investor in the Rio Grande Southern:

> I have given very close attention to the organi-
> zation of the Senate and Lower House, and as
> there was every evidence of an early completion
> of same, it was necessary for me to act promptly.
> . . . I can assure that the organization in both
> Houses, so far as the Railroad Committees are
> concerned, are in our favor. The Senate Commit-
> tee is especially strong. It consists of five mem-
> bers and they are all decidedly opposed to rail-
> road legislation. The House Committee consists
> of thirteen members, the majority of whom will
> be opposed to a railroad bill. [6]

Upon this occasion he found it necessary to go beyond organizing the legislature's railroad committees. The

impluse was so strong among the legislators to create railroad regulatory laws that Mears had to employ other
tactics. In the same letter to Coppell, he explained how he
used one such ploy:

> In addition to the railroad bills proper there
> will be Employes' Liability bills, which, if pass-
> ed, would be almost as injurious as regular rail-
> road bills. I am very hard to defeat this class of
> legislation also and have had a member of the
> Lower House present a bill, very strong in lan-
> guage, affecting every possible interest in the
> State including railroads, and I believe it is so
> strong as to bring out the proper ideas and that
> the members will never consent to its passage.
> In this connection I should say that three or four
> of the Populist members have presented as
> many bills confining the liability to railroad com-
> panies and my purpose in having presented the
> one affecting all interests was to bring out the
> true inwardness of such legislation.

His tactics were very successful and all bills concerned
with railroad regulation were defeated. Mears' 1893
political activities culminated in a trip east in the fall.
Visiting many large cities on the eastern seaboard, he
distributed material favoring a return to the silver
standard. He believed the panacea to the state's and his
own problems was a return to the standard, and he did
everything he could in the following three years to effect
this end.

In 1894, Mears took time out from his busy business
schedule and his silver standard campaign to engage in
the gubernatorial election. Selection of a winning
Republican candidate was important to him. The Populist
incumbent, Davis H. Waite, was running for a second
term and he seemed unable to solve the state's
problems. Otto wanted someone in office who, if not
competent, at least would follow the advice he and his
associates offered.

Mears also had another more personal reason for

wanting to see Waite defeated for re-election. As a member of the Board of Capitol Commissioners since April, 1889, Mears had fought incapability and corruption among the capitol managers. Waite, when elected in 1892, decided to remove Otto from his post and replace him with a Democrat. Mears refused to resign, stating that Waite had no right to replace him. The matter went to the Colorado Supreme Court. Mears, although represented by attorney Charles Hughes, presented his own defense. He argued that it was in the best interest of the people of Colorado that the old capitol managers be retained. Only they had the necessary experience to supervise the construction of the capitol building, he stated. So persuasive was Mears that the judge allowed him to retain his post. He never forgot this incident and his desire for revenge against Waite was a motivating factor in his drive to unseat him.

Mears' first task in preparation for the fall election was to find a candidate acceptable to both himself and the rank and file of the Republican party. In April he chose—as the ideal candidate—Albert McIntire, a resident of Conejos County who was virtually unknown to his fellow Republicans. Eastern born and educated at Yale, he had come to Colorado in 1876. In 1891, he was appointed to what was then his most important public office: A recommendation by Mears and Fred Walsen to Governor Routt resulted in his being appointed district judge of Conejos County. McIntire had served one year as judge when fellow party members from his district—believing him unfit for office —selected a replacement at the Republican judicial convention.

McIntire's political career was revived in the spring of 1894, when Mears selected him as his choice for Republican gubernatorial candidate. In return for support, the political boss evidently insisted that McIntire do as he ordered upon gaining office. After an agreement of some kind had been reached, Mears began the campaign for his protege in June in a county by county canvass. At this time he talked to local leaders and asked for their help.

The men of influence were told that McIntire would be the best man for the office because he was educated and because he had a million dollar inheritance to spend on the election—the latter a Mears fabrication. The candidate's other qualifications, the campaigner asserted, were fine stature and a little known reputation. It was also claimed that because McIntire had no political enemies, his selection would cause no intra-party discord.

McIntire's sponsor campaigned well. He repeated again and again to local political bosses the story about the office seeker's million dollar inheritance and thereby gained delegates for his candidate. So successful was the campaign manager that at the Republican state convention conducted on September 12, 1894, McIntire was nominated by acclamation as the party's candidate for governor.

Mears' next task was to insure, so far as he was able, McIntire's election. McIntire had two competitors for the gubernatorial post. The Populist-Democratic coalition which had elected Davis H. Waite governor in 1892 had broken up because of Democratic dissatisfaction with Waite. In 1894, Waite was running for re-election as a Populist candidate. The Democrats chose Charles S. Thomas, an experienced politician, as their candidate.

By late September, the gubernatorial race was no longer a three-way contest. The chief contenders now were Waite and McIntire, with Thomas running a distant third. Because Waite was McIntire's principal opponent, the slogan for the Republicans in the 1894 election became "redeem the state from Waiteism." Mears was able to run an effective campaign despite McIntire's poor public speaking ability. Otto worked hard for his candidate canvassing the voters of each county.

The Republicans used a more novel campaign tactic along with the usual speeches and newspaper editorials. In this ploy, men were hired to seek out members of the Populist Party heading large families, owning considerable amounts of property, and needing money. The Populists were approached and asked if they would consider selling their property. If the Populists were willing to sell, the hired men would give them a deposit, depending on the number of voters in the family. The seller was told that the remainder of the purchase price would be forthcoming from Denver in a few days. Several days later, the would-be purchaser would return and present the seller with the following letter:

> Dear Sir—If you will recall the promise we made, to loan you the money mentioned, you will remember it was conditioned on the election of Mr. McIntire. If Waite is elected, we shall be compelled to call in loans instead of extending them. After the election you can have the money if the result is as we hope for.[7]

The agent, after showing the letter, would assure the seller that the deal would be consummated after McIntire's election. This ruse induced several Populists to vote for McIntire instead of Waite. The Republican leaders had no desire to complete the transactions set up by their agents and bought votes by this method for only $2 to $5 apiece.

The shrewd Republican campaign tactics in combination with a growing dissatisfaction with the way the Waite administration was dealing with the problems caused by the 1893 Depression and the consequent labor unrest led to a decisive McIntire victory. After the election, Mears spent the next several months in Denver selecting individuals for the various offices which it was the new governor's duty to fill. After choosing most of the new officeholders, the political boss went on a combined business and pleasure trip to New York in January, 1895.

When he returned in February, Mears found himself in the role of peacemaker in a dispute between Governor McIntire and John Hecker, a prominent Longmont Republican. McIntire had allegedly promised Hecker a fish and game warden position in return for support in the gubernatorial election. Upon gaining office, the newly elected official had not honored this agreement because he discovered that Hecker was a Catholic. Knowing that

Coloradoans were assumed to be prejudiced against Catholics, the new governor believed it politically inexpedient to appoint one to office. At this juncture, the officeseeker became disgruntled and Mears, to placate him, promised him a position in the new administration.

Two months passed. In early April, Hecker, irate because he seemingly was once again passed over, stormed into the governor's office and demanded his reward for his support in the last election. When McIntire refused, Hecker complained to the *Rocky Mountain News.* The story appeared on April 19, 1895, and caused a sensation. Commenting about the facts of the case, the editor demanded impeachment proceedings be started against McIntire because it was unconstitutional to make political deals for offices. Evidently Mears and McIntire placated Hecker, because nothing more was heard about the matter.

For the next year and a half, Mears busied himself with his railroads. He did not engage in political activity until September, 1896. At that time he began preparations for the state and national elections. The political situation in Colorado was confused: Republicans had nominated William McKinley for president. McKinley was in favor of the gold standard, while his Democratic opponent, William Jennings Bryan, favored silver. The so-called "Battle of the Standards" disrupted normal political alignments in Colorado. Many Republicans—including Otto—knowing that the economic welfare of Colorado depended upon government subsidization of silver, split off from the party. These Silver Republicans "fused" with the Democrats to form a state ticket and to support Bryan. Meanwhile, the National Silver Party joined the Populists. A third political grouping comprised the minority of Republicans who supported McKinley and subscribed to their party's platform.

On September 10, 1896, the Silver Republicans met for their convention. Their purpose was to name a slate and platform in advance of the following day's joint convention with the Democrats. At the Silver Republican convention, Mears was the leader, and he obtained both the slate and platform he desired.[8] At this convention, a protege of Mears—Simon Guggenheim—was nominated for lieutenant governor in his first bid for state office.

Guggenheim, 29 years old, came from a wealthy Philadelphia family. The Guggenheims owned the Philadelphia Smelting and Refining Company of Pueblo, of which Simon was vice president and general manager. The young man was ambitious and desired a seat in the United States Senate; he allegedly formed an alliance with Otto Mears. Since Guggenheim was not old enough to be senator, Mears promised to have him elected at the appropriate time. In return, the political hopeful agreed to allow Mears to be his political mentor and to provide Republican campaign funds when necessary. He further repaid his political debt by investing heavily in Mears' railroads and other enterprises.

The Silver Republicans, having completed their slate, met in a joint convention with the Democrats on September 11, 1896. As one of the most important political leaders, Mears was kept busy throughout the convention with the formation and maintenance of an alliance between the two parties. He was omnipresent, using his wit and powers of diplomacy to soothe ruffled tempers.

Mears' work on behalf of the coalition went neither unnoticed nor unappreciated. An incident occurred which showed the esteem the delegates had for him. While the nominations committee was in the process of selecting a gubernatorial candidate, a committee member suggested that the old pioneer be chosen as nominee. Another committee member, however—knowing that the political manager did not want the nomination but that he enjoyed flattery—pointed out that in effect "Otto Mears *is* the Governor of Colorado." The political boss was so delighted by this open acknowledgement of his importance that he repeated the compliment everywhere.[9]

Due to the finesse with which Mears manipulated the delegates, the convention was short and ran smoothly. Alva Adams was chosen as the Fusion Party's candidate for governor and Simon Guggenheim as its nominee for lieutenant governor. The latter, however, was too young to serve as lieutenant governor, and his nomination was token, intended to serve as thanks to Mears for his astute management of the convention. Jared L. Brush, an experienced politician, was later chosen to take Guggenheim's place on the slate. The party's other nominees were chosen in the same spirit of conciliation and compromise as were the candidates for governor and lieutenant governor. The slate was completed with an equal number of nominees coming from each party. The platform was also an expression of concordance between the Silver Republicans and the Democrats. The main plank was the restoration of silver as the medium of exchange, with the United States government subsidizing the silver industry as it had before the repeal of the Sherman Silver Purchase Act in 1893.

Due to Coloradoans' overwhelming support of the Fusion Party platform and to an effective campaign conducted by the coalition's skilled leaders, Alva Adams and the other members of the Silver Republican-Democratic slate won office. With the campaign out of the way, Mears stayed in Denver from November, 1896, to the early spring of the next year to assist in the selection of governmental appointive officers. When the legislative session opened in January, he undertook additional duties. He served as lobbyist in the interests of large corporations. He worked against adverse railroad legislation and bills which gave benefits to the wage-earner. Passage of such measures would discourage outside investment in Colorado and would make it difficult for big businesses to raise the money to finance expansions.

For the next year and a half, Mears was out of politics but he returned to Denver in September of 1898 to participate in the Silver Republican convention. By this time, he was becoming more and more immersed in business, social and political activities in Washington, D.C. [See Chapter VII], but not wanting to relinquish his control of

SIMON GUGGENHEIM
*"His money and my brains
dovetail in together so sweet."*

142

the Colorado Republican Party, he took time out from his busy schedule to return to the Centennial State and help his party prepare for the state elections.

The political situation in Colorado had been in a state of confusion since the 1896 campaign, when many Republicans had refused to support McKinley for president and had voted for the Democratic candidate, William Jennings Bryan. In state elections, most Republicans joined with the Democrats to form the Fusion Party. Although the new party was in favor of a silver standard—something desired by nearly all Coloradoans—it was uncertain how long the Republicans and Democrats would bury their traditional rivalry. When Mears arrived in Colorado in September of 1898, it was not known if the 1896 coalition would be maintained.

On September 8, 1898, in this politically unstable situation, the Silver Republicans conducted their convention in Colorado Springs. Mears managed the convention and the slate of the Silver Republicans met his wishes. Simon Guggenheim spent $70,000 and had Mears' help in his successful bid for the gubernatorial nomination of this convention.

While the Silver Republican convention was in progress, Mears kept a close watch on political developments elsewhere. He realized that if the Democrats, the Silver Republicans and the Populists united as they ultimately had in 1896, Guggenheim would have little chance to be nominated for high office on the Fusionist slate because of his youth and inexperience. If a coalition party could be prevented from forming, the Silver Republican Party headed by Mears and Guggenheim would be in the ascendancy. And so, agents—possibly paid by Mears himself—disrupted the pre-convention proceedings of the Democrats and the Populists in an effort to disorganize the parties and prevent them from uniting.

The agents were unsuccessful, however, in preventing the formation of a Fusion Party. On September 10, 1898, delegates of the Democrats, Populists and Silver Republicans met in a joint convention in Colorado

Springs. The delegates soon came to an agreement concerning the platform and slate. The main plank of the party was the same as it had been in 1896—the maintenance of the silver standard. Mears did not succeed in having Guggenheim chosen as the Fusion candidate for governor. Charles S. Thomas, the experienced Democratic politician, was nominated instead.

Although he failed to obtain a nomination for Guggenheim, Mears did succeed in finding places on the slate for some of his other friends to fill. One of these spots was filled by John C. Bell, a Montrose Populist, who was nominated for representative from the second district. Mears had known Bell for 25 years and had encouraged him in every endeavor. During one of Bell's previous campaigns, Mears was asked by a *Rocky Mountain News* reporter why he was supporting Bell, who was a Democrat. Mears answered:

> because he was my boy. I made him. When he
> first came to Saguache he was growing so darn
> fast that his pant legs were at the top of his
> stockings and his coat sleeves half-way up to his
> elbows, but he was an awful nice boy. He did not
> know what a dance hall was. He had never been
> to one. He walked in one night and pulled off his
> hat out of respect for the ladies.

When Bell saw the article the next day, he sought out Mears and asked him why he told the reporter the untrue story. Otto replied, "I know there is no truth in it, but by Shiminy I want to advertise you. That is the way to get you elected." [10]

Upon the completion of the Fusion Party slate, Mears went East where for the next five years he tried unsuccessfully to recoup the fortune he had lost in the 1893 depression. At the end of this period, he returned briefly to participate in what was to be one of the state's most sensational political contests—the 1903 senatorial election.

7

The Ubiquitous Mr. Mears

*A*fter the sale of the Rio Grande Southern Railroad in November, 1895, Mears did everything he could to recoup the financial loss he had suffered on the venture. Desperate, he knew that his only chance to regain his fortune in Colorado would be a victory for William Jennings Bryan in the 1896 presidential election. The candidate promised, if victorious, to return the nation to bimetalism. If this occurred prosperity was expected to return to Colorado because the United States government would again subsidize the state's silver industry as it had before the repeal of the Sherman Silver Purchase Act. The railroad president awaited the fall election in Silverton where he superintended the operations of his various enterprises.

On August 25, 1896, he left the management of his business affairs to subordinates and traveled to Denver on a lucrative offer from the First National Bank of Denver. The president of the bank, David H. Moffat, had close social and business ties with Mears for decades. Moffat knew his friend needed cash and offered him a large commission if he would manage the Appel Clothing Company's bankruptcy sale. The company had been founded in 1894, and through good management soon became one of Denver's largest retail stores, but it had been forced to close when Eastern creditors, without warning, demanded money owed. The owners tried desperately to avert bankruptcy by securing mortgages on their property. The money raised on the mortgages was inadequate to satisfy the firm's creditors, however, and the First National Bank finally took over the company at the request of the mortgagees.

It was at this point that Moffat made his offer to Mears. The latter decided to accept the job and acted as agent for the First National Bank until mid-September when the Appel stock was liquidated. He sold all the merchandise in little more than a fortnight, showing his considerable sales ability during such hard times.

The salesman then turned again to politics. In early fall he stumped the state on behalf of Bryan. Although the candidate carried Colorado by a wide margin, McKinley gained the presidency. With the defeat of Bryan, Mears knew that Colorado had a bleak future. The state was still in the grips of a depression and the only areas in Colorado to experience economic growth at the time were the gold producing regions. Too enterprising to remain in an area crippled by economic stagnation, Mears began examining opportunities for investment in other localities.

In July, 1897, Mears went to British Columbia to determine if it would be profitable to invest money there. Finding that business conditions in the province made prospects for a quick return unlikely, he returned to Denver. He spent August in Silverton managing his railroads. One day in mid-month, he received a telegram from David Moffat inviting him to examine a railroad construction scheme in Washington, D.C. Otto, knowing Moffat's reputation as a shrewd businessman, left immediately for the East.

Upon arrival in Washington, Mears met with Moffat to receive an outline of the proposed venture. Everyone knew, the latter explained, about the hot summer weather in the nation's capital. All who had the time and money would leave the town and go to a resort. The others who were forced to stay in town during the summer would go to lakes in the vicinity for recreation. Those who were able would go to Chesapeake Beach, the best of the local beaches. Although only 20 to 25 miles from Washington, Chesapeake Beach was inaccessible except by a long, roundabout train trip through Annapolis or by a steamship ride on the Potomac.[1]

Enterprising individuals had tried to construct a direct railroad connection between Washington and Chesapeake Beach in the early 1890s, Mears was told. Edwin Warfield, a Maryland financier and politician, and J.L. Barbour, a Washington businessman, were the promoters of this prior project. On September 1, 1891, they had incorporated the Washington and Chesapeake Beach Railway Company in Maryland. According to their charter, the incorporators were entitled to issue one million dollars in capital stock. With the funds a railroad would be constructed between Washington and Chesapeake Beach. The incorporators could also, if they desired, build a resort on Chesapeake Beach.

The Panic and Depression of 1893, coupled with fraud and incompetence among the corporate officers, made it impossible to build any part of the railroad, Moffat explained. The promoters. unable to raise the funds necessary for construction of the line, were also unable to pay the interest due on monies already borrowed. On November 5, 1893, they consequently conveyed the property and rights of the corporation to the American Security and Trust Company. Later, Moffat became interested in the defunct corporation. Knowing a good investment opportunity when he saw one, he ordered his New York agent, Robert E. Tod, to buy the property and rights of the Washington and Chesapeake Beach Railway Company.

The transaction was completed on December 10, 1895, and Moffat soon realized that much work was necessary before he recovered the purchase price, much less a profit, from the corporation. His first step to revitalize the company was to effect a complete reorganization so that construction and management of the railroad would be facilitated. The new enterprise, called the Chesapeake Beach Railway Company, was incorporated on March 7, 1896. The charter empowered the company to construct a railroad between Washington, D.C., and Chesapeake Beach, Maryland, and to raise the sum of $500,000 for the purpose.

After the incorporation of the Chesapeake Beach Railway Company, Moffat wanted the most competent assistance possible to complete the project and thought Mears was the most qualified for the job. Moffat told Mears he needed his visitor's advice and expertise to build the railroad. To encourage his participation in the project, the guest was invited to investigate all aspects of the scheme to determine if good investment potential existed. If Mears decided to join Moffat in the venture, he could do so on advantageous terms.

After his long introductory discussion with Moffat, Mears spent considerable time and effort determining the profitability of the projected railroad. In his usual thorough way, the speculator examined all facets of construction and operation of the proposed line. During his study of the project, he found that more than 12,000 people left Washington daily during the summer for salt water resorts. On Sundays, the figure rose to between 15,000 and 20,000. During the course of their peregrinations each individual spent between $1 and $5 for transportation costs. He calculated if the Chesapeake Beach Railway was built, a round trip ride to the ocean would cost the patron only $ .50. The combination of low ticket prices and the popularity of salt water recreation would attract one million passengers annually to the new line, he decided.

In addition to profits from the passenger business, Mears believed that the proposed railroad would make money from freight rates. He estimated that fishermen on Chesapeake Beach sent 6,000 barrels of crab, 38,000 barrels of fish, and 900,000 bushels of oysters to Washington, D.C., annually. These products usually took three and a half days to reach Washington. By railroad, they would take only one and a half hours. He assumed the proposed railroad would carry at least one third of the seafood caught in Chesapeake Bay.

Although he believed that the proposed railroad would do a lucrative business hauling passengers and freight, Mears was more intrigued with the possibility of building a resort on Chesapeake Beach. He believed that the railroad's articles of incorporation permitted the building of a casino on the bay. The ambiguous wording of the charter seemed to indicate that the State of Maryland had forfeited its police powers on the beach.

The opportunity to become involved with an American Monte Carlo was probably the major factor in Mears' decision to build the Chesapeake Beach railroad. This choice resulted in a watershed in his life. During the preceding 30 years, he had been active in Colorado's economic and political life. For the next decade, however, he would be concerned primarily with economic and political activities outside of the state. To adequately understand the conduct of his Colorado business enter- prises during this period and to understand his activities in Colorado after his return in November, 1906, it is necessary to trace his career during the time he was largely absent from the Centennial State.

After deciding to become part of Moffat's venture, Mears displayed his characteristic energy. In September, 1897, he incorporated the Chesapeake Bay Construction Company. A profitable arrangement was made with Moffat: The construction company would receive $30,000 in Chesapeake Beach Railway Company stock and the same amount in bonds for each mile built. It was also agreed that the work would be divided into five sections and that the 29-mile line would be completed by July 1, 1898.

Construction of the railroad began in October, 1897. Work began at the junction of the Baltimore and Ohio Railroad in the District of Columbia and track was laid in a southeasterly direction toward Chesapeake Beach. While the crew was building the broad gauge roadbed a pier was being assembled on the beach. The 2,000-foot pier was necessary to facilitate the transfer of seafood from fishing boats to the railroad.

Initially, prospects were good for rapid completion of the construction. In Denver for a short visit in December, 1897, the railroad builder predicted that the track would be laid by March 1, 1898, and that the resort would be finished by May. Things did not go as forecast, however. The terrain between Washington and Chesapeake Bay made the work of grading and track-laying much more difficult than had been predicted.

Mears had an even more difficult problem than the obstacles presented by the country. He and the treasurer of the Chesapeake Bay Construction Company, Charles Popper, were in constant disagreement with Ambrose C. Dunn, the corporation's vice president. Dunn, an experienced army engineer and construction supervisor, believed—and rightly so—that the work was being done too rapidly and was consequently defective. The engineer also felt he was being mistreated. Mears constantly countermanded his orders, undermining his employees' respect for him. Holding the opinion that he was receiving bad treatment, Dunn retaliated by obstructing efforts to complete the railroad. The discord among the officers caused nearly a year's delay in the construction.

The dissension among the officers prevented more than ten miles of track from being completed on time. With the expiration of the contract with the Chesapeake Beach Railway Company on October 7, 1898, Mears believed the obvious changes were in order if the remaining 20 miles of track were to be laid at all. To prevent Dunn from causing further trouble, Mears decided to exclude the engineer from future management decision-making. The construction company was dissolved and its property was transferred to the Chesapeake Beach Railway Company. The railway company—with Mears in undisputed control—eventually finished the construction.

Mears' problems with Dunn were not over, however.

Not willing to be so easily ousted from an enterprise which had consumed so much of his time and money, Dunn sued the Chesapeake Beach Railway Company, claiming that there was a conspiracy of Mears and other officers to deprive him of his investment profits. The president, although finding Dunn's suit irksome, still kept his sense of humor. A letter to Moffat June 23, 1899, demonstrates:

> Everything is running along here, although a little hot. The people here complain a great deal about it, but I have been frozen up in Colorado for the last thirty years and am just thawing out, so it does not hurt me.[2]

Dunn's lawsuit was tried in New York City in early July, 1899. The plaintiff charged that his investment in the Chesapeake Beach Railway Company was jeopardized by the incompetence and mismanagement of Otto Mears. The complaint alleged that Mears had ignored Dunn's advice and as a consequence, had done a very poor job of tracklaying. The construction work, it was asserted, was done so rapidly that a fatal accident might result if the trains were allowed to operate.

Dunn's attempt to oust Mears as president of the Chesapeake Beach Railway Company was unsuccessful. The plaintiff did succeed, however, in achieving some measure of revenge for his alleged mistreatment. The publicity from this bitter legal battle was not advantageous to the railroad. Many would-be customers were deterred from using the line, thinking it unsafe.

After withstanding Dunn's legal assault, Mears returned to Washington in order to complete the shortline while the tourist season was still in progress. In early August, 1899, the railroad reached Chesapeake Beach and while much work was still necessary, the president did what he could to build up passenger traffic.

The completion of the railroad was only the first step in the speculator's plan to develop the Chesapeake Bay region. In addition to possessing track, equipment and rights of way, the company owned Colorado Beach situated on the bay. At Colorado Beach, the railroad investor intended to build a mammoth resort with an amusement park, race track and casino.

After the railroad was extended to the beach, Mears embarked on the improvements he had planned. The resort was established on a grand scale. A boardwalk was built on Colorado Beach—larger than the one at Atlantic City—7,000 feet long and 20 feet wide. Facing the boardwalk were several buildings, one of which was a small hotel. Provisions were included, if warranted by tourist monies, for the construction of five more hotels. For those desiring semi-permanent living quarters, hundreds of acres were surveyed into lots for the building of cottages.

While the land was being divided into plots, every effort was made to ensure the self-sufficiency of Colorado Beach. A 2,600-foot pier was constructed to facilitate the catching of fresh seafood for tourists. To refrigerate the fish and other food, an ice-making plant was built.

To provide diversion for the residents and transients, an American Monte Carlo was under consideration, but this was found to be illegal. As Maryland still claimed its police powers in Chesapeake Bay, games of chance were unlawful and other entertainment was provided for guests. A race track was built instead of a casino and a

minature railroad was built along the beach. Powered by a steam locomotive, this railroad was a favorite with the children.

During the development of Chesapeake Beach, Mears found time for a full social life. He had to make some adjustments, however, to be fully accepted in the highest eastern society. He shaved his full beard, leaving only a moustache. He became a fastidious dresser who sported the latest fashions. With his stylish dress and his irresistable charm, Otto was soon moving in Washington's highest social circles.

In keeping with his new social position the Coloradoan purchased a yacht. To enhance his enjoyment from salt water sports, he joined Washington's Capitol Yacht Club and invited businessmen, prominent politicians, and young ladies to join him for a good time on his yacht.[3]

The entrepreneur found time for politics as well as social life. His political objectives in Washington and Maryland were similar to those he had had in Colorado. He participated in Eastern politics on the same scale as he had in his home state. His political alliances—as in the Centennial State—were motivated by friendship, wishes for power, profit, and revenge.

Mears' most significant foray into politics during his first years in the East was his attempt to engineer the defeat of incumbent Republican Sydney Mudd of Maryland in the 1900 Congressional election. Mudd first had been elected to Congress in 1896 from Maryland's fifth district and had shown so much ability that he was chosen a member of the House's powerful railroad committee. Initially, he and Mears were political allies. The latter, desiring to ingratiate himself with a powerful member of Congress, contributed much time and money to help Mudd's Maryland friends in the 1899 campaign.

The Mears-Mudd alliance did not last long, however. It became apparent to the former that a right-of-way into Washington, D.C., was necessary for the survival of the Chesapeake Beach Railway. Passengers became tired after taking a succession of street cars from Washington

City to the railroad's boarding site. Efforts to improve the street car connection failed and the only solution was to lay track into Washington itself.

To obtain permission for a right-of-way into the capital city, Mears asked for a hearing before the House railroad committee. After listening to the pleas of the railroad president, the committee members refused to give approval to his request because Sydney Mudd allegedly convinced them that if a right-of-way was given to anyone, it should be to the Congressman himself. Mudd, who was also involved in a railroad scheme, received permission to build into Washington, whereas Mears did not.

Enraged by the lack of support from his former ally, Mears wanted revenge. Knowing that Mudd was up for re-election in 1900, the railroad president did what he could to assist Mudd's Democratic challenger. Mears used every trick he knew in an attempt to defeat Mudd. One ruse was to permit women to travel free on his railway. When asked why he did this, he stated:

> I am after Mudd, and "the hand that rocks the cradle, rules politics."[4]

In addition to his attempts to influence women, the political boss endeavored to persuade another bloc of voters to vote against Mudd. He allegedly bribed hundreds of Negros to cast their ballot for the Democratic candidate. Mudd, however, was said to have outbid Mears and induced the bribed voters to support the incumbent instead. Successfully countering his rival's tactics, the candidate was returned to office in the fall election.

After his bad luck in the Maryland state elections, Mears entered national politics. In the 1900 election year, in addition to his unsuccessful attempt to defeat Mudd, he participated in the presidential election. He left Colorado politics "strictly alone" that year, believing that with the Republicans and Democrats in the state banding together according to their views for or against silver as a medium of exchange, the situation was "foolish." Although the boss had exploited the political chaos in the state, he was tired of it by 1900. He also realized that although the silver standard issue was paramount in his former home, it was becoming a dead issue in other parts of the country and he had neither the time nor inclination to support lost causes.

In 1900, William Jennings Bryan was the Democratic presidential nominee. Mears had supported him in the 1896 campaign, but in 1900 he reasoned that the incumbent William McKinley would be re-elected by a landslide. Otto resolved, therefore, to change his allegiance to McKinley.

Mears threw himself wholeheartedly into McKinley's presidential campaign. With this candidate's victory in November, 1900, he was rewarded for the time, money and energy he had expended on the election. He was repaid for his assistance by a high honor. He was appointed to the committee in charge of planning the inaugural ball.

The new appointee became the most active member of the inaugural committee. The other members, impressed by his dynamism and diligence, permitted him to assume their duties. Given a free rein, the Coloradoan outdid himself. In a January 20, 1901, interview he predicted that the occasion would ''be the biggest thing in the history of inaugural balls.'' His confidence was based on the elaborate plans he had made and on the participation of the 150 policemen who would be in attendance.

The inaugural ball lived up to Mears' expectations and marked the high point of his Washington stay. Moving in the highest political and social circles gave the Russian immigrant much satisfaction. After a half-century rags to riches struggle, he was hobnobbing with presidents. He was so pleased, in fact, with Washington life that he wanted to make the city his permanent home. His plans, however, were contingent upon the financial success of the Chesapeake Beach Railway, which had been losing money but had good prospects for the future.

Many obstacles had been overcome in an attempt to put the railroad on a paying basis. Because of the various problems, the Chesapeake Beach Railway was the most difficult project upon which the railroad president had ever embarked. His difficulties had been threefold: faulty workmanship during the railroad's construction; inability to obtain permission to build into Washington City; and the numerous lawsuits involving the railroad.

The easiest problem to deal with was the replacement of defective materials and equipment. The fills, which had been done improperly due to the hasty construction, were sinking because of an influx of clay and water, and were rebuilt. In addition to the fills, the trestles also presented a problem. In Colorado, trestles lasted eight years. In Maryland and Washington, the corrosive sea air prevented the trestles from lasting longer than two or three years. Because of the repair work on the fills and the replacement of the trestles, the Chesapeake Beach Railway incurred much unforeseen additional expense, which put the corporation further in the red.

The most serious problem of the corporation was the absence of right-of-way into Washington City. As connections between the city and the railroad were poor, many would-be passengers were lost because of the inconvenience. Everyone involved with the operation of the railroad realized that permission had to be obtained for entry into Washington to assure optimum passenger traffic. Adequate connections with the capital city were not acquired, however, until near the end of Mears' presidency. His failure for so long to provide the right-of-way probably constituted the principal reason for Mears' later removal from the presidency of the company.

Less serious but more vexatious than the frustrating attempts to build into Washington City was the constant litigation which plagued the company from 1898 on. In late March of that year, the corporation's legal troubles began. The Washington and Potomac Railroad brought suit in Maryland claiming that the Chesapeake Beach Railway Corporation was using without permission its track and right-of-way—a two-mile stretch of track from northeast District of Columbia to the Maryland line. The court action was described by the March 28, 1898, issue of the *Washington Evening Star* as "one of the hardest fights in Washington railroad history." The issue was finally settled when the Chesapeake Beach Railway Corporation acknowledged the title of the Washington and Potomac Railroad to the two-mile segment. For its part, the Washington and Potomac Railroad agreed to lease the two-mile section to the rival railroad.

Fourteen months later Mears was again in court. In July, 1899, as previously described, Ambrose Dunn unsuccessfully tried to take over the railroad. In less than six months in January, 1901, the railroad president had to withstand another legal assault. On January 9, 1901, C.R. and John Meyers of Atlantic City filed suit in the chancery court of Trenton, New Jersey, applying for a receiver for the railway. The brothers claimed that because the railroad was $70,000 in debt, their holdings on Chesapeake Beach, involving the race track and other concessions, were in danger of being attached by the railroad's creditors. The court, however, did not appoint the receiver as requested because the brothers could not prove that their property was in danger.

Although Mears had successfully withstood four years of lawsuits, the constant litigation helped undermine his control of the Chesapeake Beach Railway. The other stockholders became disgruntled and refused to give him the necessary support and the funds he needed to expand operations. His chief opponent was ironically David H. Moffat, who had first interested him in the railroad scheme. A successful Colorado financier, Moffat was involved in other projects in addition to the Chesapeake Beach Railway, and was even considering a new project — the Denver, Northwestern and Pacific Railroad. The new scheme entailed the building of a railroad from Denver to Salt Lake City. Moffat realized that much time and money would have to be expended to make his projected railroad a success and that his other ventures would have to be put aside under competent subordinates for the time being.

Moffat decided that the Chesapeake Beach Railway was his most nagging worry. The investor considered the line badly managed, was tired of the many lawsuits which he believed could have been avoided, and was disgusted with the poor workmanship displayed in the construction of the railroad. He was also disappointed in the road's financial returns. Accordingly, he began buying up shares of the corporation's stock so that he could assume control of the railroad. Upon gaining control of the railroad, he reasoned he could depose Mears and appoint a person more competent to the presidency.

Throughout 1901 and early 1902, Moffat pursued this plan. Having purchased $1,500,000 worth of stock by the summer of 1902, he was the majority stockholder and in a position to demand Mears' resignation. Rumors about the president's expected dismissal began circulating among railroad personnel and he wrote Moffat in a last ditch effort to retain control of the operation. This was the most revealing letter Mears ever wrote. His pride, reputation, financial standing, and social position were being threatened and the long letter indicates his state of mind:

> All my life I have been unfortunate in one respect and that is that I have worked out schemes that have paid and made money and some else [sic] get [sic] the benefit of my work. I have now gone to work and got this property in a position where any one [sic] can take hold of it and, as far as the road is concerned, can make it pay. But even after all this I have heard it rumored that I am to be kicked out and the management of it turned over to some one else.
>
> This property here is now all improved and if you will only be patient until fall you will see that I am right. Now, Mr. Moffat, you know that if you had told me that you wished me to get out and let someone else take hold here I would have done so at once, and not only that I would have gladly helped the gentleman whoever he might

be in any way that I could by giving him my ideas in regard to the property, that is if he wanted my ideas. But you know that at my age, when I have spent the last five years of my life here working night and day studying and figuring and worrying about how to get a profit out of this property that it is very disappointing and hurtful to my pride to be told to get out just at the time when I feel that I have at last succeeded in realizing the reward of my work, when the turning point has just been reached and the undertaking is on the eve of success.[5]

This letter did not have the desired effect. In August, 1902, Mears and the other company officers were asked to resign. Moffat selected Sylvester T. Smith, a Chicago railroad man, to replace the former president; Fred W. Moffat, his brother, as treasurer; and Arthur C. Ridgway of Colorado as the new general manager.

Removal from the presidency of the Chesapeake Beach Railway was a severe blow to Mears' pride. Overcoming many human and natural obstacles, he felt he had put the line into a position where in the future it would pay a handsome return. After his resignation he was very bitter. For the second time in his career, he had lavished time and money on a railroad project only to lose the benefits himself.

After relinquishing control of the railroad, Mears' first inclination was to sell his stock and to retire to Colorado. Disillusioned at first, his optimism soon returned and he became philosophical about his dismissal. His stoic attitude was exemplified in an October 4, 1902, letter to Fred Walsen. The theme of the letter was summarized by the statement that "you can never tell what changes will come to pass in a man's life that will change the entire future."

Resigned to his bad luck, the Coloradoan spent the early fall of 1902 closing out his Washington affairs. Keeping his promise to Moffat, he assisted the new management in its takeover of the operation. When he could offer no further help to the new officers, he returned briefly to Colorado.

Not content to force Mears from the presidency of the railroad, Moffat wanted to rid the railroad completely of his influence. Motivated by sound business reasons and perhaps by jealousy, spite, or a sense of injury, the financier sought to force the ex-president to relinquish control of his stock in the enterprise. The opening salvo in the battle to force Mears out entirely was begun in late June, 1905. A longtime president of Denver's First National Bank, Moffat directed the bank's attorneys to bring suit against his former friend for $75,000. The plaintiff claimed Mears had borrowed the money in several installments in 1899 and that the principal and interest had been due since April 1, 1905. By bringing suit, the bank president hoped that the defendant would be forced to sell all or part of his Chesapeake Beach Railway stock to repay the loan.

The defendant found out about the lawsuit when he visited Colorado in late June, 1905. When told about the proceedings against him, he told a *Rocky Mountain News* reporter, "I do not owe the bank one cent, but if I did, I will say that I am always ready to pay any legitimate debt." He asserted Moffat was motivated by spite.

Mears' supposed financial plight aroused much sympathy from the Colorado press. The editor of the *Denver Post,* for example, asserted that the pioneer had always been generous with money. Although Otto was a heavy gambler and had won and lost large sums, he was always munificent. When a winner at the tables, he was particularly lavish, distributing money freely and thus forming many new friendships. The editor implied that it was unfortunate that an individual who had done as much for others as Mears would have no one to help him now.

Dave Day offered commiseration as well in the *Durango Democrat* and added the following humorous comment about his friend's financial woes:

Otto Mears is $75,000 ahead of the First Na-

160

tional Bank. He is not only a pathfinder but a doughfinder. Otto was at Atlantic City last summer with "Simiah" Guggenheim. Otto stooped down on the board walk and apparently picked up something. Simiah saw him and wanted half of it. "What was it, Otto?" asked Simon. "Wadding," replied Otto, "but I'd like to pinch dot fellow who can spit so much like a quarter."[6]

The sympathetic reaction of the Colorado press toward Mears did not deter Moffat from making further moves to acquire his Chesapeake Beach Railway stock. On June 26, 1905, the financier's attorneys filed suit for $1,222,800 in the Supreme Court. It was alleged that a promissory note had been made in December, 1904, stipulating that the amount should be paid on demand. The plaintiff, however, admitted that the assets of the Chesapeake Beach Railway did not amount to the sum asked in the suit. He hoped to force his rival to sell his shares of stock so that they could be purchased at a premium.

When notified of this lawsuit, the defendant claimed it was motivated by revenge. He admitted directing Mrs. Mears to sue the Chesapeake Beach Railway Company for $11,000 she had advanced for construction purposes. Moffat had retaliated in turn, it was alleged, by bringing his suit.

Moffat was subsequently successful in forcing Mears to sell his shares of stock in the railroad. The financier purchased the stock at a sale in the fall of 1905. The forced sale of his railroad stock caused Mears to suffer a large potential financial loss. The Chesapeake Beach Railway Company—which operated for another 30 years—was eventually to prove profitable to its stockholders and would have helped Mears regain part of the fortune he had lost in 1893. It would be years before he again had the opportunity to recoup his losses, and the chance came only after he experienced several more failures.

Back in the summer of 1903, two and a half years before he lost his court battle with Moffat, Mears had cast about for new business opportunities. Ousted from the presidency of the Chesapeake Beach Railway the previous summer, he had returned to Colorado to determine if business conditions warranted the investment of time and capital there. Although business conditions were improving from the depression years, he found it difficult to raise money for new railroad projects. Monied men wanted more evidence of a return of prosperity before they risked their funds. Hoping that a new railroad project would turn up elsewhere, he returned east.

Back in Washington, Mears soon became interested in a new railroad scheme. The plan was to build a line between Monroe and New Iberia, Louisiana, a distance of 195 miles, and to later extend the railroad from New Iberia to New Orleans. The projected railroad, called the Louisiana Central, would run through timber lands, of which 109,000 acres were owned by the promoters.

The timber owned by the company was the inducement Mears needed to invest in the project. As a Colorado railroad and mining man, he was aware of the value of timber in the Rocky Mountains. In high altitudes, above timberline, lumber had to be imported at great expense. He hoped to ship the timber from Louisiana to Colorado, where it could be sold at a high profit.

In order to obtain approval from the state legislature for the new railroad, Mears was forced to become what he called a "Louisiana Democrat." Concealing the fact that he was still an important Colorado Republican political boss, he changed his politics to promote his business interests. His shrewd tactics achieved the desired result and the state assembly awarded him the charter for the Louisiana Central Railroad in early 1904.

In March, 1904, Mears journeyed to Washington, D.C., on behalf of the new railroad. He used his political connectidns to receive permission from the War Department to build bridges over the Red River. The railroad builder then returned to Louisiana and relaxed at the Mardi Gras before construction began.

In late April or early May, 1904, grading began. W.

Decker of Newport, Arkansas, president of the Louisiana Construction Company and Mears' partner in the Louisiana Central, supervised the work.

Even with Mears on the scene to offer advice, construction progressed slowly. The swampy terrain made it difficult to build the grade and to transport food and supplies to the laborers.

An even more serious difficulty than the terrain arose which prevented the completion of the railroad. The management's elaborate plan for the operation of the line depended on obtaining a right-of-way into New Orelans. A competitor, however, outmaneuvered Mears. The directors of the New Orleans, Crowley and Western Railroad succeeded in receiving permission to build into the city. The owners of the New Orleans, Crowley and Western then sold the right-of-way to the Kansas City Southern Railroad Company. The deprivation of the outlet made it unprofitable to continue building the Louisiana Central and work was abandoned on the line.

When the decision had been made to stop construction, 32.96 miles of track had been laid at a cost of $387,164.39. The line began operating in late spring 1907, and at the end of its first year of operation it had hauled $68,135.96 worth of freight and passengers, and returned a net profit of $7,307. By the following year, traffic had increased two and a half times and the management found it necessary to employ 157 workers to service the customers.

During the period in which the new railroad had been under construction the railroad builder had lived in Louisiana at least six months of the year, making his home at Marksville. He became intrigued with the distinctiveness of the southern state. In particular, he loved the Mardi Gras, which seemed to embody all that was attractive about southern civilization and culture. So enthralled was the newcomer with the Mardi Gras that he volunteered to manage the celebration in 1905.

During his three-year residence in Louisiana, Mears became immersed in politics. Once he had made it known

163

that he was a Democrat and for appearance sake had participated in a few party functions, political bosses cultivated him, being impressed with his savvy and charmed by his magnetic personality. He claimed he soon began to cut such an important figure that his advice was sought by important state officials on local and national issues.

While the Louisiana Central project was in its developmental stages, Mears decided to engage in yet another transportation venture. Realizing the future importance of the young automotive industry, he purchased a major interest in the capital stock of Mack Brothers Motor Car Company, and became president of the firm on April 29, 1905.

Incorporated on February 1, 1905, in Allentown, Pennsylvania, the Mack Brothers Motor Car Company was organized by John, Augustus, William and Joseph Mack; three Brooklyn businessmen: Louis Meyer, William E. Butler and Willis H. Heath; and Leo E. Schimpff, an Allentown silk manufacturer. The newly organized Mack Brothers operation at Allentown was actually an outgrowth of an old Brooklyn, New York, wagon business which brothers John and Augustus had taken over in 1893. But it was no doubt the display of their first 16-passenger sightseeing bus at the New York Automobile Show in January, 1904, that attracted the proper financial backers, including Otto Mears, to the Mack automotive venture.

The automotive industry was developing very quickly by 1904, with the second commercial vehicle service contest being conducted successfully in New York City during May of that year. With growing orders for motor buses in addition to their local wagon business, it was suggested by Joseph Mack that the motor vehicle operation be moved to a large vacant foundry complex he knew about in Allentown. During 1904, Mears had ordered a "railroad automobile" to run on his Colorado narrow gauge railroad lines. The rail car was named the "Mary M"—after Mears' wife—and had to be shipped to

ONE OF OUR PRODUCTIONS.

The above cut represents our 15 passenger car, built expressly for public and private use. Its construction is the best and is mechanically perfect; is handsome in appearance.

It is equipped with a 24 horse power horizontal motor, four cylinders double opposed, sliding gear transmission, three speeds forward and reverse. Double chain drive, bearings on countershaft, thrust bearings and axles are roller bearing; double band brake on countershaft, and emergency brake direct to rear hubs. Turner Solid Tires and Springs of special design, which make the car ride easy.

This car will ascend a 12 per cent. grade, fully loaded on the high gear with ease; normal speed 12 miles per hour, but can be run 20 miles if desired. Average gasoline consumption, one gallon to every seven miles.

Price $5,500, complete, f. o. b. New York; to order only.

Will design and build cars to carry from 10 to 30 passengers, and guarantee them to do the work.

We do all kinds of machine repairs, rebuild bodies, make canopy tops, wheels, springs, etc.; in fact, everything pertaining to an automobile. Our prices are low, consistent with good work. Correspondence solicited.

THE MACK BROTHERS CO., 532-540 Atlantic Avenue, BROOKLYN, N. Y.

THE MACK BROTHERS' SIGHTSEEING VEHICLE
An Intriguing Harbinger of a New Age

165

Allentown for completion when the Brooklyn automotive operation was transferred in December, 1904.

During the nine months Mears was president of the Mack Brothers Motor Car Company—from April 29, 1905 to January 9, 1906—he made a significant contribution to the success of the struggling commercial vehicle builder. Through several mergers, the firm eventually became the internationally known Mack Trucks, Inc. Mears not only headed the Allentown-based operation, he also helped form and became first president of the Mack Brothers Manufacturing Company, which was set up on February 2, 1906, to continue the Brooklyn operation of the original Mack Brothers Company. He resigned as president of the Brooklyn operation on November 30, 1906, because, it was recorded, "interests in the West would demand practically all his attention."

In the rail car Mary M, Mears wanted a unit of moderate size that could operate over the steep grades of his Colorado rail lines more efficiently than contemporary steam motive power. The Mary M was a true rail car, having flanged wheels, and equipped with one of only three six-cylinder, 90-horsepower, gasoline engines built in the Mack shops during 1904-1905. According to suggestions by Mears, it was designed to pull a second car, which was reported to have been adapted from a Brooklyn horsecar. After initial testing, the Mary M was consigned to the Silverton Northern Railroad at Allentown on August 22, 1905. It was hoped that a successful demonstration of the rail car in the rugged Rocky Mountains would create a market for the new "railroad automobile."

Despite heavy publicity, this first railroad automobile never made it to Silverton in 1905. It spent several months on display at Coney Island—much to the chagrin of curious Silvertonians—and on its maiden trip over the Cumbres Pass route of the Denver & Rio Grande, it broke down just out of Antonito, and was returned to the shops in Alamosa for more work.

Dissatisfied with this original model's performance

and unsuccessful in impressing would-be customers with the machine's efficiency, Mears decided that the machine had to be perfected before it would be a marketable commodity. After the test, therefore, the innovator used the vehicle on his Silverton shortlines so that further experimentation could be made.

In the summer of 1908, after three years of testing, Mears built a new model of the railroad automobile. The new machine was given so much publicity by the inventor that Dave Day of the *Durango Democrat* was impelled to inspect it as it was being sent to Silverton for testing. He made the following humorous report to his readers:

> Otto Mears' sideboard and chip rock, scientifically known as a railroad automobile, passed through Durango last evening enroute to Silverton, having undergone repairs on the outside. It is equipped to withstand snowslides, landslides, waterspouts and various other mountainous castrophes [*sic*] without disturbing the game.[8]

Day's sarcasm did not detract from the ingenuity with which the railroad automobile was designed. Built at the Stover Company plant at Freeport, Illinois, the vehicle incorporated the most advanced automotive technology of the day. Equipped with a four-cylinder, thirty-horsepower, water-cooled engine, the machine accommodated ten to twelve passengers in comfort with room for more if necessary.

This railroad automobile arrived in Silverton for testing on the evening of June 2, 1908. Mears was so pleased with the vehicle's performance en route to the mountain village that every day for a week after it arrived, he took it on short runs to nearby towns. Although initially successful, the machine became more an object of curiosity than of utility, being unable to operate efficiently for long periods at high altitudes.

In November, 1906, a year and a half before he began experimentation with the second model of the railroad automobile, Mears decided to retire to Colorado. His presidential connection with Mack Brothers had come to

168

an end. He had been out-maneuvered in his attempt to extend the Louisiana Central and deprived of a New Orleans outlet. When it became apparent that no more construction would be done on the railroad, he left subordinates in charge of the line and returned to Colorado where he was needed to manage his enterprises.

Mears—drawing the characterization "ubiquitous" from the Denver press—had been away from the Centennial State, except for brief visits, for a decade. When he left his adopted state in 1897, he had hoped to recoup his losses on the Rio Grande Southern. Instead of making money, he had lost heavily on such ventures as the Chesapeake Beach Railway and Mack Brothers. The Louisiana Central, while profitable, could not begin to repay the hundreds of thousands of dollars he had lost on earlier schemes. He consequently returned to Colorado a comparative failure rather than a success. It was not until 1911 that the speculator succeeded in amassing another fortune. And it would be gained through mining and not transportation.

RICHARD A. RONZIO COLLECTION

A LATTER-DAY TRAIN CROSSES DALLAS DIVIDE
Mears Peak [Far Left] Graces the Rugged Uncompahgre Backdrop

8

The Master of Hounds

*M*ears interrupted his decade-long stay in the East to return to Colorado for the 1903 senatorial election, a contest in which he had a personal interest. The principal candidates before the state assembly were Edward O. Wolcott and Henry Teller. The contest between the two candidates and their supporters would be one of the most sensational political confrontations in Colorado history. This campaign was so striking to contemporaries it was talked about for years afterward.

Edward O. Wolcott, an attorney, had first been elected to the United States Senate in 1889. He had gained the office through the sponsorship of the Denver and Rio Grande Railroad—his client—and other interests. At that time his main supporter among the Republican political bosses was Otto Mears, who assisted Wolcott in his bid for the Senate because of his usefulness to the party in previous campaigns. Wolcott was re-elected to the Senate in 1895, again with Mears' support.

In the Senate, Wolcott's ability soon manifested itself. His capacity for leadership, his oratorical skill, and his sound political judgment made him a standout. He soon established himself as one of the leading members of the Republican Party on the national scene. His political stature was such that in 1900 he was chosen as temporary chairman of the Republican National Convention in Philadelphia.

Wolcott's national prominence did not help him win a third term, however. In 1901, he was defeated for re-election by Thomas Patterson, owner of the *Rocky Mountain News* and a Democrat. Wolcott was unable to muster enough votes to gain re-election because the legislature was under Democratic control. Even more harmful to his cause was the enmity of Otto Mears. Wolcott had incurred the political boss' wrath through what Mears regarded as ingratitude and double-dealing. The latter, whose usual philosophy was to let deceivers hang themselves, was roused to retaliation when Wolcott bested him in a Rio Grande Southern stock manipulation.

Two years later, Wolcott appeared again as a candidate for a third senatorial term. He was desperate. He was aware that another defeat would end his political career. His key opponent was one-time Republican Henry Teller. Teller, in the capacity of United States Senator and Secretary of the Interior, had been prominent in national politics for a quarter century. In addition to his reputation and record, Teller had another asset—the support of Otto Mears.

Otto decided to back Teller because he believed Teller was most likely to defeat Wolcott. The contest between the two political factions headed by Wolcott and Teller reached epic proportions. The candidate battle was so bitter that the Republican Party in Colorado was almost destroyed. During the height of the contest—the week of January 19 to January 28, 1903—the central government of the state was paralyzed as elected officials awaited the outcome of the election. Residents of the state afterward would remember the events of this tumultuous week as among the most momentous in Colorado's political history.

The parade of exciting events began on January 19, 1903. In the morning of that day the House and Senate met separately in Denver, preparatory to the senatorial election. Unusual events began in the House at once. To gain a clear majority, the Republicans previously had agreed in caucus to expel 17 Democrats. At first all went as planned and six Democrats were unseated for alleged election frauds. When the Republicans tried to unseat eleven Arapahoe County Democrats, however, they met unexpected difficulties. Three Republicans—for some reason called "Mexicans"—split from the majority of their party and voted that the eleven should be seated. The so-called "Mexicans" presumably acted in accordance with a secret agreement with Teller and Mears. The eleven were promised that they would be allowed to take their seats if they voted for Teller in the senatorial election. This agreement was necessary because it was obvious that if the Arapahoe County legislators were expelled and replaced with Republicans, Wolcott would have more than enough votes to gain the senatorial seat.[1]

The three "Mexican" votes in conjunction with the Democratic votes were enough to seat the Arapahoe County legislators. The "Mexicans'" double-dealing caused consternation in the Republican ranks and the resulting acrimony became so bitter that the proceedings in the lower chamber were bogged down.

The Senate proceedings were even more disorganized. The executive session of the Senate was immediately taken over by the Democratic majority, bent on party revenge. The Democrats were irate over the expulsion of their six fellow party members in the House. To retaliate and to restore the original balance between the two parties, the Democrats took over the Senate chamber. With the help of armed thugs, according to newspaper accounts, the Democrats succeeded in preventing some Republicans from joining the "rump." The Democratic "rump," in rancor against the House, then began the process of unseating Republican senators. Two Republicans—Jesse F. McDonald of Lake County and J.P. Dick of Huerfano County—were unseated.

The Republican members of the Senate prevented from participating in the Democratic "rump" began proceedings of their own. Meeting in the rear of the Senate chamber, they began expelling Democratic members.

The split between the Democrats and Republicans, engineered by Mears and Teller, caused a unique situation whereby two Senates were meeting simultaneously in the Senate chamber. The chaos continued all night. Both factions refused to vacate the Senate chamber for fear they would not be allowed to re-enter. The senators spent the evening hours playing whist and telling stories, resting from the day's activities.

While the senators were amusing themselves, the capitol building was being surrounded by plain-clothed Denver police and Democratic ward heelers. The display of force was an attempt by Mears and his cohorts to intimidate the Republican members of the legislature who disagreed with the attempts to re-organize the Senate and House to procure more votes for Teller.

During the early morning hours of January 20, Governor James H. Peabody debated whether to call out the militia to dispel the disorderly throng surrounding the capitol building. National guard units were assembled in the meantime at the Curtis Street Armory. In addition, every available uniformed Denver policeman was taken off street duty in case the governor decided to act. As dawn approached, Coloradoans were faced with two state Senates and the possibility of three United States Senators being elected and a possible national guard order to empty the capitol building.

The governor decided to let events take their course. Later in the day both houses met to begin the election for United States senator. In the House, the Republicans voted for Wolcott and the Democrats voted for Teller. As no candidate had a clear majority, a deadlock ensued. Proceedings remained confused in the Senate with both the Democratic and Republican "rumps" occupying the Senate chamber. In the Senate, as in the House, the Democrats supported Teller and the Republicans voted for Wolcott. Neither candidate had the backing of a majority of the whole number of the senators.

174

As both houses were deadlocked and no clear majority could be obtained in the senatorial election, state law required that the election proceedings be continued in a joint session. United States Senator Thomas Patterson, possibly at Mears' behest, convinced Governor Peabody to delay the joint session until the chaotic conditions in the legislature could be brought under control. Peabody received permission from the legislators and postponed the start of the joint session until January 23.

Peabody had been tricked, as events were to show. The Democrats of both Houses did not use the two-day postponement to settle their differences with the Republicans. The Democrats instead met in a "rump" joint session. With the Republicans excluded, Mears believed that it would be easy to elect Teller and then get Peabody to certify the election.

The "rump" joint session of the Democrats conducted its first meeting on January 21, 1903. With all the Democrats in attendance, Teller received unanimous approval for the senatorial office. Although Teller had received the support of the Democrats, he did not have the backing of a majority of the total number of legislators. As it seemed unlikely that Teller would receive substantial Republican support, Otto began grooming Simon Guggenheim, his protege, as a "dark horse" candidate. As long as Wolcott was denied a third senatorial term, Mears did not care who became senator. If Guggenheim was selected instead of Teller, it was so much the better from his point of view. Guggenheim, a multi-millionaire, would give him much more money as a reward for election than Teller could afford. And he needed the money.

The Democratic "rump" joint session adjourned after voting for Teller so that the leaders could plan further action. That night, with political bosses discussing the situation among themselves, the Wolcott forces attempted to take over the capitol building. Rumors circulated that Wolcott and his campaign manager, Lieutenant Governor Frank Howbert, had amassed a force of 150 armed men. The rumors seemed substantiated when two or three ladders were found propped against the outside of the capitol building. It appeared that the ladders were to be used to gain forced entry into the building to enable the Wolcott gang to expel the Teller forces. To protect themselves against what seemed to be an imminent attack, the anti-Wolcott forces armed themselves with Colt .45 revolvers and repeating rifles. The arming of the Teller gang forestalled the planned night attack. The constant threats of a Wolcott capitol building takeover, however, caused the legislators to remain armed until January 23, when the joint session opened.

During the period before the joint session's scheduled commencement, newspaper editors were exhorting their readers to pressure their assemblymen to restore normal conditions in the legislature. The editor of the *Rocky Mountain News*, for example, made this January 23, 1903, editorial comment:

> In Colorado we have heard much of "misrule" and of "failure to enforce the laws," but never in all the history of the state has there been such openly illegal action and such brazen resort to bludgeons and threats of violence as have marked the past three days under the direction of the Republican leaders of the different factions. The wildest anarchist conceives of nothing worse than resort to physical violence to overthrow law and order, and the men responsible for the disgraceful condition of affairs at the state house have descended to the level of the anarchist.

> Colorado Republicans may well ask themselves what malevolent spirit possesses their leaders—a spirit that is willing to blacken the good name of the state and to run the risk of staining the halls of the capitol with blood to gratify ambitions gone mad.

Editorials of this kind had no effect on Mears and the other leaders of the Republican factions. Political bosses still did everything they could to achieve their goals, despite the illegality of the method used. The Mears-Teller combination, for example, prevented the joint session of the legislature from meeting by urging Democrats to continue their joint "rump" session. Pleas from Governor Peabody, legislators, newspaper editors and concerned citizens did not deter the Democrats from holding their joint "rump."

The Democratic joint "rump" met daily from January 21 to January 25. Although the Democrats had selected Teller on January 21 as their candidate, the votes which had been cast still numbered less than a majority of the total number of legislators. To gain more votes for Teller the Democrats allowed the anti-Wolcott Republicans to join the Democratic "rump." On January 24, enough Republicans were admitted to the "rump" to equal a clear majority of the total number of assemblymen. The "rump" went through the pretense of having a second election in which Teller was again declared the winner.

So blatantly illegal were the proceedings of the "rump" that it was unclear at first whether Governor Peabody would direct Secretary of State James Cowie to issue Teller a certificate of election. Peabody was induced to certify Teller's election, but it was expected that Wolcott's lawyers would contest the Colorado election before the United States Senate, the final authority in disputed senatorial elections.

Wolcott, however, did not wait until the United States Senate examined the election to gain revenge. After losing the senatorial contest he decided that Mears and principal supporters should be thrown out of the Republican Party. On the evening of January 26, 1903, Wolcott convened the Arapahoe County Republican Central Committee. At the meeting Wolcott supporters charged that Mears and fellow bosses Philip B. Stewart, Isaac N. Stevens and Frank C. Goudy had treacherously turned a sure Republican victory into a disastrous defeat. Due to the efforts of Mears and others, Wolcott—his party's choice—not only had lost the election, but the dissension caused in Republican ranks rendered it impossible to implement the party's legislative platform. To placate the Wolcott supporters, the central committee voted 106-19 to suspend Mears, Stevens, Stewart and Goudy from the Republican Party for two years and to notify the newspapers and President Theodore Roosevelt of the decision.

Otto was not to be outmaneuvered, however. On the following day, he asked Frank C. Goudy to appeal the decision of the Arapahoe County Central Committee before the Republican Union Club. Goudy stated at the hearing that he and the other accused men had not been allowed to defend themselves. The members of the Union Club decided, in consequence, that the matter should be investigated further and selected a committee of their membership to do so. The Union Club's decision was a victory for Mears and his cohorts. Action on the charge was deferred which meant that nothing would be done to punish the offenders.

Although Mears had managed to escape punishment for his so-called betrayal of the Republican Party, he was not content to let matters stand. He realized that the acrimony caused by his conduct would have to be dispelled if he were to retain his hold on the party. He therefore began hosting a series of banquets in which Republican Party members were the guests. His object in holding the banquets was to restore amity and concord in the party.

One such banquet was particularly notable. On the evening of March 6, 1903, Otto hosted a $10-a-plate dinner in the ballroom of the Adams Hotel in Denver. Thirty-five of the forty Republican members of the House attended. An elegant dinner was served to the guests who were seated at tables arranged, appropriately, in a double cross. After the banquet the guests were presented with a set of glasses. While the glasses were being distributed, Mears and other speakers exhorted the audience about the value of party loyalty and the importance of concord among Republicans. So effective was the banquet and the after-dinner speeches that observers were confident that the discord among the various Republican factions would soon be ended.

During the period in which Mears was giving the successful banquets to restore amity among Republicans, the legislature was still in session. In this assembly Mears served as a professional lobbyist. He was the agent-in-chief of the Guggenheim interests. The Guggenheims, owners of numerous smelters, hired him to defeat any bill which, if passed into law, would affect their business operation.

Mears worked diligently as a lobbyist. Colorado was entering an era of reform, and legislators had introduced many bills designed to correct the abuses of big business and government. The first of these reform measures introduced into the Fourteenth General Assembly, which Mears ultimately helped defeat, was the initiative and referendum. The bill, as introduced into the Senate, stipulated that eight per cent of the voters participating in the previous gubernatorial election be allowed to initiate legislation or vote on the desirability of those measures already approved by the assembly. He realized that if the bill was passed, the autocratic control over state government by the political boss would be ended. Both his own political position and that of big business such as the Guggenheim smelters were threatened. Companies could now be controlled by laws initiated from the populace. He therefore worked to have the bill killed when it arrived in the House. Upon the bill's consideration, representatives influenced by Mears and other lobbyists immediately removed the initiative clause. The representatives further crippled the measure by changing the percentage necessary for referendum from eight to twenty per cent.

After helping defeat the initiative and referendum, Mears' next effort was to prevent the passage of a constitutional amendment allowing the University of Colorado to maintain a medical school in Denver. Although the regents deemed the medical school a necessary adjunct to the university, he and other lobbyists prevented the ratification of the amendment.

The lobbyists believed that their political position depended upon the weakness of the assembly. If the legislators discovered that with the approval of the voters they could amend the state's constitution at will, they would feel a sense of strength which would make a professional lobbyist's job that much more difficult. For a lobbyist to be effective, Mears believed, common identity and common interest must be discouraged among the legislators.

Mears next helped defeat a tax reform measure. This bill would have amended the current law which allowed a $200 tax exemption for furniture by changing the permitted deduction to $200 on personal property of any kind. He lobbied to defeat the measure; if the poor were allowed to pay less tax, corporations would be assessed more by the state to obtain the needed revenue.

When it became evident that the House would not pass the tax reform bill, Mears concerned himself with other bills inimical to the operation of big business. One of the measures most potentially damaging to big business was a proposal for an eight-hour work day. To operate at capacity, smelters and other big businesses found it necessary to require employees to work twelve-hour or longer working days. If the eight-hour bill became law, big businesses would have to either pay their employees more money to work longer, begin a shift system, or cut their operating time. No matter what expedient business would adopt, a loss of revenue would occur. Although there was much labor agitation against current working conditions, Mears lobbied successfully against the bill at this and the second session of legislators in July, 1903.

After preventing the passage of the first eight-hour bill Mears lobbied against the Belford amendment. The Belford amendment declared that the smelting industry should be regulated by a commission, in the same manner as were railroads and common carriers, since the industry was so important to the welfare of Colorado. He collaborated with other lobbyists and successfully prevented the measure's ratification.

180

THE PATHFINDER   "Py heavens, when a man is bought I like him stay bought."

THE DENVER PRESS VIEWS THE UBIQUITOUS LOBBYIST
Otto Never Lost Interest in Colorado

181

With the defeat of the Belford amendment, Mears utilized his time to lobby against several other bills which, if passed, would have been personally harmful. The first of these was the anti-gambling bill. This proposal declared gambling a felony. Enjoying gambling as much as he did, Mears helped prevent the ratification of this measure by lobbying against it. A disgruntled legislator who had been in favor of the bill charged publicly that bribery was used to kill the measure.

The revelation of the bribery charges caused a furor and several legislators demanded that restrictions be placed on lobbyists. Throughout the controversy, however, the political boss remained undistracted and continued to implement his lobbying program. At this point, he was most interested in preventing the passage of measures that would undermine his and other bosses' control of state politics. In conjunction with other interested lobbyists, he pressured legislators to kill the primary control bill. The measure provided for nomination of regular party candidates in supervised primaries. If approved, the bill would have done away with the current system allowing political bosses to control conventions.

Mears' next objective was to defeat the so-called assessor's bill. This measure provided for the tax assessment of railroads and other corporations on the basis of the market value of the company's stocks and bonds instead of having the corrupt state board of equalization make the tax assessment. In financial straits, Otto could not afford to pay more taxes on his railroads and so he effectively helped lobby against this measure.

Mears was also able to devote his attention to another project very important to him at this time. Since 1899 he had been trying to have his achievements commemorated in the state capitol building. Otto, according to newspaper reports, was very egotistical about his role in Colorado development. He realized how difficult it was to have a memorial dedicated to a person still living. He consequently used all of his considerable powers of persuasion to induce legislative approval of his plan.

During 1899, Mears had begun lobbying in his own behalf. At that time, in his capacity as capitol manager, he had occasion to participate in the selection of pioneers honored in the dome of the state capitol. He decided after studying the qualifications of the various individuals who had a role in Colorado's development that his own accomplishments equaled or excelled everyone elses. He realized his portrait could not be placed in the dome, as the dome area was reserved for deceased pioneers. If he was to be honored, a special place in the capitol building would have to be found. Moreover, his powerful political enemies would succeed in defeating the proposal if he did not work in his behalf. He began a self-advertising campaign during his visits to Colorado from Washington during the summer and fall of 1899. During this period, he presented his case in newspaper interviews, distinguishing himself as the state's "original pathfinder." [2] At one point while the capitol managers had over 100 names in consideration, a frustrated Mears made the following statement to the press:

> The idea of the board seems to be to put in this gallery the portrait of anybody who drove an ox across the plains in '59, and if that is going to be the programme, the best plan would be to put them in a bag, shake them up, then take out the numbers needed and let it go at that.[3]

Otto did more than engage in a publicity campaign for himself. He evidently prepared a petition or caused one to be prepared which asked the legislature to provide a gallery for living pioneers and suggested that he be the first to be so honored. The petition was circulated in Silverton. After hundreds of signatures had been affixed, the petition was sent with other memorials to W.S. Buckley, the senator from San Miguel County. Mears presumably arranged matters so well that it seemed a spontaneous outpouring of sentiment had been generated on his behalf.

The next step was to have Buckley turn over the petition and letters to the Senate when the Thirteenth General

Assembly met in Denver in January, 1901. Buckley, after turning over the material to the Senate, made an eloquent speech about Mears' role in the state's development. The senator then arranged for a concurrent resolution to be introduced in both the Senate and the House providing for a picture of Mears to be placed in an appropriate spot in the capitol building.

The concurrent resolution passed in early February, 1901. It was now up to the board of capitol managers to decide when and where in the capitol building the plate glass on which Otto's portrait was to be painted would be hung. An impasse was soon reached. John A. Thatcher, a capitol manager since 1900, was antagonistic to Mears. It is not known whether this was due to jealousy, a political feud, or simple objectivity. After the legislature had voted to have Mears' portrait placed in the state capitol, Thatcher did everything he could to frustrate the move. As the portrait subject was frequently out of the state for business reasons, Thatcher was able to induce the other capitol managers not to act on the concurrent resolution.

Thatcher prevented the implementation of the legislature's directive to honor Mears for two years. Thoroughly piqued, Otto finally took action to offset Thatcher. In March, 1903, near the end of the first session of the Fourteenth General Assembly, Mears—technically a non-resident of the state—lobbied successfully for the legislators to again approve the 1901 concurrent resolution.

The legislature's approval of the 1901 measure created too much pressure for the capitol managers to resist. They allowed the plan to honor Mears to go forward. In April, 1903, Otto posed for the glass glaziers of the Copeland Glass Company. By July, the plate glass window was finished. Thatcher, however, prevented the portrait from being installed for an additional 13 months.[4]

The stained glass portrait was finally hung in late summer of 1904. Placed on the outside corridor of the second and third floors, the portrait was to be the first in a gallery of pictures of living pioneers. For years, Mears' portrait was the only one in the special gallery overlooking the Senate chamber, a tribute to his accomplishments. Probably no other pioneer had enough political influence to be so honored. Mears did not achieve this singular honor without much hard work, something he never publicly admitted. He preferred to pose as an unsolicited recipient of the honor.

For the year following the installation of the portrait, Mears stayed out of Colorado politics. He was too occupied with his business enterprises in Louisiana and with court battles with David Moffat over ownership of the stock of the Chesapeake Beach Railway. Otto's legal encounters with Moffat went so badly that he lost his stock in the railroad. Despairing over his financial reverses, he decided to give up politics in the summer of 1905. When interviewed by a reporter from the *Denver Republican,* he declared that:

> I am out of politics. I have had my share. My skin is about as thick as you make 'em, but I find that it feels better to be out of it and making money. Do you know that I am getting old?

Mears' political retirement was short-lived it seems. By September, 1905, he had been recruited by Simon Guggenheim to assist him in the 1907 senatorial election. Otto had been Guggenheim's friend and political mentor since 1896 when Guggenheim had attempted to gain nomination as the Republican candidate for lieutenant governor. At the time Mears had promised he would assist his protege in a senatorial bid. In 1903, the young aspirant had been groomed as a ''dark horse'' candidate in case the deadlock in the legislature resulted in neither Wolcott nor Teller being selected to fill the vacant Senate seat.

Appetite whetted by the 1903 contest, Guggenheim was willing to do anything and spend any amount of money to secure his election to Thomas Patterson's seat, which was to be vacated in 1907. Guggenheim's extensive preparations for the 1907 senatorial election began as early as March, 1904, a year and a half before Mears joined his campaign staff. At that time, the office seeker announced the first step in his campaign—the appointment of Richard Broad, Jr., an old time political boss, as his campaign manager.

The next step in the senatorial aspirant's bid for office occurred in August, 1904, when he let it be known that he would contribute generously to the Republican election fund. Nineteen hundred four was a state and national election year and Guggenheim hoped to gain support in his own party by liberality.

In addition to contributions to his party's election fund, the smelter king endeavored to gain support by the purchase of newspapers. By mid-October, 1904, Guggenheim had purchased the *Leadville Herald-Democrat,* the *Victor Record* and the *Pueblo Star Journal.*

When Mears joined the Guggenheim machine in September, 1905, the latter already had purchased everything money could buy to help him gain the Senate seat. But it was Otto's consummate political skill combined with his friend's great wealth that achieved the desired result. The political juggler's acumen and judgment were held in such esteem that the leadership of Guggenheim's forces devolved upon him and campaign manager Broad assumed a secondary importance.

In order to be of the greatest assistance to his protege, Mears had to re-establish his Colorado residency. He had not been a legal resident of Colorado since 1897 when he had gone east to build the Chesapeake Beach Railway. Seven years later he moved to Louisiana where he had been overseeing the Louisiana Central construction and various business ventures. In May, 1906, he satisfied Colorado's residency requirement by purchasing a home in Silverton, allegedly his ninth legal residence at the time.

Although it was recognized that the pioneer's establishment of residency was only to fulfill a legal requirement, he was welcomed back by the San Juan press. Dubbed the "Harbinger of Prosperity" by his old critic Dave Day, now editor of the *Durango Democrat,*

Mears did little in 1906 to deserve the name. He was interested primarily in Guggenheim's campaign. After renovating and furnishing the Reese Street house in Silverton, Otto returned to Louisiana.

The remainder of the summer and early fall of 1906 Mears spent in Louisiana closing out his business interests. He returned to Colorado in November to make sure that everything was in readiness for the January senatorial election. Allegedly Guggenheim had been paying the election expenses of certain legislators for years in return for promises to vote for him for senator. Both manager and candidate remembered the 1883 senatorial election which Horace Tabor lost when promised support did not materialize. Guggenheim and Mears wanted to avoid a recurrence of the mishap.

The cautious approach of Mears and Guggenheim appeared successful. By late December, 1906, the mentor and protege were openly confident. Joviality prevailed in the Guggenheim headquarters on the eighth floor of the Brown Palace Hotel. It was alleged that Richard Broad Jr. was using Room 823 as an "oil" room in which money was dispensed to legislators. Upon one occasion, Broad was asked about this and he replied "oil nothing, we don't need oil in this campaign—except possibly for our hair." Otto was so amused at the witticism that he insisted that Broad repeat the joke to everyone who had not heard it. So self-assured were the Guggenheim campaign managers that, at a political rally on the evening of December 28, 1906, at the Brown Palace, they asserted that "we've got 'em already."

The political bosses' predictions of the senatorial election's outcome were justified. On January 1, 1907, a Republican caucus was conducted at the Brown Palace Hotel. Guggenheim received 68 of 70 votes for senator. As there was a Republican majority in the legislature, the *Rocky Mountain News* was able to forecast an easy victory on January 15 for the smelter king.

When the near certainty of Guggenheim's election became apparent, reactions were quickly filed by the editors of the state newspapers. The industrialist's most important Republican opponent among the editors was Clarence P. Dodge, editor of the *Colorado Springs Gazette,* the oldest Republican newspaper in Colorado. On December 26, 1906, Dodge asserted that

> Simon Guggenheim in the United States Senate would be a joke, but a most discreditable joke on Colorado. He would be simply a dollar mark placed there to show that another state had sold out.

The opinions expressed in the *Gazette* were echoed in the *Rocky Mountain News*, the state's most influential Democratic paper. Describing the inevitability of Guggenheim's election as the "triumph of the machine," the editor asserted that the smelter king had "gone after the senatorship as he would go about the purchase of a desirable piece of property." The outrageous manner in which Guggenheim and his "cabal" had dealt with the legislators was "without parallel in the history of senator-making in the United States." [5]

The reaction of the state's Democratic and liberal press was best captured by Durango's picturesque paragrapher Day. He opined that Guggenheim's senatorial candidacy was "an insult to honor, integrity and intelligence in the state." The editor warned that

> With Simon Guggenheim as senator and Otto Mears as master of the hounds, the common herd will be in for a warm chase. Colorado would be headed for an administrator. [6]

Mears and Guggenheim appeared unruffled by the newspaper criticism. They continued with the course of action that had already been planned. While waiting for the legislators to vote for senator, they scrutinized all bills introduced into the legislature to determine if any pertained to the regulation of big business. Mears was particularly worried about the possible passage of a railroad regulation act. The Republican legislators had promised at the state convention to frame a strong railroad commission law. By forcing railroads to reduce rates and give better service Republican assemblymen hoped to gain support for future elections.

When it became apparent that the Republicans would keep their promise and introduce a railroad regulation bill, vigorous lobbying to defeat the measure began. On January 3, 1907, the eve of the day when the railroad commission bill was to be considered by the Sixteenth General Assembly, railroad passes were left on the desk of each legislator. The assemblymen received passes from the following railroads: the Denver & Rio Grande; the Colorado Midland; the Colorado & Southern; the Colorado Springs & Cripple Creek; the Midland Terminal and Florence & Cripple Creek; the Denver, Northwestern & Pacific; the Silverton; and the Silverton Northern. In addition to the pass distribution, it was rumored that other favors would be granted by the railroad companies.

The use of passes in lobbying was an effective bargaining device. Passenger rates were so high on the state's railroads that a man with an average income could not afford to travel. State law provided that legislators would receive a fifteen-cent mileage allowance for one trip to Denver and back during the legislative session. If an emergency arose and a lawmaker had to return home, he would have to do it at his own expense.

Usually the railroad passes were accepted without comment by the legislators. The assemblymen believed that it was a favor justly due them. After all, most could not afford to attend the legislative session without more financial remuneration than provided by the state. Occasionally, an honest legislator would object when a pass was offered and a sensation would be caused when the unethical attempt to influence legislation was exposed. This occurred during the 1907 session when Rep. O.M. Kem of Montrose complained about the practice. Kem, a Democrat, objected to receiving items from lobbyists. He believed it to be felonious to give or to receive gratuities. In no other state, he claimed, was politics as thoroughly dominated by big business.

Kem was so indignant about the attempted bribe that he reported the incident to the newspapers and wrote letters to each railroad president, deploring the current lobbying practices. His letter to Mears was as follows:

Yesterday was handed to me by the clerk of the house two railroad passes, good for one year (unless otherwise ordered), one over the Silverton Railway company's lines, the other over the Silverton Northern railway, both signed by Otto Mears, president.

In acknowledgement of the receipt of the same, accept my thanks for the compliment, also please accept the return of the passes.

I desire to say in connection herewith that I return these passes in no captious mood, but as a matter of principle. The state convention of the party I have the honor of representing in part in the house declared emphatically against the pass system, and my county convention declared the giving or accepting of a pass to be morally a felony, and, believing, as I do, that it should be made a felony by law, I can do nothing but return them to you with my thanks and kindest regards.[7]

The revelation of unethical railroad lobbying practices contributed to the popular demand for railroad regulation. Sentiment was so strong that the legislators finally passed a law which created a railroad commission.

Although Mears could not prevent passage of the railroad bill, he later maneuvered a clause to exempt his railroads from regulation by the newly created commission. He went to court and contended that the railroad bill did not apply to shortlines. Judge Greeley Whitford, who was presiding over the case—allegedly unduly impressed by the petitioner's political influence—ruled in favor of Mears. Dave Day pithily summarized the proceedings: "A political judge can always be relied upon to skim skimmed milk."[8]

Back in early January following the revelation of the railroad lobbying, Simon Guggenheim's senatorial campaign seemed to be going badly. The early optimism exhibited in the smelter king's camp had melted away. Guggenheim had bragged openly that he would achieve election because of bargains made with individual legislators. Some legislators who had allegedly agreed to Guggenheim's terms were said to have changed their mind because of his braggadocio. The senatorial aspirant had so little popular support that many legislators were afraid of endangering their political career by voting for him. After Simon's admission, any lawmaker who voted for him would seem to have been bribed. Other legislators who had not made any commitment to the would-be senator but who might have voted for him were disgusted by his cynical remarks.

The aversion of some legislators to Guggenheim's campaign methods was made manifest on January 11, 1907, four days before the election. Senator John H. Crowley, a Democrat from Otero County, introduced a resolution in the state senate condemning the office seeker. He charged that Simon Guggenheim had purchased Republican votes by bribery. Not only were illegal campaign methods used, Crowley claimed, but the senatorial aspirant had admittedly broken other laws as well. The candidate had shown his unfitness for office by his confession of bribery in an interview with Frederic Lawrence of *Ridgway's Magazine*. In the interview, Guggenheim also admitted to accepting rebates in his smelting business. Crowley asserted that Guggenheim was morally unfit to be senator. After an acrimonious debate, the resolution was tabled. It was also decided to expunge Crowley's accusations from the Colorado Senate minutes.

Although no official record existed of Crowley's resolution, it was not forgotten. Democrats were angry about the election fraud and the majority of Republicans, anxious to avoid an investigation, hoped that no more formal presentations of charges would be made.

Although the atmosphere was made increasingly bitter by charges and counter-charges, Mears was able to rally enough support to insure Guggenheim's election. He reminded legislators who were reluctant to vote for the would-be senator that Guggenheim had been the source of most of the Republican Party's campaign funds for several recent elections. If Simon was not elected, he warned, no more money would be forthcoming from the industrialist. The political bosses' threats were taken to heart and Guggenheim was elected to the U.S. Senate by a wide majority of the state legislators.

The date of the senatorial election, January 15, 1907, seemed to mark the beginning of the end of Otto Mears' active participation in Colorado politics. The old timer in several recent interviews had apparently implied that if his protege was elected to office he would retire from politics and let him run things. The first indication that the pioneer was stepping down from his powerful position in the Republican Party was a May 18, 1907, announcement by the new senator. In the statement, almost a proclamation, Guggenheim arrogantly asserted that he would not only select Colorado's next U.S. senator, but would choose the Republican delegates to represent the state at the national convention. More an ultimatum than an announcement, the statement revealed the power-hungry young man's ambitions to control the state's politics by usurping the power of his mentor and other bosses.

From this point on, Mears appeared to be in the background of the state's politics. He ran no more campaigns for gubernatorial or senatorial candidates. He even quit serving as a lobbyist-in-chief at future meetings of the legislature. Except for the Eighteenth Session of the legislature convened in 1911, there is no record of the veteran campaigner even attending sessions after 1907.

No matter how it looked to contemporaries, however, Mears had neither lost interest in politics nor had surrendered one iota of his political power to his friend. The younger man, to satisfy his ego, was allowed to have the trappings of power, while in actuality, he was being manipulated by his political teacher. In a 1904 interview, Mears had been candid about this relationship:

192

Simon Guggenheim he vollow my adwice all der dimes. Der vos a schmart young man . . . If Zimon vos dere twendy years ago, I vould own der sthate now. You see his money und my prains dovetails in dergetter so sveet. [9]

During the six-year term of his protege, the political boss was, in consequence, the power behind the political throne. With Guggenheim's retirement from office in 1913, however, Mears' only connection with politics was through the Board of Capitol Managers. By this time, Otto's wife Mary was in such bad health that frequent lengthy vacations in Southern California were needed to restore her health. He had neither the time nor the inclination to maintain the supremacy he enjoyed in the party.

Mears' one remaining link with politics was very important, however. The Board of Capitol Managers by this time was politically the most important state governmental agency. It was allocated hundreds of thousands of dollars annually and the money was used to provide jobs for the supporters of elected officials. The board had been formed in 1883 to supervise the construction of the capitol building, and had been moribund until Mears had been appointed a member in 1889. Within six years after his appointment, enough had been constructed of the building to allow Governor McIntire to move in. The last touches of the capitol building were finished 13 years later, when the dome was gilded.

As more of the capitol building had been completed, there became less for the capitol managers to do. At the monthly meetings of the board little was done to justify its continued existence and its high budget. Occasionally improvements on the capitol were considered, and toward 1910, plans for a new museum building were discussed. During this period, Mears helped make the board a dispenser of political patronage. The board evolved into a clearing house where jobs were found for supporters of the dominant party. Many individuals were appointed to positions which required little or no work and many appointees did nothing except collect their pay checks. [10]

At this point, some members of the Board of Capitol Managers—aware of the corruption around them—decided to take advantage of the situation. The dishonest managers awarded contracts to those who would extend the largest bribe, rather than those who presented the lowest bid. The illegal activities of some of the managers involved more than the acceptance of bribes. Supplies allocated for use by the board were misappropriated. Stamps, stationery and other items were taken for personal use.

The corrupt board was intolerable to the progressive reformers of the time. In an era when government was being reformed in Colorado and throughout the United States, popular sentiment was against any corrupt or inefficient governmental agency. The board managed to withstand attacks until 1914 when Governor George A. Carlson assumed office. Carlson, a Republican, was against the high cost of state government.

In order to decide how best to make the operation of government less wasteful, Carlson ordered his auditor, Harry E. Mulnix, to investigate several state agencies. In his investigation of the Board of Capitol Managers, Mulnix found evidence of both inefficiency and corruption. The findings of this investigation were turned over to a grand jury appointed by District Judge John A. Perry.

The grand jury empaneled on February 5, 1915, was able to make a partial report within two weeks. The substance of the report was that a recommendation should go to the Twentieth Session of the legislature, then in session, to abolish the board because of the incompetence and dishonestly of its members.

The grand jury report spurred some legislators to action. Senator William C. Robinson, for example, introduced a bill—endorsed by Carlson—which provided for the abolishment of the agency. During debates on this measure additional data was uncovered which was to shed more unfavorable light on the agency. It was reported, for example, that the board had never announced the completion of the construction of the capitol building even though it was evident to all that the building was in its final shape. It was also disclosed that a capitol architect was allegedly receiving a salary of $1,200 annually to write monthly reports stating that the capitol dome was still in place.

Robinson's bill was killed on its second reading on March 11, 1915, when a coalition of Democratic and Republican senators voted against it. The uneasy alliance was formed to protect the political patronage the board controlled. Undaunted, Robinson introduced a new bill. This measure, while providing for the continued existence of the board, reduced the revenue allocated to it by cutting the half-mill tax levy which supported the agency.

Vigorous lobbying was employed by legislators and board members to prevent the passage of Robinson's new bill. Both houses, however, approved the measure with each chamber recommending a different sum for operating expenses. In order to complete the process of making Robinson's bill a law, it was necessary to resolve the differences concerning the amount of money to be allocated to the agency. At a conference attended by House and Senate leaders, it was agreed to reduce the funds allocated each year by approximately $110,000. The new annual allocation was now about $90,000. The cut in the board's budget was expected to greatly diminish the amount of patronage the capitol managers could dispense. The board consequently lost its tremendous political importance. Its primary functions became the maintenance of the capitol building and control of the construction of the state museum.

Once the power of the Board of Capitol Managers had been weakened by the fund cut, Governor Carlson demanded the resignation of its more dishonest and incompetent members. Mears, however, was allowed to stay on the board. Throughout the scandal, his name was not mentioned in connection with any dishonest activity. In his capacity as capitol manager, he had displayed only honesty and efficiency and it was known that he had not participated in graft. It was recognized that he may have had a large part in building up the patronage power of the agency, but it was believed that patronage was the legitimate prize for those in office. His part in developing this aspect of the board by lobbying for larger allocations was therefore condoned. He was allowed to retire when he wished. He remained on the board for five more years and resigned because of ill health in May, 1920. When his resignation was tendered, he was presented with a beautifully engraved book in appreciation of his 31-year service with the agency.

Otto Mears' retirement from the Board of Captiol Managers marked the end of his incredible political career. In one of the longest careers in the state's history, he had been politically active for more than a half century and a major Republican party boss for 45 years. As a politician—and in keeping with the morality of the time— he worked to gain his own ends at the expense of the welfare of others. He saw progressive reform as a threat to big business and a threat to the realization of his ambitions. He therefore did much to prevent the passage of reform legislation. Ruthless, Mears did whatever necessary to gain his ends. Contemporaries, who were generally aware of his political strategy and tactics, seldom criticized him. Far from condemning his "end justifies the means" philosophy, they admired him for his consummate skill and for his political longevity.

9

The Man of the World

$\mathcal{A}$lthough Otto Mears was extensively involved with transportation projects and other enterprises in the East in the decade between 1897 and 1907, he did not neglect Colorado transportation development during this period. His most important venture in the Centennial State at this time was the construction, operation and extension of the Silverton Northern Railroad.

The construction of the Silverton Northern had long been contemplated by the ubiquitous entrepreneur. The idea of a railroad between Silverton and Mineral Point had germinated in the mid-1880s while Mears was building the Silverton and Animas Forks Toll Road between the two points. Profits on this toll road had remained high during the period when the falling price of silver and the resultant mine closures had decreased the income on his other roads and railroads. The repeal of the Sherman Silver Purchase Act had not affected the price of gold, and several mines producing gold-bearing ore continued operations along the toll road. Two such mines—the Silver Lake above Waldheim and the Sunnyside in the Eureka area—produced so much ore that he believed they warranted railroad service.

If a railroad were built, additional profit could also be

made from the smaller gold mines in the region. So much mining was going on in the area that Mears estimated the proposed railroad would haul 500 tons of ore daily. Not only would gold ore shipments be a source of income, but if the local silver mines were reopened additional revenue would be obtained. Prospects of a good return upon investment were so encouraging, he resolved to build the line in the summer of 1895.

The feasibility of the railroad had been established by Mears from the 1889 and 1890 surveys of the proposed route. One was not built at the time because all available monies were used to build the Rio Grande Southern. He did not have the funds necessary for construction of the Silverton Northern until November 30, 1895, when he sold his bankrupt Rio Grande Southern to the Denver & Rio Grande for a relatively high price.

So anxious was the developer to begin the Silverton Northern Railroad that as soon as he was assured of a good price for the Rio Grande Southern, he started construction. He built the first two and a half miles from Silverton to Waldheim in the summer of 1895. Since the Silverton Northern Railroad Company was not yet organized, the new line was considered an extension of the Silverton Railroad for legal purposes.

The Silverton Northern Railroad Company finally was organized by Mears in the late summer of 1895. Old time business associates Fred Walsen and Alexander Anderson were co-founders as were two Denver merchants, Jerome B. Frank and Thomas L. Wiswall. The company was incorporated on November 4, 1895. According to the charter the corporation had a 50-year life and could issue $150,000 in capital stock.

The first stockholders' meeting was conducted on December 20, 1895, in Denver. At the meeting, the stockholders decided to raise $300,000 for building costs by selling bonds. The five per cent bonds would be issued on January 1, 1896, be due 50 years later, and the International Trust Company of Denver was to be the trustee.

Other important decisions were also made at the

meeting. The Silverton and Animas Forks Toll Road was purchased for $149,400 for use as a roadbed, which had the effect of 1,494 shares of Silverton Northern stock winding up in Mears' hands, the remaining six shares going to the other stockholders. Finally, arrangements were made for the transfer of the first two and one-half miles of track from Mears' construction company to the Silverton Northern Railroad Company for $40,000 in Silverton Northern bonds.

With the financial arrangements completed at the December meeting, Mears was able to go ahead with the construction of the new railroad. On March 4, 1896, he announced that track would be laid to Eureka as fast as weather would permit. Eureka, a camp rich in gold and silver deposits, was nine miles north of Silverton. Charges for hauling ore out of the mining town were exorbitant, ranging from $3.50 to $5 a ton. So much ore was transported by pack animals that the railroad president anticipated filling two trains a day upon the extension of track to the town, saving prospective customers between $2 and $3 a ton on freight charges.

C.W. Gibbs made the final survey between Waldheim and Eureka in late April, 1896, and a crew began grading soon after. Work was pushed at such a rapid pace that the tracks reached Howardsville in late May. By mid-June workers were laying track at Middleton and Maggie Gulch, points a few miles south of Eureka. Within days the track was completed to Eureka and the townspeople celebrated the important event in true frontier style. The driving of a golden spike by Mrs. Edward G. Stoiber, the wife of the Silver Lake's owner, signaled the start of the festivities. A barbecue and dance followed the ceremony.

The Waldheim-Eureka extension of the Silverton Northern was the last piece of Colorado railroad construction Mears was to undertake for several years. A year later he went to Washington to build the Chesapeake Beach Railway. For the following decade, concentrating mainly on projects in the East, he had little time to devote to schemes in his adopted state.

While the promoter was in the East building the Chesapeake Beach Railway, his Colorado short lines were operated by Alexander Anderson. Born in Scotland in the early 1860s, Anderson was a competent railroad man. He became an employee of Mears sometime after 1889 and proved so knowledgeable and trustworthy that after the summer of 1897 he served as the superintendent of the Silverton Railroad and as the general manager of the Silverton Northern Railroad.

The employee and employer had a good personal relationship. The former made the everyday decisions while the latter made the long-term policy on monthly visits. The principal concern of the owner was the cutting of expenditures on his Colorado lines because all available money was needed to build the Chesapeake Beach Railway. The resulting rigorous retrenchment policy implemented by Anderson is shown by this letter from the general manager to John L. McNeil, dated September 16, 1897:

> One of our engines struck a milch cow yesterday on Northern about a quarter of mile above station. Butcher will not buy the cow. I have had her appraised and seen the owner. I can settle claim for thirty dollars which is less than appraised valuation. If you approve of it I will make payment and get release.[1]

Besides overseeing the operation of the Silverton shortlines, Anderson had the responsibility of keeping his employer informed about San Juan developments and suggesting possible investment opportunities. In the summer of 1898, for example, Anderson advised Mears to build a railroad from Silverton to Gladstone. Gladstone—located eight miles north of Silverton up a third canyon as yet untouched by any Mears projects—had several rich gold mines such as the Occidental, Gold King, Sampson and Smuggler. The superintendent believed these mines had sufficient ore deposits to make the proposed railroad a good investment.

Mears acted upon his employee's recommendation

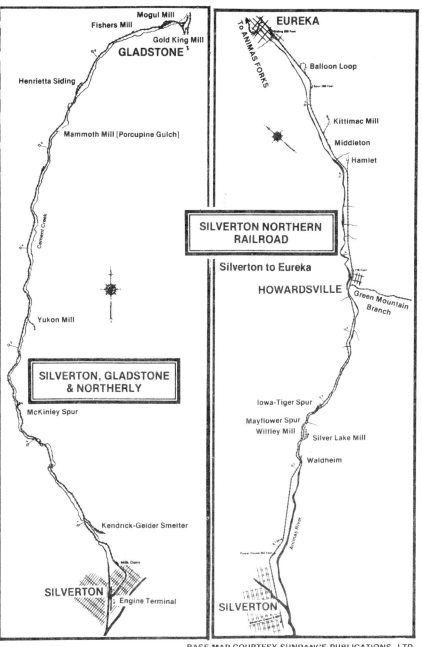

Mogul Mill
Fishers Mill
Gold King Mill
GLADSTONE

Henrietta Siding

Mammoth Mill [Porcupine Gulch]

Cement Creek

Yukon Mill

McKinley Spur

Kendrick-Geider Smelter

Milk Dairy

SILVERTON
Engine Terminal

TO ANIMAS FORKS
EUREKA
Siding 600 Feet

Balloon Loop

Spur 200 Feet

Kittimac Mill

Middleton

Hamlet

SILVERTON NORTHERN RAILROAD

Silverton to Eureka

HOWARDSVILLE
176 Feet
Green Mountain Branch

SILVERTON, GLADSTONE & NORTHERLY

Iowa-Tiger Spur

Mayflower Spur
Wilfley Mill
Silver Lake Mill

Waldheim

Animas River

Power House 342 Feet

SILVERTON

BASE MAP COURTESY SUNDANCE PUBLICATIONS, LTD.

201

without delay. In late July, 1898, soon after receiving Anderson's letter, he arrived in Colorado for his monthly visit. In addition to his regular business, he visited Gladstone to examine the mining town's prospects. Finding conditions favorable, he ordered a survey of the route of the proposed Silverton to Gladstone railroad. While the survey was being conducted, the railroad president attempted to find backers for the line. He could not find anyone willing to advance the $45,000 necessary to build the railroad. Neither able to finance the project himself nor able to raise the amount needed, he gave up the scheme. A year later, Cyrus W. Davis of Maine and F.A. Jones of New Brunswick were to build a railroad between Silverton and Gladstone—which Mears would ironically lease a decade later.

The promoter could not utilize his own funds for the Silverton-Gladstone railroad in 1898 because of his unfavorable financial position. Most of his ready cash was being invested in the Chesapeake Beach Railway. In addition he was suffering a financial drain on his Silverton Railroad operation. The railroad had been losing money since 1897 because of the closure of several mines along its route. To pay operating expenses on the line he had to divert funds from the Silverton Northern, including an apparent $500 a month payment for the use of Silverton Railroad locomotives and rolling stock.

Mears hoped that if he could hold out long enough conditions would improve in the Red Mountain District and his Silverton Railroad would not only avoid bankruptcy but would again be profitable. He had reason to believe that some Red Mountain mines would reopen in the summer of 1899. In June, 1899, in anticipation of a good year for the railroad, he replaced the defective rails and ties at considerable expense.

The replacement of the ties and rails proved unnecessary. The Red Mountain mines slated to reopen did not, and those few in operation were closed because of a strike by workers who wanted shorter hours. Because none of the mines along its route were in operation, the

Silverton Railroad in early June, 1899, was in the worst financial condition in its history. Unable to meet either its expenses or the interest due on its bonds, the railroad went into receivership to protect its assets from the creditors, at a time when Mears was arguing before the State Board of Equalization that the line should not have to pay taxes because it was covered with snow.

In July, 1899, Alexander Anderson, who had been the railroad's superintendent, was appointed its receiver. After his selection by the court, Anderson operated the Silverton Railroad in a manner most beneficial to his long-time employer. With his Colorado interests so well supervised, the railroad's president was able to return to Washington, D.C., to complete construction of the Chesapeake Beach Railway.

The Chesapeake Beach Railway was finished in early August, 1899. It was not until mid-October, however, that Mears found the time to visit Colorado. On that occasion he made a brief inspection trip to Silverton. Discovering that Ouray was unexpectedly prosperous, he also visited the mountain town to evaluate the business prospects there. He found the mining camp rapidly recovering from the 1893 depression. Money had been invested in the area and many producing mines had been developed. Mines such as the Wedge, El Mahdi, Delmonico, Black Girl, Atlas, Calliope, Slide, and Army and Navy were producing high-grade gold ore. The owners of the Camp Bird Mine were the most successful. They boasted that $6,000 in gold ore was extracted daily from their mine.

Because the mines in the Ouray region were shipping so much ore, Mears decided to revive a scheme he had conceived in the fall of 1891—the construction of an electric railroad between Ouray and Ironton. Although Mears had incorporated a company to build the railroad in November, 1891, the line was not built because of the following year's closure of the silver mines.

The entrepreneur believed that it would still be relatively easy to build the electric railroad. He still had in his possession the 1891 surveys of the route; further surveys would be unnecessary. Mears had already researched the engineering techniques required to construct an electric railroad in the high mountains. He also had a promise from Colonel Charles H. Nix of Ouray that a power plant large enough to supply the needs of the proposed railroad would be built. He even owned the right-of-way he would need. He could use his old Ouray and San Juan Toll Road as the roadbed. He had everything required except the funds for construction.

As he could spare only a few days away from his Chesapeake Beach Railway, he was forced to return to Washington before he could implement the electric railroad scheme. He stopped in Chicago on the way East, however, to raise money for the new project. But he discovered that monied men were reluctant to invest in the venture because Colorado had acquired a bad reputation from its labor agitation. Potential investors feared a repetition of the June strike, which resulted in the closing of mines and smelters in the Silverton-Durango area.

Mears could readily understand the refusal of the Chicago financiers to underwrite the electric railroad project. In a June, 1899, interview he expressed their sentiments:

> We are always fighting something out here. How can a man make a living by his work if a certain element says to him that he shall not work and he quits? We have got to get out of this foolish habit, or prosperity will never bless us.[2]

The promoter devoted what time he could spare to the venture until February, 1900, when he gave it up for good, as the necessary funds were not obtainable.

After the abortive electric railroad scheme, Mears had no more time for new Colorado transportation projects until November, 1902. At that time he had returned to Colorado after being removed from the presidency of the Chesapeake Beach Railway by David Moffat. Soon after his arrival in the Centennial State, his frustration and depression resulting from his ouster vanished. The reason for the return of his buoyancy and optimism was a new railroad plan—the extension of the Silverton Northern Railroad to Lake City.

Otto had contemplated the proposed 35-mile extension for years but had been unable to raise the construction money. In November, 1902, he revived the plan because monied men would be more likely now to invest in the project because of the revival of prosperity in the San Juan Mountains.

Mears spent only a few days in Denver after his return to Colorado and then went to New York and Philadelphia in an attempt to raise funds for the Lake City venture. In early December, 1902, he was back in the San Juan giving a number of prospective Eastern investors a tour of the Lake City region. During the tour he emphasized to his guests the potential of the new line. The Denver & Rio Grande Railroad had built a branch from Sapinero to Lake City in 1888, he pointed out, but the mine owners in the remote high country between Eureka and Lake City had difficulty in hauling their ore to either railhead. With the building of the Silverton Northern extension, the tour guide asserted, mine owners in the more remote areas would be able to ship the lower grade ores thrown previously on dumps. Mears also claimed that in addition to the money earned by hauling ore out of the mines, the railroad would be profitable because revenue would be made from transporting machinery and goods to the residents of the mountainous district.

Mears' powers of persuasion failed him on this occasion. The prospective investors believed that the terrain between Eureka, as the terminus of the Silverton Northern, and Lake City was too precipitous for a railroad. Even if the steep Engineer Pass could be negotiated, which they did not believe possible, the construction costs would be so prohibitive and the return so small that investment in the scheme would be unjustifiable.

Although the promoter had failed to raise the money for the Lake City project, he was not discouraged. He was soon engaged in another Silverton Northern extension plan—the building of a line as far as the booming mining town of Animas Forks. The Animas Forks branch had first been considered in 1899 but the construction had to be deferred because the necessary funds could not be raised.

An important gold strike in Animas Forks in the spring of 1902 made this Silverton Northern extension plan more attractive. On April 14, 1902, Alexander Anderson wrote his employer, informing him about the discovery of large ore deposits and the resulting influx of miners. He suggested in the letter that a branch be built to the town because the returns on the investment would be high.

Busy with other projects, Mears could not act upon Anderson's recommendation until the following spring. At that time he interested monied men in the idea and raised the necessary funds. With the cash in hand only a final survey of the route was required to complete preparations. Engineer Thomas H. Wigglesworth was ordered to conduct the survey. Beginning in early June, Wigglesworth finished the job by June 26, 1903.

Wigglesworth had conducted the survey rapidly, overcoming many difficulties. For nearly a month the crew had worked on the east side of the Animas Canyon. The grade was so steep on that side the engineer reported to Mears that the western side, which already had a wagon road, would be better to use. To the surveyor's surprise, as the story goes, Otto answered, "Vell, vy not, it's mine; I built it; go ahead and take it if you want it!"[3] Consequently the trailblazer's old Silverton and Animas Forks Toll Road provided the roadbed for much of the new extension.

Upon the completion of the survey, grading on the four-mile branch began. The 400 men employed to do the grading were billited in four boarding houses—one at Eureka, one at Animas Forks, and two others located between the two towns. One hundred and twenty-five Navajo Indians were in the force and proved extremely difficult to supervise. Mears, who happened to be visiting Silverton at this time, decided to utilize his past experience with Indians in an endeavor to make the Navajo workers more productive. He arrived while a big

Burns Gulch

Crown Mt.

ANIMAS FORKS IN ITS PRIME
Lofty Objective for the Silverton Northern

fill was under way and tried to direct the Indians by means of hand signals. The Navajos—thinking the newcomer humorous—laughed at him, whereupon the latter began windmilling his arms in anger. Now thoroughly amused, the Indians stopped work and mimicked him. Frustrated Otto gave up his attempt to supervise the Indians and left the grade in disgust.

In spite of the problem with the Navajo laborers, grading went rapidly on the new branch and was completed in mid-August, 1903. Tracklaying, the next step, was deferred to the next year since rails were unobtainable. Rails became available the following spring and tracklaying began in mid-May, 1904. Forty men were employed to lay the tracks on the four-mile stretch. By late summer the last rail had been laid. The cost of the construction had been very high, more than $10,000 a mile. Contrary to expectation, the Eureka-Animas Forks branch did not pay well. Mears, however, was more than reimbursed for the building costs. The Silverton Northern Railroad Company purchased the extension from the builder's construction company for $80,000 in first mortgage bonds and $27,000 in cash.

The new extension did not return a profit because normal railroad operation was impossible on the steep grades. From Eureka to Animas Forks, the grade was between 7 and 7.5 per cent—so steep that only a coal car and an empty freight car could be pushed to the latter point. Another problem occurred during the early stages of operation because there was no turntable at Animas Forks. Unable to turn around, the engine backed down on the return trip, a dangerous procedure because the cars could not be effectively controlled.

To ameliorate the situation, Mears moved the turntable at Corkscrew Gulch on the Silverton Railroad to Animas Forks. With the turntable, the locomotive could be turned around and by working against gravity effectively brake the cars on the return trip. Even with the turntable— installed in 1905 or 1906—only three box cars could be hauled on the downhill trip between Animas Forks and

Eureka. In spite of such conditions, the Silverton Northern had an outstanding safety record. The only accident of any consequence on this stretch occurred on August 4, 1906, when the train overturned.

The precautions taken to make the Eureka-Animas Forks run safe were not sufficient to keep the branch operable. Service was curtailed in a few years because the steep grades made operation so difficult that it was economically unfeasible to run trains on the line.

During the short period that trains were run to Animas Forks, the mining town grew rapidly. The influx of people was so great that a Silverton editor predicted in 1904 "Animas Forks is to be on the map again." The newspaperman's optimism was justified on the short term. The railroad helped stimulate mine owners to rework old properties and to discover new lodes of ore. Another important development brought about by the coming of the railroad was the building in 1906 of the Gold Prince Amalgamating and Concentrating Mill. Equipped with machinery of the most modern design, the mill soon became one of the most productive in the state.

During the early years of the century, while the Animas Forks extension was being planned and built, Mears was engaged in another Colorado project. This scheme involved paying off the indebtedness of the Silverton Railroad. To raise money, he decided to form a new corporation and, as an inducement to the future stockholders, he used the Silverton Northern as the collateral for investment.

In order to reorganize his Colorado shortlines, the railroad president needed the permission of the two principal creditors of the Silverton Railroad—Charles Graham of Philadelphia and Fred Walsen. The latter, a long-time friend and business partner, was particularly cooperative, and helped in every possible way to bring his business associate out of his financial difficulties. For example, in January, 1900, Walsen allowed Mears to have his option on the Silverton Northern as the collateral for investment.

Even with Walsen's cooperation Mears found it difficult

to effect a merger of his Silverton lines. His first attempt to do this was in the spring of 1900 when he traveled to St. Louis, Kansas City and Chicago in an endeavor to interest would-be investors in the scheme. On March 20, 1900, the prospective underwriters reviewed the plan in Chicago but refused to advance any money because of the depressed state of the San Juan economy.

Unable to interest monied men in his project, the promoter cast about for ways to make the idea more palatable to investors. Finally, he hit upon an ingenious solution. If he could lease or purchase a silver mine on Red Mountain and operate it profitably, other mines in the area — closed since the drop in silver prices in the early 1890s — would be reopened. With a revival in Red Mountain silver mining he would have no trouble securing the needed financing for his Silverton Railroad reorganization plans.

In accordance with Mears' plan, Alexander Anderson was directed to negotiate for a mine on Red Mountain. In late October and early November, 1900, he accordingly tried to buy a mine for $20,000. The owner, however, wanted $50,000 and the offer was withdrawn.

Unable to revive Red Mountain mining, Mears turned in desperation to Simon Guggenheim, his friend and political protege, for assistance in his reorganization plan. The smelter king, however, refused to advance the necessary funds because he believed that he had already invested too much money in the San Juans. He had recently purchased several Red Mountain mines, including the Guston, Yankee Girl, Liberty Bell and Paymaster. These mines were not yielding the expected return and the industrialist believed that investment in the Silverton Railroad was unjustifiable, even for friendship's sake.

During the years that Mears' repeated attempts to reorganize his shortlines failed, the Silverton Railroad sank deeper into debt. Nineteen hundred was the line's last year in the black. Through extremely careful management, the net profit was $427.67. In 1901, the railroad was not even able to make the token profit it had made in 1900 since its only regular customer, the Silver Ledge Mine, no longer shipped ore. With the loss of its only important shipper there was no longer any reason to adhere to regular service. By 1903, trains were run so infrequently that service sometimes ceased for months at a time. In the summer of that year traffic hit an all time low, with only one carload of ore being shipped out of the entire Red Mountain district.

By 1904 the total debt on the railroad, accumulated since 1899, was $4,000. Mears had no money to spare for upkeep, and so it was difficult for Anderson to keep the roadbed and tracks in good physical repair. At this juncture the railroad president, with bankruptcy imminent, was able to save the line from disaster by adroit maneuvering and achieve the long-sought reorganization.

He convinced William S. Jackson of Colorado Springs and M.D. Thatcher of Pueblo—both merchants and railroad men—that a corporate reorganization of his shortlines would be very profitable to those underwriting the scheme; they agreed to invest $100,000. The funds were to be used to organize the Silverton Railway Corporation. The new company would purchase the Silverton Northern, and pay the debts of the Silverton Railroad Company. When all preparations had been made, the Silverton Railway Corporation was incorporated on November 3, 1904, ending the receivership of the Silverton Railroad. But the reorganization did not keep the line financially solvent for long. Eventually, the railroad was abandoned as there was not enough business to justify operation.

The completion of the railroad consolidation left Mears' Colorado interests solvent for the moment and enabled him to engage in another Silverton Northern extension project. The new branch was to be a 1½-mile line from Howardsville to Green Mountain, where the Green Mountain Mining and Milling Company was erecting a mill. The milling company promised to be such a good customer that its freight shipments were expected not only to repay the cost of the extension but to bring a good profit as well.

Mears had the branch surveyed in the summer of 1904 when he first heard that the mill would be built at Green Mountain. It was to be some months, however, before he was able to raise the funds required for the extension. In early 1905, all the necessary arrangements were made. Grading began in May of that year and construction was completed a few months later at a cost of $75,000.

When the final preparations had been made for the construction of the Green Mountain branch, the railroad builder addressed himself to the realization of an old dream—the extension of the Silverton Railway into Ouray. He had attempted to reach the mining town by rail since the late 1880s. He had already found that a steam railroad could not negotiate the steep grades between Albany—the old Silverton Railroad terminus—and Ouray, and he contemplated constructing an electric railroad between Ironton and Ouray instead. Although an electric railroad was feasible and the returns would have made the venture very worthwhile, he could not raise the money for construction during the 1890s.

In 1905 the mines near Ouray were still producing heavily. Intent upon reaching the rich mining region and with the prospect of adequate financial backing, Mears contemplated a new approach to the problem of negotiating the rugged terrain between Red Mountain and Ouray. By using a cog railroad similar to the kind used on Pike's Peak, it would be possible to negotiate the 10 per cent grades. The scheme called for building a 12-mile cog line on the mountain passes along the route. Not only would the cog railroad be profitable, it would allow the builder to keep the Ouray and San Juan Toll Road open. If tracks were laid for either a steam or electric railroad, the toll road would have to be torn up and used for the trackbed. The toll road, however, was used so frequently by the San Juan's residents that they would not tolerate its closure. Although the proposed cog railroad between Red Mountain and Ouray was attractive, huge building costs precluded its construction.

Mears was unwilling to give up the idea of connecting

Red Mountain and Ouray. After the unfeasibility of the cog railroad scheme was shown, he contemplated another plan involving the use of his railroad automobile. During the summer of 1905, Mears was testing the experimental model of the railroad automobile made at the Mack Brothers factory in Allentown, Pennsylvania. The automobile, powered by a gasoline engine, could carry 28 passengers. The machine had flanged wheels to enable it to operate on railroad tracks, and it was supposed to be cheaper to operate and more efficient on steeper grades than steam railroads.

Already in possession of a railroad auto, all Mears had to do was to lay the tracks between Red Mountain and Ouray. Rails would be laid on the roadbed of the Ouray and San Juan Toll Road and, theoretically, the vehicle would easily negotiate the steep grades while pulling a freight trailer. The plan, however, depended upon two factors for its realization: the cooperation of the people of Ouray County, who would have to approve the destruction of a major traffic artery, and the successful operation of the experimental model of the railroad automobile.

Assuming he could overcome any obstacles preventing the implementation of his newest idea, Mears widened the Ouray and San Juan Toll Road throughout the summer of 1905, so that it would accommodate the railroad automobile. That fall, ties were scattered along the four-mile stretch. The builder, however, was not willing to lay the rails until he received support from the people of Ouray. He had raised the $400,000 necessary for the project but wanted the townspeople to buy $8,000 to $10,000 worth of stock in the enterprise to guarantee their patronizing the railroad automobile.

But the residents of Ouray were unwilling to invest in the enterprise. They did not want to underwrite such a risky venture. The railroad automobile was new to Colorado and they wished to see it tested at length before advancing funds for an untried scheme. The caution of the inhabitants of the mountain hamlet proved well advised, as the initially successful railroad automobile performed so poorly on subsequent occasions that Mears had to drop all transportation plans involving the machine.

It was at this same time that Mears contemplated the construction of a $100,000 tourist hotel in Silverton in connection with the railroad revival plans and, even though he raised half the funds, the hotel was never built.

In 1906, undaunted by the failure of the railroad automobile, Mears planned two new projects involving his Colorado lines. The first was a revival of the 1902 plan to extend the Silverton Northern to Lake City. That mining camp was still booming and the promoter believed that he could—this time—raise the large sum necessary for construction. In early June, 1906, he accordingly ordered a survey crew to plot a route between Animas Forks and Lake City. Nothing came of the owner's wish to extend the Northern, however. As in 1902, it was impossible for him to convince would-be investors that the steep grades along the proposed route could be negotiated by a steam railroad.

Unable to raise the funds required for the Lake City extension, the railroad president focused his attention on another Colorado project—the experimental full-time winter operation of the Silverton lines. This idea was probably borrowed from the snow-fighting plan of the Denver & Rio Grande Railroad. In the 1880s, the railroad had erected a snowshed in the Animas Canyon three miles south of Silverton. Ever since, the snowshed had prevented avalanches from covering the track. Mears believed that similar construction would enable him to operate his shortlines throughout the year and to more than double the income from these lines.

In a newspaper interview, Otto described how he proposed to build and operate the snowsheds:

> The roof will be constructed of heavy timbers, stretching in tiers over the track and sloping to the ground on either side on a grade conforming to the mountain slope, so that slides from any direction will glide over the sheds without harm. There will be a station built in each shed and sec-

tion hands will live there during the winter and keep the road clear between the sheds.[4]

This interview was greeted with scorn by many readers, but in the following issue the Silverton editor was critical of those who could so easily dismiss the innovator's idea without giving it a fair test. The editor asserted that the plan, if implemented, would be "the crowning act of a useful and well spent life."

Unfortunately, Mears' detractors proved to be correct. By December all of the necessary arrangements had been made and several sheds had been built in the Animas Canyon along the route of the Silverton Northern. The sheds were up for only a short time, however, when heavy snowslides carried them into the Animas River. The project was abandoned.

During late fall of 1906, when the Animas Canyon snowsheds were being built, Mears re-established his Colorado residency. For a decade he had spent most of his time in the East, hoping to regain the fortune he had lost on the Rio Grande Southern. Unsuccessful and going further into debt, he finally returned to the Centennial State. He hoped that his luck would change, that he would be able to pay his debts, and that he could accumulate enough money to retire.

Once again a full-time resident of Colorado with the purchase of his Silverton home, Mears embarked on a series of new projects which he hoped would be lucrative. The San Juan country was booming and he wanted to capitalize on this prosperity. The surest guarantee of a profit, he believed, would be to extend the Silverton Northern to some of the busy mining camps. Some of these extension schemes were more feasible than others. One of the least practical involved the building of a branch from Animas Forks to Mineral Point.

Mineral Point, according to the Silverton Northern articles of incorporation, was to have been the original terminus of the railroad. By 1907, however, Mears had succeeded in extending the railroad only as far as Animas Forks. The terrain was so precipitious north of the town that huge sums would be required to do any further building. In spite of the obstacles, Mineral Point remained an objective worth reaching. The *Silverton Standard* of July 11, 1903, for example, reported that in a one-mile radius from the camp, $3,000,000 worth of ore had been extracted and that there was "enough ore within this radius, if properly opened up, to keep 1,000 stamps pounding the remainder of this century." [5]

The long-contemplated Mineral Point extension began to materialize in the spring of 1907. Mears could now be assured of the necessary funds. Simon Guggenheim, out of gratitude for his mentor's help in the 1907 senatorial election, was allegedly willing to subsidize any reasonable transportation project of his friend. In April, 1907, to promote the venture, the railroad president joined Silverton's Boosters Committee of One Hundred.

A few months after joining the boosters' group, Mears commissioned a survey of the proposed Animas Forks-Mineral Point branch. When the surveyors brought back a discouraging report about the feasibility of building a railroad between the two points, he decided further confirmation was necessary to substantiate their findings. In 1909, accordingly, another survey was taken. When it affirmed the results of the 1907 survey, the Mineral Point extension plan was dropped.

While the 1907 Mineral Point survey was being conducted Mears ordered a second corps of surveyors to plot a route from Animas Forks to Ouray. This was his almost annual attempt to bridge the gap by rail between Silverton and Ouray. It, too, ended in failure when the surveyors again reported the terrain was too rugged between Animas Forks and Ouray for a rail connection.

The results of the two Mineral Point surveys and the Silverton to Ouray survey finally convinced Mears that the geographical obstacles were too great to extend either of his Colorado shortlines. He never again attempted to lengthen his San Juan railroads. In the future, he would support himself on revenue from the Louisiana Central, the Silverton Northern and various mining ventures.

After the disappointing results from the 1909 Animas Forks to Mineral Point survey, Mears believed he would never again be called upon to do any extensive railroad building. That fall, however, he accomplished perhaps the most important railroad construction of his career. By repairing track destroyed in a series of natural disasters, he saved the San Juans from potential ruin.

The trouble began in early August, 1909, when heavy rains lasting for days caused rockslides which demolished track in some places and covered it with debris in others. All railroads in the area were put out of commission, and Silverton was cut off from the outside. After putting his own lines in working order, Mears offered his services and those of his men to the management of the Denver & Rio Grande Railroad so that the blockade of Silverton could be lifted and normal service restored. The officers of the railroad accepted the volunteer's assistance and signed him to a contract. [6]

At the contract signing it was decided to form two construction crews: One, based in Silverton with Mears in charge, was to work south towards Durango clearing and repairing track; the other, supervised by P.B. McAttee of the Denver & Rio Grande, was to begin working north from Durango. The two crews were to start work simultaneously and meet at some point between the two towns.

With the rallying cries of "push ahead" and "back to the grade," Mears began the difficult task of rebuilding the Denver & Rio Grande branch. Work progressed rapidly but about 15 miles from Silverton, at a spot near Needleton, the workers were baffled by a gigantic rock fall. At Mears' suggestion, the old track was left covered and a new roadbed was constructed at a five per cent grade eight feet over the old one.

Two weeks later, Mears' crew, after very arduous work, had cleared the track as far as Cascade, a hamlet a few miles below Needleton. The situation at Cascade involved

    the clearing away of thirteen heavy rockslides,
    the rebuilding of that portion of Mineral Creek
    bridge which was swept away, the filling and

grading of miles of washed out roadbed and track, and the cutting of a new roadbed through hundreds of feet of rock in the cliffs some distance above Cascade.[7]

In the meantime, superintendent McAttee's crew rapidly worked north from Durango and restored the tracks to Tacoma. At this point—about five miles south of Cascade—was the largest slide. "A heavy rock cut from 150 to 200 feet in length through perpendicular cliffs over fifty feet high in places" was required, according to the *Durango Democrat*. The men were slowly working through the slide when Mears' crew arrived on the scene. Using his decades of experience on the grade, the old timer was able to cut through the slide on September 24, 1909, and meet up with the Denver & Rio Grande crew. On the following day, the 46-day blockade of Silverton was ended when a train steamed into the mining camp from Durango. When the blockade was lifted at Silverton, there were 83 fully loaded railroad cars waiting to be hauled to the smelter.

The arrival of the train evoked feelings of relief from the townspeople, who had been waiting a month and a half for rail serivce to resume. To express their gratitude, the inhabitants paid Mears one of the highest accolades ever accorded a resident of the town in appreciation of his good work. The Silverton Cornet Band, headed by Professor Estabrook, led a large group of people across the city to the pioneer's Reese Street residence. Mayor B.B. Allen knocked on the door and invited him to come out. Stepping outdoors, Mears was surprised to find scores of people. He was serenaded and when the singing was over, a deeply moved Mears was given three cheers by the crowd. When the throng quieted down, John T. Joyce, the publisher of the *Silverton Standard*, presented the man of the hour with a silver punch bowl. The inscription:

Presented to the Hon. Otto Mears, by the people of Silverton in recognition of his earnest and faithful work in opening the Rio Grande Railroad to traffic, September 25, 1909. [8]

Near tears, the recipient of the honor mumbled his thanks to the gathering, and the crowd dispersed.

Just three weeks after being honored by Silverton, the pioneer was again called upon to help a San Juan town. All railroad traffic to Telluride had been stopped by a September 5 storm which had washed away the Rio Grande Southern track south of the town. After the washout, the residents of the mining camp were charged exorbitant rates for supplies of food and fuel which had to be freighted in. With the approach of winter, the town was "on the verge of a coal famine of serious proportions," and unless the track could be cleared, the residents would probably find it necessary to evacuate.

During the period of the Telluride blockade, the Rio Grande Southern management seemed paralyzed and appeared to be unable or unwilling to restore the track. Grading companies were sent to the scene but nothing could be done because of the lack of men and supplies. After most of the fall was wasted the townspeople became frantic. Finally, the management of the Rio Grande Southern decided that the only way to have the repair work done properly was to hire Mears to do the job. They offered him a lucrative contract to restore the damaged roadbed. Still recuperating from his arduous efforts on behalf of Silverton, he decided to accept the restoration job. He needed the money and he did not want to see the residents of Telluride starved out.

After recruiting a construction crew in Silverton and Durango, Mears left for the beleaguered town on the evening of October 13, 1909. Dave Day described his old friend as he was leaving Durango:

> He was enthusiastic as a boy and yet Otto is well toward 70 years of age, but younger now than 30 years ago. He was all smiles at a chance to tackle the Southern and went out with the usual energy characteristic of the man.[9]

After boarding the train at Durango, Mears and his crew went to the main washout north of Trout Lake. A dam had burst there and 2,000 feet of track and roadbed had been washed away. With the men working two shifts of ten hours each daily, the damage was repaired in two weeks.

When it became apparent that the restoration of railroad connections would be imminent, the residents of Telluride decided to plan a large celebration to honor Mears, who was largely responsible for saving their town. On Friday, October 23, 1909, several townspeople met and preparations for the festivities were made. All the inhabitants of the town were encouraged to attend and "Welcome to Otto Mears" buttons were distributed.

Telluride was ready on October 25 when the first train in 50 days arrived. When Mears climbed down from the train, he was greeted by a large crowd and the city band. He was escorted to the luxurious New Sheridan Hotel, where 20 prominent citizens hosted a dinner. A public reception followed the banquet. The guest of honor's exploits were told to those present by ex-Congressman Hirschel M. Hogg. Attorney L.W. Allen presented Otto with a decanter inscribed: "Otto Mears, Telluride, October 25, 1909."[10]

The pioneer returned to Silverton on the following day, stopping at Durango to call on Dave Day. The editor reporting on the visit to his readers stated that his visitor was as "happy as a lark" after the restoration work. Day asserted that his friend thrived under adverse conditions and was "never happy unless surrounded with trouble and a lot of men working him out." Within the same week, in admiration of Mears' achievements, Day stated that "Otto Mears remains the 'Pathfinder.' He always will. We got in by paying toll."

After his Durango visit, Mears returned to Silverton for a short stay. After completing some unfinished business, he decided to go to Denver where he planned to remain most of the winter. He also planned to take an ocean cruise during his vacation to recuperate fully from his grueling fall season; whether or not he went is not known.

In Denver, Otto soon tired of his indolence. Eager for more activity, he negotiated a contract on January 7,

220

MEARS AND GUESTS AT GLADSTONE'S GOLD KING MILL
Looking to Breathe Life into an Old Giant

1909, with the management of the Silverton, Gladstone & Northerly Railroad. The agreement provided for a ten-year lease of the railroad by the Silverton Northern Railroad Company. The transaction was approved by the stockholders of the Silverton Northern Railroad Company on January 10, 1910. On February 24, 1910, the stockholders of the Silverton, Gladstone & Northerly Railroad Company also assented to the lease.

Mears' newly leased railroad operated on a nine-mile stretch from Silverton north along Cement Creek to the Gold King Mine at Gladstone. The line had been built in 1899 by Gold King backers when the mine was yielding tremendous amounts of gold ore. In July, 1898, about a year before construction of the railroad began, Mears had contemplated a line to Gladstone but could not raise the funds for the venture.

The railroad builder had maintained his interest in Gladstone during the 12 years following his abortive attempt to construct a line to the mining camp. During that period, the Gold King had been producing less and less ore, and by 1910 the owners of the mine believed that most of the ore had already been extracted. The Silverton, Gladstone & Northerly reflected the condition of the Gold King. With its builder and principal customer shipping little ore, the railroad was unwilling to keep the line in good repair and was anxious to sell it at any fair price.

In order to prevent the sale of the line to absentee owners who might put their own welfare above that of the residents of southwestern Colorado, Mears assumed control of the railroad. He had realized long before that only if the San Juan region was growing and prosperous could he make any money from his Silverton shortlines. By leasing the Silverton, Gladstone & Northerly, he would be in a position to foster the region's growth, he believed, because he would now control all the in-San Juan County railroads.

In addition to leasing the Gladstone line, Mears promoted San Juan development by becoming an advocate of improved surface automobile roads. When president of Mack Brothers, he had learned that techno-logical advances would make the automobile efficient enough to render horse-drawn vehicles obsolete. Roads in southwestern Colorado were adequate for horse and buggy but difficult for automobile travel. To reach its potential, he believed the San Juans would have to prepare for the future and improve roads to facilitate automobile travel.

The pioneer pathfinder used his celebrity status to promulgate his opinions about the importance of good roads at a time when such proposals were not popular. Taxpayers were not willing to have their funds allocated for roads which only the rich would use. Mears perceived, however, that automobiles would soon be manufactured cheaply enough to be purchased by most middle-class families. The visionary consequently used every con-venient occasion to suggest the routes that the new roads should follow and to indicate how cheaply they could be built. The plans he developed at such times reveal the great amount of thought he had given these ideas and show how much in advance of his time he was.

The most interesting proposal set forth by the good road advocate during this period was a plan whereby Denver would emulate ancient Rome in road building. He hoped to convince legislators to approve an ambitious three-pronged construction program. The road network would include a north-south highway extending from Denver to Trinidad, a road from Pueblo to Ouray by way of Lake City, and a road beginning at Salida and reaching Routt County. The counties would be encouraged to build their own roads to reach the three main state highways. Using convicts who were just "eating their heads off in the penitentiary," he estimated this network could be built cheaply for only $100,000 and could be completed in just eight years. When completed, the system would make Denver—like ancient Rome—the hub of the sur-rounding hinterland.

Although Mears lobbied whenever possible for im-proved surface roads, it was not until the summer of 1910 that anything was done to carry out the ideas. The chain of events which led to the implementation of some of his proposals began on July 7, 1910, when Thomas H. Tulley, the son-in-law of Dave Day, visited Durango. Tulley, a state highway commissioner, was on a tour of inspection to determine the best automobile route between Denver and Durango.

In addition to the selection of a route, it was Tulley's duty to determine if the counties through which the proposed road would be built would appropriate two-thirds of the construction cost as stipulated by law. To ascertain if the money would be forthcoming from south-western Colorado, he convened a meeting of the commissioners of La Plata and San Juan Counties.

The meeting was conducted on the evening of July 7, 1910, in Durango. Tulley opened the proceedings by stating that since he was the San Juan representative on the State Highway Commission, he would do all he could to implement any workable idea presented at the meeting. Attorney W.N. Searcy of Silverton then took the floor and suggested that the proposed road between Denver and Durango be extended to Silverton and from there built to Ouray and Grand Valley. The lawyer argued that the scenic attractions along his proposed road would justify the construction cost. So many tourists would use the highway because of the spectacular scenery, he claimed, that enough money would be brought into the area to pay for the road.

Searcy's proposal was supported by Mears, who also attended the meeting. In a short speech the San Juan booster stated that the road could be built at a minimal cost because his old toll roads would serve as the roadbed for the state highway. If the road were built, he asserted, not only would tourism be promoted in southwestern Colorado, but settlement and commerce would also be affected.

So impressed was Tulley with Searcy's and Mears' arguments in favor of the Denver-Durango-Grand Valley highway that he persuaded the State Highway Commission to build the road. With the state putting up one-third of the required funds, the counties which the road would traverse now had to decide if they would pay the remaining costs.

San Juan County made its decision on funding the road on July 26, 1910, when the county commissioners invited the members of Silverton's Commercial Club to a joint meeting. After the formalities were over, Mears asked for permission to speak. He argued persuasively that the money for the road ought to be raised. He repeated his arguments, advanced at the July 7 meeting with Tulley, that good roads would encourage tourism, settlement and commerce in the area. He asserted that Silverton would benefit from the highway because residents would no longer be required to pay the exorbitant freight charges of the Denver & Rio Grande Railroad for household commodities. The railroad president was so persuasive that the county commissioners decided to appropriate the necessary construction funds.

Just a month after the meeting of the San Juan County commissioners, Mears exploited one of the most important automotive feats in San Juan history to advertise the need for improved roads. In late August, 1910, the first automobile negotiated the rugged roads between Del Norte and Silverton, having come all the way from Denver to publicize auto travel's potential. When the automobile entered the city, Mears was on hand to congratulate the successful motorists—David L. Mechling and Louis Wyman. The next day, at a party celebrating the event, Mears made an effective plea for improved roads.

That December, the pioneer again used his prestige to gain support for the good road movement. He offered to formally relinquish his old Ouray and San Juan Toll Road when the county commissioners began rebuilding it. He had sold the toll road to Ouray County in 1891. Although no longer owner of the road, Mears believed that favorable publicity would be gained if he were on hand for the ceremony marking the beginning of the road's

THE FIRST AUTOMOBILE IN SILVERTON

226

renovation. Not content to help advertise the road building, he had some suggestions on how the construction should proceed. He recommended that the old toll road be widened and that turnabouts be built for the safety and convenience of automobile travelers.

Three months later, on February 5, 1911, to further promote improved surface roads, Mears—accompanied by several members of the State Highway Commission—took an automobile excursion to Canon City. The tourists were invited that evening to attend a banquet at the Strathmore Hotel. After the dinner several members of the party made speeches emphasizing the need for good roads. The speakers also endorsed the proposed Rainbow Route State Highway. The so-called "Rainbow Route," then under consideration by the legislature, was a proposed highway from Pueblo to Leadville through the Arkansas Valley. From Leadville the road would extend to the western state line, following the Eagle and Grand [or Colorado] Rivers.

Mears was very much in favor of the Rainbow Route. In his speech at the Strathmore Hotel banquet, he cited the advantages of the proposed highway. Connected to the old toll roads he had built, the highway would help form a road network in southwestern Colorado. As the shortest possible route between Denver and the Western Slope, it would save travelers hours in driving time in comparison to present roads. Besides being practical, the road would also be relatively inexpensive and would be easy to build. The day before, he said, the excursionists traversed the proposed route; the only construction problem they could foresee would be the 12-mile stretch between Parkdale and Cotopaxi. The speaker concluded his remarks by stating that he believed so strongly that the road should be built that he would exercise what influence he had to induce the legislature, then in session, to approve the highway's construction.

The day following the banquet, Mears returned to Denver to lobby in the Eighteenth Assembly for the road bill and other measures helpful to the San Juans. Working with other lobbyists, he succeeded in persuading the legislators to approve the road measure. After the legislature adjourned in early April, he took a well-deserved six-week vacation from business and politics.

Well-rested Mears was back in the San Juans in mid-May, 1911, ready to embark on a busy season supervising his mining and railroad interests. He also continued his efforts in behalf of good roads and promoted the area's development whenever possible. He used the future highway to lure monied men to the region. To would-be investors he gave glowing reports of the region's potential. He gave standing invitations to wealthy individuals to visit Silverton as his guests, so that they could see for themselves the great potential of southwestern Colorado.

One of the tours he typically gave to men of means occurred in mid-July, 1911. At that time, he hosted a delegation of the members of the Denver Chamber of Commerce, who visited the Western Slope to investigate investment possibilities. He accompanied the delegation on an excursion on the Silverton Northern. To impress his guests he took the occasion to boast that the railroad was "the highest commercial railroad in the state of Colorado." He stopped the train to allow the party to pick some columbines on a mountain side. Upon completion of the trip, he gave the sightseers a ride on the Silverton, Gladstone & Northerly. The host did such a good job of promoting the San Juans that the visitors declared themselves infatuated with the area and were quite enthusiastic about the district's future.

After a busy summer, during which he had supervised his railroad and mining ventures and had promoted southwestern Colorado whenever possible, Mears was ready for his usual extended winter vacation. His plans were interrupted, however, when disaster again threatened the San Juan region as it had in 1909. Several weeks of unusually heavy precipitation had culminated on October 5, 1911, with a 36-hour downpour.

The rainstorm produced the largest and most damaging

COLUMBINE PICKING AT ANIMAS FORKS
Capitalizing on Another Mountain Resource

SAN JUAN COUNTY HISTORICAL SOCIETY
WARREN PROSSER COLLECTION

229

flood in the history of the area. Every stream became a torrent. Farms, ranches, and personal property were washed away. Railroads were damaged. In order to reduce the loss, the management of the Denver & Rio Grande and the Rio Grande Southern Railroads took immediate action. To prevent bridges from being washed away, freight cars filled with iron and rock were placed on the endangered structures. But the timely move saved very few bridges from the raging flood.

Unsuccessful in the attempt to save their bridges, the management of the San Juan railroads tried to preserve the equipment and track. This proved impossible. The destruction caused by the flood was so great that each of the area's railroads sustained crippling injuries. The Denver & Rio Grande Railroad, for example, experienced a $143,000 loss in roadbed and equipment. The Rio Grande Southern Railroad was even harder hit.

By October 10—five days after the storm—communication was still disrupted between the towns serviced by the Southern, and nothing had been heard from the stations east of Dolores. Under these conditions no trains could be operated.

Mears' Silverton lines suffered storm damage similar to that of the Denver & Rio Grande and Rio Grande Southern. He estimated that it would cost $25,000 to repair the Silverton and Silverton Northern. The Silverton, Gladstone & Northerly was also in bad condition, but the line had so few customers that repair work on it was deferred.

As soon as weather permitted and a construction crew could be formed, Mears was on the grade repairing his railroads. It required seven days of work on the Silverton and Silverton Northern to restore the roadbed and track. When it became apparent that restoration work on the Silverton lines would progress well, the railroad president made an agreement with the Denver & Rio Grande management: In return for a high fee he would help supervise the track repair work between Silverton and Durango.

On October 14, 1911, a day after he signed the contract, Mears began work on the Silverton branch of the Denver & Rio Grande. Two hundred men divided into two crews began work at Silverton. Repair operations began simultaneously at Durango, supervised by George Logan, an employee of the Denver & Rio Grande. Because of the immediate danger of a food and fuel shortage that coming winter for Silverton's residents, work was pushed as rapidly as possible.

To facilitate the work, Mears treated the members of his construction crew fairly. From long experience he knew that employees would work harder if properly motivated and therefore, contrary to the employment practices of the time, he was fair and even generous to his underlings. In keeping with his policy of keeping workers contented he paid a $3 daily wage, twice the amount the Denver & Rio Grande customarily paid its crew members.

George Logan, supervisor at the Durango end, did not emulate Mears' policy of creating good working conditions and he consequently had labor problems. His construction crew went on strike, angered at their low wage of $1.50 per day. Policemen had to be called to the scene to keep order, and repair work on the Durango end stopped. A division superintendent in Durango sent a telegram to Mears in a fit of jealousy, angered at the work stoppage and piqued at the excellent progress made by the latter's crew. The superintendent suggested that Otto quit work, claiming the latter's assistance in repairing the flood damage was not needed. Mears wired back that he had been hired by E.T. Jeffery, the president of the railroad, and would continue to take his orders from him.

Because of good treatment, Mears' crew worked hard. By November 10, track had been restored as far as Needleton, a distance of approximately 15 miles from Silverton. Years later Mears would recall an amusing incident that occurred about this time. One day he was on an inspection trip in a canyon. Pressed for time, he thought that engineer "Pete" Meyer, normally a daredevil, was going too slow. Finally losing patience, Otto exclaimed, "Vhat's the matter—'fraid?" Meyer replied that he was not; he said the track was too unsafe for traveling any faster. The engineer, however, was piqued and began going dangerously fast. Now worried, Otto cautioned, "Vell, it's all right if you stay on the track, but if you go off, v'here are you?" [11]

Another story has been told about Mears' experiences at this time. To hasten the work, he obtained coal from mine owners and merchants to supply his engines. Even housewives were called upon to conserve coal, and coke and cord-wood were used in the homes instead. It was not until mid-November that Silverton's fuel shortage was over, but the townspeople endured their hardships without complaint, knowing that their sacrifices would enable Mears to finish the repair work faster.

The confidence Silverton residents had in Mears was well placed. The facility with which a 71-year-old man solved the tremendous problems encountered in the repair work amazed everyone, including Mears himself. His strength and endurance were astonishing. His own description of a typical work day exemplifies this:

> I get up at 5:30 in the morning and at six I go to the depot, ready for starting work. The fresh air I get going to the depot, sometimes the temperature below zero and sometimes in a snowstorm, is very invigorating and tends to lengthen a man's life. This is espcially [sic] true when I get down on the grade, where the men are often scattered over two or three miles and I take a walk over the line and then walk a couple of miles ahead with the Engineer, to lay [out] the work for the next day and then return to the track-laying gang. By that time it is about lunch time and I take my dinner bucket and sit down on a rock or log and eat a hearty dinner, after which I rest until 12:45, which is our time for resuming work in the afternoon. To do this makes a man of my age feel good. Meantime my Asst. Supt. keeps walking up and down the line the whole day, telling the gang bosses that the salvation of

ANIMAS CANYON FLOOD DAMAGE IN 1911
A Rude Interruption from Mother Nature

Silverton lies in our getting through by Dec. 1st, and impressing it upon them that it will ruin the camp if we don't get through by that time.

The only trouble I have is getting a sufficient number of ties. When I get home between six or seven in the evening, I take a hot whisky toddy, eat my dinner, read the three day old papers and go to bed to dream about ties.[12]

Mears used his stamina to good advantage. In the first week of December his crew met Logan's between Needleton and Elk Park and the repair work was finished. The completion of the reconstruction job on the Denver & Rio Grande trackage marked a turning point in his life. From this point on, because of advancing age and the unprofitability of his railroads, Mears was to spend most of his nine remaining summers in Colorado concentrating on mining schemes rather than transportation projects. His contribution to the development of transportation in southwestern Colorado had been considerable. His 400 miles of toll roads and three railroads, besides being engineering triumphs, played a considerable role in the area's growth. Through bad luck he had not made the money he had hoped from his road and railroad building, and now in his old age he needed to earn enough to support himself during his retirement.

10

Amen Corner

*M*ining, which was to become Mears' primary business interest in the second decade of the 20th century, was of only secondary importance to the pioneer in the years immediately preceding 1910. Transportation projects—uppermost in his mind after his return to Colorado in November, 1906—were gradually shelved due to insurmountable geographical and financial problems. Only when railroad extension ideas proved impossible did he engage in his first mining venture in the Centennial State since the early 1890s.

The leasing of the Iowa-Tiger Mine in the summer of 1908 was the new mining investment. Initially, Mears' friends thought the mine was a bad financial risk. It had been closed recently because not enough ore had been extracted to pay expenses. In an unsuccessful attempt to avoid bankruptcy, the previous operators had mortgaged the mine, and the principal as well as the back interest on the loan was due. The Iowa-Tiger's financial condition was so unsound, in fact, that its stock was worthless.

Relying on 50 years of mining experience, Mears believed that the Iowa-Tiger would be a lucrative investment with good management and accordingly leased it for three years. Besides luck, he had discovered

235

that the most important factor in the success of a mining operation was the work habits of the miners. If improperly motivated, employees would not work up to their potential; poor management would thus be reflected in lower profits.

To insure that the mine would be worked properly the new operator selected his best miners and offered them a share of the eventual profits related to the efficiency of their production underground. Mears' motivational techniques—far ahead of their time—caused the miners to work harder and the Iowa-Tiger began to show high profits. By the summer of 1909 the mine was returning 20 per cent a month on a $15,000 capitalization.

In July, 1910, the character of the Iowa-Tiger operation was transformed. A very profitable investment turned into a bonanza. Since 1908, silver and lead had been extracted from the mine, but in the summer of 1910 a very rich vein of gold ore was discovered. The vein had been found by the foreman on July 13, 1910, on the fourth level. The foreman, by habit, had "picked" into the tunnel walls while making a tour of inspection. In the darkness he chipped a piece of what appeared to be iron pyrite. Leaving the mine, he re-examined his ore sample and was startled to find that it contained gold.

Excited about his discovery, the foreman ordered a crew to search the location where the gold had been found. The miners found a vein of gold ore at least two feet thick. Twenty sacks of gold ore—worth $1,200 a ton—were extracted the first day. It was estimated that the vein extended through the five levels of the mine. So large was the amount of gold-bearing ore calculated to be in the mine that the strike was hailed immediately as one of the largest and most important in southwestern Colorado history.

So much ore was found, in fact, that the debts of the Iowa-Tiger were paid, the mortgage extinguished, and the mine owners were able to declare a dividend on what was formerly worthless stock. Although high royalties were due on the lease, Mears earned enough profit from

236

this venture to repay the debts he had accumulated since 1893 and to become a millionaire.

The Iowa-Tiger enterprise proved so lucrative that Mears invested in other mining projects. In mid-August, 1911—thirteen months after the discovery of the Iowa-Tiger deposits—the speculator leased the Gold King Mine at Gladstone. By operating the mine he hoped to stimulate business on the Silverton, Gladstone & Northerly Railroad, which he had leased in January, 1910. He had assumed control of the railroad in order to promote growth in Gladstone, but he had been unsuccessful and had lost money in the attempt. By operating the Gold King, he expected to revive the economy of Gladstone, which had been dealt a crippling blow when the owners had earlier decided to close the mine. If valuable ore could be found, so much the better. Any profit from the mine would be used to help pay the railroad's debts.

The pioneer was taking a big risk by taking over the Gold King. At the time when he assumed control the mine was in very bad shape. The workings had been abandoned for so long that much repair work was necessary before ore extraction could begin. The shafts, for example, were dangerous for the miners because the supporting timbers were rotting away. Not only was the mine unsafe, but the mill posed hazardous working conditions as well because its roof was ready to cave in. In addition to the large sums required to repair the mine shafts and to fix the mill roof, a further $5,000 to $6,000 would have to be spent to remodel the miners' boarding houses that were unfit to live in. As Mears was obligated to pay $4,500 a month royalties whether or not the mine was operational, the necessary repairs were completed as fast as possible.

In spite of the large cash outlays required to make the Gold King operational, Mears was confident about the venture. He was convinced that the mine still contained enough ore to justify investment. He understood, however, that it would be necessary to properly motivate the miners to realize the mine's potential. By inaugurating a profit-sharing plan, he estimated that overall production would increase by 56 per cent. As in the Iowa-Tiger operation, the best miners were included in the plan in return for insuring efficient work from their colleagues.

At first, in spite of the extensive preparations, the venture seemed on the verge of failure. A preliminary test of 30 tons of concentrates in early October, 1911, showed that the ore was worth on an average only $19 per ton. The results of the assay were so discouraging that James R. Pitcher, Jr., Mears' son-in-law, threatened to close the mine if the owners did not reduce the royalties due.

When the owners agreed to Pitcher's demand, Mears was able to keep the mine operational. The following summer, the latter's persistence in the unprofitable scheme was rewarded when high yield gold ore was discovered at all levels in the mine. The richest part of the strike seemed to be in the Sampson vein, which was reported to be "literally covered with free gold." The ore extracted from this vein was said to compare favorably with the highest yielding ore ever mined in the district.

After the gold discovery, six to eight carloads of ore were shipped from the mine daily. So much ore was extracted, in fact, that it was necessary to repair the Silverton, Gladstone & Northerly Railroad—then in very bad condition—to expedite ore shipment to the smelter.

In 1915, three years after the discovery of rich ore deposits at the Gold King, Mears decided that the continued high production of the mine justified the purchase of the Silverton, Gladstone & Northerly Railroad, which he had leased since 1910. The owners of the line were bankrupt and the railroad was taken over by creditors who were going to sell it to the highest bidder at a foreclosure sale. In June, 1915, the entrepreneur obtained permission from the stockholders of the Silverton Northern Railroad to buy the bankrupt railroad. The stockholders decided to allocate $40,000 plus expenses for the purchase of the shortline. The acquisition of the line at the foreclosure sale in Denver on July 10, 1915, enabled the pioneer to control a large share of the intra-San Juan County railroad traffic.

Back in November, 1911, before the success of the Gold King prompted Mears to buy the Silverton, Gladstone & Northerly, he organized a company to facilitate the operation of the mines he had under lease. On November 23, 1911, he had incorporated the Iowa-Tiger Mining Company. Headquartered in Silverton, the corporation was capitalized by 100 shares of stock worth $100 apiece. In addition to the old timer and his son-in-law, J.R. Pitcher, Jr., the directors of the new company were three Silverton mining men—J.H. Slattery, Matt Delsante, and Louis Quarnstrom. In time, the new company gradually assumed control of all Mears' mining investments.

A month after the formation of the Iowa-Tiger Mining Company, Mears embarked on a new mining project. On December 27, 1911, he signed a lease allowing him to operate the Gold Prince Mine and Mill at Animas Forks. The Gold Prince had been closed because there was not enough ore extracted to justify operation. The new lease-holder hoped that by operating the Gold Prince he would earn money from the mining and milling operation and, in addition, would add another shipper to the Silverton Northern. The investment, however, did not prove lucrative. The San Juan newspapers, quick to report any local mining success, did not carry any further reports about the mine after his takeover.

After unprofitably operating the Gold Prince for the 1912 season, Mears was ready for more lucrative ventures. The next year found him engaged in the most ambitious mining project of his life. He had decided to form a partnership with A.R. Wilfley in order to process tailings of various San Juan mines and mills. Arthur R. Wilfley, 53 years old in 1913, was the inventor of the famous Wilfley table. This table, used in ore refining, had been introduced in 1896 in a mill at Kokomo, Colorado. So successful was the device that the inventor had become well known among mining men of several continents.

By 1913 Wilfley had invented a more advanced table which was so efficient that he believed it would be profitable to treat low-grade ore left on dumps. In order to test the new table, he decided to lease an old mine or mill having tons of tailings on the premises. Southwestern Colorado had many tailings dumps and the inventor believed it best to buy or lease a mill in that area. He needed funds for this test, however, and because he had a history of heart trouble, he needed a partner who knew something about mining and milling to help supervise operations. In Otto Mears, he found not only an individual who could supply or raise the necessary funds and provide the assistance he needed to test the new table, but a man who also had numerous contacts among mining and milling men of the San Juan region.

In August, 1913, Mears and Wilfley visited Silverton in order to examine abandoned mines and mills and to select the one most appropriate for the test. After a thorough inspection of the area, they chose the old Silver Lake Mine and Mill as most suited to their needs. The Silver Lake had begun operations in the early 1890s under the direction of owner E.G. Stoiber. To refine the ore extracted from the mine, Stoiber had built a stamp mill on the shore of Silver Lake, located in a basin high above the Animas River. A subsequent 50-stamp mill built in the Animas Canyon below both the mine and original mill was ultimately reached by Silverton Northern sidings, facilitating operations and enhancing the value of the property.

More attractive to Mears and Wilfley than the railroad connection were the thousands of tons of tailings in the lake. Stoiber, a shrewd businessman, had been credited with the belief that a method would be discovered to treat the mill tailings his operation was depositing in the lake. Although too far ahead of his time in his belief that a profit could be made from the tailings, Stoiber still made millions from the Silver Lake Mine and later sold it for an excellent price.

After the mine passed from Stoiber's control, it suffered a decline with less and less ore being taken out each year. The operation became so unprofitable that the new owners finally decided to close the mine. By the time Mears and Wilfley became interested in the Silver Lake, the American Smelting and Refining Company—a Guggenheim corporation—was glad to get rid of the property, being unable to make money from it.

Although the Guggenheims were unable to make a profit from the Silver Lake, the mine was ideally suited to Mears' and Wilfley's needs. The attractions of the property to the partners were the large amount of tailings in Silver Lake itself, the connection with the Silverton Northern Railroad, and the abandonment of the mine by the owners, which was expected to assure a low lease price. Mears' long-standing business, social and political ties with Simon Guggenheim made for friendly lease negotiations and in October, 1913, an agreement was reached. As there were enough tailings in the lake to require five years of treatment by Wilfley's table, Mears agreed to lease the mine until 1919.

When it was certain that the lease would be signed, the partners asked for and received permission to begin building the new mill housing the Wilfley tables on the Animas River below Silver Lake. Construction began in mid-September, 1913, on the west bank of the Animas, next to the tracks of the Silverton Northern. When completed the following summer the new mill had several interesting features. Designed to attain maximum efficiency, the mill contained three Wilfley tables in a 40 by 60 foot plant.

In a 24-hour period, five to six hundred tons of tailings could be treated. To facilitate the Wilfley process an ingenious method was devised to transport the estimated half million tons of tailings from Silver Lake down to the mill. The method involved the pumping of tailings from the lake, with the material then being channeled into Arastra Gulch. A flume, built at grades from 6 to 9 per cent in the gulch, carried the tailings to the plant.[1]

During the mill's construction, Otto was compelled to leave Silverton earlier than he had planned, due to his wife's failing health. Mary—in ill health for years—suddenly became very feeble and her husband decided to take her to the Hotel Maryland in Pasadena, California,

241

where the couple had been spending the winters. The mild southern California climate had its usual and expected salutary effect. Mary's condition improved so much that her husband was able to make arrangements to return to Silverton during the summer of 1914.

Mears' plans changed unexpectedly, however. He was forced to return to the San Juan earlier than he had anticipated to attend the funeral of his long-time friend David Frakes Day. The retired newspaper editor had died in Durango on June 22, 1914. Grief-stricken, the pioneer immediately left Pasadena for Colorado. At the funeral, conducted in Denver, Mears gave a moving graveside tribute to his deceased friend.

After observing a period of mourning, Mears went to Silverton to spend the summer supervising his mining and railroad interests. When he arrived in the mountain town, he conducted a tour of inspection of his holdings. He was interested particularly in the progress of the Wilfley Mill still under construction. Upon examination, he found that the building was going well and that the mill was expected to be ready for operation in late summer.

The mill was finished in mid-August slightly ahead of schedule. Operation began immediately and, to take advantage of the remaining months of good weather, the tailings were processed day and night. The workers were employed in three eight-hour shifts a day. In each 24-hour period, four to six hundred tons of tailings were treated. The new Wilfley tables functioned well and required only an occasional adjustment, even with the heavy work load.

The successful Mears-Wilfley mill operation was a good augury for San Juan development. More mine tailings were to be found in that area than in any other part of the state. Efficient and profitable tailings reduction meant increased prosperity for mining camps with numerous low-grade ore dumps. The *Silverton Standard* predicted that besides Silverton, Ouray and Telluride stood to benefit the most from the new process.

Before the Wilfley method of tailings treatment came into widespread use in the San Juans, a newer process called flotation superseded it. Flotation involved the use of chemicals instead of the Wilfley table in the treatment of ores. The newer process had been introduced in San Juan County in the summer of 1914 through the efforts of Louis O. Bastian, a local mining man, and D.L. Thomas, a mining engineer who specialized in ore reduction.

In order to familiarize himself with the new process, Bastian visited the Butte Montana Copper Company plant. Upon his return to Colorado, the engineer imparted his knowledge to Mears and John Slattery. The glowing reports of the success of the new method prompted Mears and Slattery to invest in a plant which would use the process. They decided to remodel the old mill at the Gold King Mine in Gladstone because of the large supply of tailings in the vicinity and attempt a flotation experiment.

In October, 1914, the first flotation mill in the San Juans accordingly began operation. From the beginning the new process was successful, proving more efficient and profitable in reduction than the Wilfley table. From 60 to 95 per cent of the ore in the tailings was salvaged by the new process.

The success of the Gold King experiment encouraged Mears to convert other mills to the process. The Wilfley Mill below Silver Lake was equipped with flotation machinery. Wilfley, aided by his sons Elmer and George, installed the equipment in the mill in July, 1915. After the conversion to the new process, the mill immediately began showing higher profits. Five hundred tons of tailings, with an average value of $2.60 per ton, were processed daily. After treatment, four to six carloads of concentrates were sent to smelters each week.

A tragedy prevented Mears from being on hand for the opening of the Silver Lake flotation plant. His oldest daughter, Laura Mears, died of a brain tumor in June, 1915, in Seattle. Although she had been in failing health for some time, it was not known that she was dying. Upon learning of her demise, Mears rushed to Seattle. In accordance with Laura's last wishes she was cremated and her father accompanied the urn to

244

Colorado. Her ashes were scattered on the San Juan Mountains where she spent her childhood.

His daughter's death was the worst misfortune Mears had ever experienced and he attempted to forget his grief by hard work. After Laura's remains had been disposed of, he returned to Silverton where he decided—after consultation with J.M. Hyde, a nationally known flotation expert—to build a flotation mill for the Iowa-Tiger Mine. The mining magnate had renewed his 1908 lease on the Iowa-Tiger in 1911 and, as there were several years before the expiration of the new agreement, he thought it advisable to construct a plant that would process the thousands of tons of tailings near the mine.

Hyde was hired to supervise the construction of the mill and designed the machinery to accommodate his version of the flotation process. His refinement of the standard flotation technique resulted in more marketable concentrate being extracted from the tailings. When the mill opened in late August, 1915, it proved profitable due to the success of the Hyde process.

Mears' next mining investment was to be as lucrative as the Iowa-Tiger Mill. In mid-July, 1916, he, John Slattery and J.R. Pitcher, Jr., leased the Mayflower Mine from G.H. Malchus of Silverton. The Mayflower, located in Arastra Gulch below Silver Lake, contained seven valuable claims. In the upper tunnel, for example, a vein of copper-lead ore one hundred feet long and six feet wide had been found the year before by the American Ore Flotation Company, the previous lessees of the mine. The ore extracted from this vein was worth between $20 and $100 a ton.

When Mears and his associates assumed control of the mine, they hired a crew of miners to begin work at once in the upper tunnel. Within five months a body of ore worth $25,000 was found, a discovery so large that the *Silverton Standard* predicted the mine would become one of the largest producers in the San Juans.

The Mayflower was the last new mining venture upon which the old pioneer ever embarked. In the remaining four years before his retirement he supervised his railroad and mining interests, content with the remuneration he was receiving. A major source of his income at this time was the new Silver Lake Mill. By 1917, 80,000 tons of tailings had been processed, at a net worth of approximately a quarter of a million dollars. Three hundred thousand tons of tailings remained to be treated and, to facilitate the extraction of the concentrates, the mill was remodeled in 1917 and new machinery installed.

So efficient was the new equipment in the Silver Lake Mill that by 1919 most of the recoverable tailings had been processed and the mill was closed. On April 15, 1919, Arthur Wilfley transferred his share of the plant to his partner and then retired to work on the centrifugal pump which would prove to be the foundation of the Wilfley family fortune.[2]

At this juncture, Mears—like his former partner—was also pulling out of the San Juans. Failing health, coupled with a disastrous fall in the market value of metals following the end of World War I, persuaded the entrepreneur that it was time to retire to California. In an effort to liquidate his Colorado holdings he entered into negotiations with the Sunnyside Mining and Milling Company to determine whether a good price could be had for his three Silverton railroad lines.

Unable to obtain an acceptable offer, Mears retained the railroads. Still determined to sever his Colorado ties, he sold his Silverton home in May, 1919. The Reese Street residence—which is still standing—had been a home for 13 years, but he saw no reason to retain possession when his retirement was imminent.

The following year, the pioneer continued to close out his Colorado interests. In May, 1920, he resigned from the Board of Capitol Managers, a position he had held for over three decades. In early July he arrived in Silverton to wrap up his affairs there. During what was to be his last summer-long visit in the mountain community, he terminated what mining leases he still held. With the approach of fall he returned to Pasadena, being too frail to spend extended periods in high altitude. The remaining decade of his life would be spent in California, except for two short visits to the Centennial State.

Mears' absence from Colorado did not affect the operation of his short lines. Only the Silverton Northern had enough traffic to return any profit at all. The Silverton, Gladstone & Northerly and the Silverton Railroad had so few customers that the railroad president decided that it was economically unjustifiable to keep them running. The Silverton Railroad, in particular, was in very bad financial condition. No profit had been made on the line in a decade, and with the accumulation of large debts, no regular service was offered on the railroad after 1921.

Since there were no prospects for a Red Mountain mining revival, Mears decided to obtain permission from the Interstate Commerce Commission and from the Colorado Public Utilities Commission to terminate service on the Silverton Railroad and to tear up the track. The government agencies considered his petition and decided to conduct a public hearing in order to determine whether or not to give consent.

A joint hearing on the subject began on February 2, 1922. P.F. Gault of the Interstate Commerce Commission presided over the proceedings in the federal building in Denver. The attorney for the railroad, Frank L. Ross, in his opening statement, asked that the management be permitted to terminate service on the line and to dismantle the track. Ross' proposal was bitterly opposed by several other attorneys representing influential groups and agencies. The first objection to Ross' motion was made by Barney L. Whatley, an attorney for the Colorado Metal Mining Association, the Colorado Metal Mining Board and the Red Mountain Mines. Whatley claimed that the dismantling of the railroad would do irreparable harm to Red Mountain mining as the mine owners would have no way to transport ore cheaply to the smelters.

E.W. Walters, representing the interests of Silverton and the Silverton Commercial Club, was also against the abandonment of the railroad. He testified that the railroad was not only essential to the mining operations of his district but was an important tourist attraction which brought much needed cash to the San Juans. A representative of the State Highway Commission also lobbied in favor of keeping the railroad in operation. He argued that a termination of service on the line would necessitate the use of trucks to haul the ore from the Red Mountain mines. So much ore would have to be shipped by highway, he claimed, that it would be impossible for other traffic to use the road.

Defeating the adverse testimony of the anti-abandonment parties, Mears received permission from the Interstate Commerce Commission in July, 1922, to dismantle the line. On September 16, 1922, the Colorado Public Utilities Commission also consented to the railroad abandonment. Obtaining the necessary approval to abandon the short line did not motivate the railroad president to tear up the tracks immediately, however. He would not act until every attempt had been made to save the railroad he had worked so hard to build and had labored so long to keep in operation.

For the next 15 months the owner would continue to try to find a buyer for the short line. In October, 1923, the long-delayed order to begin abandonment was finally given. Mears ordered James R. Pitcher, Jr., the vice president of the Silverton Railway Corporation, to execute a quit claim deed to the San Juan County Commissioners. The deed authorized the county board to take over the roadbed, right of way and easements of the railroad. After the county assumed control an occasional train was run until the tracks were torn up by a contractor in 1925 or 1926. After the tracks were removed, the engines and freight cars were used on the Silverton Northern.

In 1926 the same contractor who had torn up the track of the Silverton Railroad dismantled the track of the Silverton, Gladstone & Northerly Railroad. Three years earlier regular service had ceased on the Gladstone line. At the time the discontinuance of service was expected to be only temporary. There was speculation that the Gold King Mine would be reopened and that the new lessees of the mine would also lease the railroad. The would-be mining magnates, however, could not raise the funds to lease the mine. Having no shippers on the railroad and no prospective buyers for the line, Mears decided to tear up the tracks and sell them for salvage.

Unlike the Silverton, Gladstone & Northerly and the Silverton Railroad, the Silverton Northern Railroad prospered during the 1920s. The fortunes of the railroad seemed at this time to parallel that of Mears and his descendents. In the 1930s and 1940s, when business declined on the short line, family fortunes were also at a low ebb. The close-knit family was torn asunder by the deaths of Mears in 1931 and his daughter, Cora, 17 years later, and by the liquidation of the family assets. The operation of the railroad was consequently intimately connected with the welfare of Mears and his family, and a short sketch of the railroad's decline is necessary to fully understand Mears' last years and to comprehend the economic predicament of his descendents in the years after his demise.

Business was so good on the Northern in the post-World War I years that the line was kept in good condition until 1931, the last full year regular service was offered and the year of Mears' death. In 1932 the management decided to curtail service because of the closure of the Sunnyside Mine, its biggest shipper. The highly profitable mine was closed down for a combination of unusual reasons. The chain of events which led to the mine closure began when the miners threatened to strike unless working conditions were improved. A representative of the Boston owners was sent to the San Juans to investigate the situation. Upon arrival he slipped and fell on some ice. Thoroughly piqued, he recommended that the mine be closed.

His advice was taken by the owners because they had been unable to expand operations of the mine as they had wanted. Believing that a vein of rich ore lay underneath the current workings, the owners planned to build a tunnel 16,000 feet long to the spot. To construct the tunnel it was necessary to cut across ten claims. Permission was received from the owners of all but one claim—the last. Two brothers who owned the tenth claim, in the midst of a family feud, refused to sign the same document. Unable to negotiate the right-of-way for the tunnel, the Sunnyside owners had to forego the proposed expansion[3]

The circumstances surrounding the Sunnyside closure were so odd that J.R. Pitcher, Jr.—who assumed the presidency of the Silverton Northern after his father-in-law was declared mentally incompetent due to advanced age in 1930—believed that the mine would soon be reopened. Pitcher was so optimistic about the mine's future that in 1932 he borrowed $1,500 from the Reconstruction Finance Corporation to help keep the railroad operational. The loan prevented the railroad from sliding into bankruptcy but was not sufficient to pay for both the upkeep of the equipment and the salaries of the employees. To economize, the crew was paid half wages with the promise that their full salary would be restored when conditions improved.

Pitcher's high hopes would not be immediately realized. It was to be five years before the Sunnyside owners resumed operations. The mine was reopened in the early summer of 1937 and by October enough ore was being mined to warrant the resumption of full-time railroad service. Regular service on the Northern continued until June, 1938, when the mine was closed for the last time. With the loss of its last big shipper, the railroad was forced to cease operations. In January, 1939, the final run was made; it was necessary to bring in an empty coal car abandoned on a siding.

The railroad had not been in operation long enough in 1937 and 1938 to bring in sufficient funds to repay the debts that had accumulated since 1931. By 1937, for example, there were four years of unpaid taxes due, and because there were no funds available, it was necessary for the management to enter into an agreement with the

San Juan County Treasurer and the San Juan County Commissioners. The contract called for giving the county half the monies derived from selling the surplus track of the railroad in lieu of back taxes.

In addition to half the profits from the sale of some hundreds of tons of track, James R. Pitcher, Jr., agreed to transfer the right-of-way on the Eureka to Animas Forks branch to San Juan County. The Eureka to Animas Forks stretch had been unused for at least 25 years and he was glad to obtain some return from it. The county commissioners were quick to order a contractor to pull up the tracks on the historic section, which is the basis for today's jeep road connecting the two ghost towns.

After completion of the negotiations with the San Juan County Commissioners, Pitcher reinstituted the policy of financial retrenchment that was in force between 1932 and 1937. From 1938 until early 1942, the management did everything possible to cut expenses. The majority of the employees were laid off and those retained suffered drastic salary cuts. Money was so scarce that president J.R. Pitcher Jr. and auditor Norman F. Bawden received salaries of only $15 a month.

Financial retrenchment was not the long term solution to the railroad's problems. Without revenue the short line would have to be either scrapped or sold as the Pitcher family could not afford to continue to pay taxes and wages. During the summer of 1941, in order to determine whether or not it would be advisable to retain family ownership of the railroad, Robertson Pitcher—Mears' grandson—was sent to Boston.

In Boston, Robertson Pitcher interviewed the Sunnyside Mine owners. At the meeting he stated that if the mine was not reopened his family could no longer afford to keep the railroad in operation. To stop the drain on the family finances the short line would have to be either sold or scrapped, he warned. The mine owners were advised to either begin operations immediately or to purchase the Northern and save it from destruction.

Pitcher pointed out that if the mining magnates bought

the railroad they would save money on freight charges if the Sunnyside was reopened. If the railroad was scrapped, however, it would be virtually impossible, the Coloradoan asserted, to transport large amounts of ore cheaply from the mine to the smelters and it would not be feasible to reopen the mine. Pitcher's eloquence and logical arguments were to no avail. The mining magnates could not be persuaded to commit themselves to any definite course of action.

Undaunted, Pitcher returned to the San Juans where he tried unsuccessfully to interest the Denver & Rio Grande Railroad management in the Silverton Northern. When the offer was refused the family decided to retain the railroad for a short while longer in hopes that a buyer would be found. In order to avoid unnecessary expense a verbal contract was made with the San Juan County Commissioners. The latter agreed to wait for payment of the taxes due since 1938 provided that the Pitcher family promised not to sell the short line for scrap.

The commissioners were amenable to an agreement favorable to the Pitcher family because they strongly believed that the economic welfare of Silverton was dependent upon the continued existence of the railroad. The line had always played a significant role in San Juan County development, but during the early years of World War II its importance seemed to increase. This was due to its supposed impact on the future of mining in the region.

In 1941 one of the few mines in the Silverton area still in operation was the Shenandoah-Dives, located along the Silverton Northern route. The mine returned only a marginal profit and revenue could be increased only by an expansion of operations. Iron was necessary, however, to lengthen the tunnels and, due to the wartime scrap drive, the only available local source for the metal was the rail surplus possessed by the Silverton Northern.

If the railroad were scrapped and the rails used for the war effort, it would be impossible to expand the workings at the Shenandoah-Dives and the mine would probably be closed. If, on the other hand, the railroad remained intact and its surplus rails were sold to the mine owners, it would be possible to tap the large ore deposits known to exist. Once the mine began extracting large amounts of ore, the San Juan County Commissioners reasoned that a general mining revival would occur in the area.

Several months after the verbal agreement had been made between the Pitchers and the San Juan County Commissioners, Robertson Pitcher joined the Navy. With the rest of the family in Pasadena, no one was on hand to supervise Silverton Northern affairs. With the Pitchers gone, someone saw the opportunity to take advantage of the family. A scrap dealer was accused by the Pitcher family of promising to give the commissioners a substantial bribe if the railroad was put on auction at a tax sale. With scrap metal so valuable because of the war, the dealer stood to make a large profit by purchasing the railroad in spite of the alleged bribes he had already promised.

The alleged offer made by the scrap dealer was so attractive that the San Juan County Commissioners decided to break their agreement with the Pitcher family and to sell the railroad at an auction, claiming that the money from the sale would be used to pay the back taxes. The county officials made every effort to keep the July, 1942, auction secret but Cora Pitcher—Mears' daughter —learned of their machinations.[4] To forestall the auction, she raised the $17,000 owed in back taxes by borrowing the money from a Denver bank.

With the funds in hand, Cora notified Ida L. Grimes, the San Juan County Treasurer, that the money owed was being rushed to the Western Slope. The former's timely action resulted in the payment of the taxes before the deadline and, consequently, the auction was prevented.

To avoid a repetition of this problem, the Pitcher family decided to sell the railroad immediately. Negotiations with prospective buyers were begun at once and continued throughout the summer of 1942. The highest bid was offered by the Dulien Steel Products Company of Seattle, and an agreement was signed on October 15,

1942. The purchase price was not revealed, but was probably $40,000—the 1941 value placed on the short line by the Colorado Tax Commission. After the sale, the rolling stock was dismantled, sent overseas, and used in the allied war effort.

Back in the early 1920s, before the dismantling of his three Silverton lines, Otto Mears spent his retirement at the Hotel Maryland in Pasadena. He thoroughly enjoyed the Southern California climate and his surroundings were enhanced by the companionship of many of his former Colorado friends who were living in retirement in Los Angeles. Some of these old-timers habitually met with Otto in the "Amen Corner" portion of the Hotel Maryland and reminisced about their mutual frontier experiences.

In addition to socializing with old friends Mears met many new people as well. His loyalty, honesty, ability as a raconteur, and his interest in Southern California development made him very popular. Of the new friends he made, the closest were D.M. Linnart, the builder of the Hotel Maryland, and hotel manager H.M. Nickerson.

A tale is told that exemplifies how much pleasure the old pioneer received from his Southern California social life. In the early 1920s he caught pneumonia. During his period of recuperation he found out that several close friends had planned a party. Not wanting to miss what promised to be so much fun, he divested himself of his ice packs and got up. Dressing immaculately in a latest fashion suit, he attended the party. When the festivities were over he returned to his sick bed.

As much as he enjoyed living in California, Mears missed Colorado and hoped to visit the Centennial State before his death. His wife's precarious health, however, prevented him from doing so. In the summer of 1922, for example, he received an invitation from the Western Slope Fair Association to attend the Montrose County Fair and to participate in an Old Timers' Day. This invitation was declined with regret as he could not leave his wife's bedside, and he expressed an earnest wish that circumstances would soon permit a Colorado visit.

Mears' hopes about an improvement in his wife's health were unfounded. Mary's condition worsened and by the summer of 1924 she was on her deathbed. After years of illness, she finally died on August 6, 1924, of pneumonia and hardening of the arteries. In accordance

OTTO AND MARY MEARS
A Golden Years Portrait

with her last wishes, she was cremated at Mount View Cemetery in Pasadena three days later.

The widower was profoundly saddened by the loss of his wife. He had been married for 54 years and although Mary had been in delicate health for decades, he was stunned by her loss. Unfaithful upon occasion, he still worshipped his wife and was a family man.

Mears spent the next two years in deep mourning. He was so grief-stricken that his three quarters of a century old passion for traveling was forgotten. He was too resilient, however, to remain paralyzed by grief. By the early summer of 1926 his old wanderlust returned and he decided to visit Colorado. He resolved, in spite of his high-altitude breathing problem, to see his old friends once more and to visit the beautiful San Juan Mountains where he had lived off and on for 50 years. In addition to his desire to see once-familiar people and places, he wanted to attend a ceremony in late August at which a tablet honoring his achievements would be unveiled.

In early July, 1926, Mears returned to Silverton after an absence of six years. He renewed old acquaintances and visited his daughter's family. He especially enjoyed seeing his grandson Kingsbury—Robertson Pitcher's brother—who was a Silverton resident. Mears was forced to shorten his delightful visit. While on the eastern train from Los Angeles, he had caught a cold. With the cold worsening and aggravating his high-altitude breathing problem, he decided to return to Pasadena. He left Silverton on July 15, 1926, and was disappointed that he could not remain longer and be present for the August unveiling ceremonies. He was driven back home to California by Otto Mears Pitcher, his third grandson.

During mid-summer 1926, while the old pioneer was recovering from his bad cold, preparations went forward to place a tablet in his honor at Bear Creek Falls on the Silverton-Ouray road. The idea of a San Juan monument commemorating his achievements had first been suggested by David F. Day. In 1909 the editor had proposed that a monument be placed at Sheridan Junction to honor the pioneer for building the Silverton Railroad. Although Day was a frequent and influential advocate of a Mears memorial, nothing was done, and after the editor's death the idea fell into abeyance.

For almost a decade after Day's death, the idea of a Mears memorial was stillborn. Finally, in 1922, Day's son and successor on the *Durango Democrat*—Rod S. Day—revived the proposal. In a summer editorial he suggested that the new state highway from Ouray to Silverton would not be complete without a tribute to Mears. Not only had the pathfinder constructed the first roads in the San Juan, the editor stated, but decades later he had also used his considerable political influence to gain legislative approval for various road building and improvement projects.

If a monument were built, Rod Day suggested that it be erected over Bear Creek Falls a few miles from Ouray. The site was appropriate, he asserted, because it was the most picturesque spot on Mears' old Ouray and San Juan Toll Road. He argued the location was also suitable because the old road, incorporated into the new state highway, was the most impressive toll road achievement in North American history. The editor proposed that a campaign to raise the necessary funds for the memorial be started immediately.

In spite of the eloquence of Rod Day's impassioned plea, nothing was done immediately to implement his proposal. Two years later—in 1924—the editor of the *Silverton Standard*, indignant over the obscurity surrounding Mears' achievements, started a subscription drive to raise the funds necessary to build a memorial. The *Standard* editor believed that the memorial should be erected and dedicated in the pioneer's lifetime. Not only would the commemoration ceremony give the pathfinder much pleasure but the gesture would repay the debt owed to the old man by the San Juan residents. Another advantage to his plan, the editor asserted, was that Silverton would establish a useful precedent. If the town honored Otto Mears, other localities would perhaps also pay tribute to their pioneers.

THE YEARS BEFORE REDICULATION SETTLEMENT

The editor's suggestion was considered a good one by his readers. His idea was given support by such influential local newspapers as the *Alamosa Empire*, the *Durango Democrat* and the *Montrose Daily Press*. By the summer of 1926 enough money had been subscribed to warrant the designing and construction of the memorial.

The monument was a tablet three feet high, four feet wide and eight inches thick, made out of Salida granite. The tablet was engraved as follows:

> In honor of Otto Mears, Pathfinder of the San Juan, pioneer road builder. Built this road in 1881. Erected by a grateful people, 1926.[5]

In late July, 1926, Cora and James R. Pitcher, Jr., accompanied by some of Mears' old friends, took an automobile trip over the Silverton-Ouray segment of the new state highway in order to select the most appropriate spot for the tablet. After examining the route, the excursionists decided to follow Rod Day's recommendation and have the monument placed at Bear Creek Falls.

A month later, on August 29, 1926, the unveiling ceremonies were conducted. Long before the 11:00 a.m. starting time, cars were lined up and down the narrow highway. By the time the master of ceremonies, editor C.E. Adams of the *Montrose Daily Press*, introduced John C. Bell, the first speaker, hundreds of people were in attendance. Bell, a protege of Mears, outlined his mentor's Colorado career, stating that the motivation of the pioneer was always to do something that others thought to be impossible.

After Bell finished, the tablet was unveiled. The silk flag covering the memorial, donated by Bell, was presented to Mears' daughter. After the presentation of the flag, formal acceptance of the monument on behalf of Ouray County was made by James H. Doran, Ouray County Commissioner. Upon the conclusion of Doran's remarks, Silvertonian B.B. Allen—as the representative of Governor Clarence J. Morley—gave an appreciation of the trailblazer's achievements. The ceremony was concluded with a few statements by Otto Mears Pitcher,

Mears' grandson. On behalf of his absent grandfather, the boy movingly expressed the absentee's regrets about not being present and his gratitude for the great honor bestowed upon him.

During the ceremonies, James H. Doran, caught up in the emotion of the moment, promised that "not only will the present board of commissioners jealously guard the tablet, but I pledge to you that all future commissioners will do likewise."

Needless to say, Doran's promise was not kept. Decades later the memorial was removed by a highway construction crew. This ultimately came to the attention of James G. Schneider, president of Kankakee Federal Savings and Loan Association of Kankakee, Illinois. Schneider, an amateur historian interested in South-western Colorado, thought it deplorable that the only San Juan area monument to Mears had been removed. Due to his efforts, the tablet was replaced at its former spot on U.S. 550 in a short ceremony conducted September 26, 1970.

In the mid-1920s, after the original placement of the memorial, Mears was anxious to return to Colorado, see the monument and thank the people who made it possible. In the summer of 1929, he therefore decided to return to the Centennial State. He was 89 and still in very good health for his age. He was in such good condition that he made the trip from the coast by automobile rather than by train and he arrived on the Western Slope in mid-August, 1929. His first stop was in Montrose, where he visited John C. Bell. He also made a social call at the office of the *Montrose Daily Press* and thanked editor C.E. Adams for his efforts on behalf of the Mears memorial.

In his conversation with Adams, the old timer made it clear that he was still a San Juan booster. He predicted that the area's mines would be reopened and that Montrose would be the beneficiary of the increased activity. From Montrose, the visitor and his chauffer-grandson Otto Mears Pitcher drove to Silverton, observing the monument en route. In the mining camp the

OTTO VISITS HIS MONUMENT
The Pathfinder's Last Colorado Call

261

pioneer called on his many old friends. His visit was cut short after a few days, however. Unable to adjust to the 9,300-foot altitude, he had difficulty breathing normally. He left Colorado in late August, and never returned.

In the spring of 1930, less than a year after his return from Colorado, Mears' health began to fail rapidly. He became senile and could no longer take care of his personal needs nor manage his business interests. He was in such bad condition by May, 1930, that Cora Pitcher, his daughter, decided that he would have to be committed to a sanitarium in order to receive the personal care and medical attention he needed. The pioneer, accordingly, was institutionalized in early June at Kimball Sanitarium in La Crescenta, California.

Mears' commitment caused legal problems for his family. According to California law it was necessary to have court permission for the commitment of a relative. To make sure that her father would continue to receive the medical care he needed and to insure that the family assets would be properly managed, Cora Pitcher decided to undergo the humiliating and degrading legal process which would result in her being appointed her father's guardian.

On June 11, 1930, Cora accordingly filed a petition with the Los Angeles County Clerk requesting that she be appointed guardian of her father and his property. The hearing was conducted on June 19, 1930, in the court of Judge C.S. Crail. At the hearing Cora proved, in a normal procedure, that her father had been served with papers seven days previously notifying him that his competency was in question and that he would have to defend himself in court on the appointed date. After the judge had ascertained that Mears had been given adequate notice and was incapable of appearing, he ordered the appointment of his daughter as guardian of his limited estate. By this time Mears had distributed his assets to his heirs except a lot in Durango and his Civil War pension. He still retained management control over the family possessions, however. This maneuver represented an attempt to obviate the necessity for leaving a will. The old timer was profoundly distrustful of lawyers and would do anything to avoid hiring one.

In the weeks following the court hearing, the pioneer's condition deteriorated. By late August, 1930, he was reported to be very ill. A month later he was said to be dying from the effects of old age. The old timer rallied, however, and his strong constitution kept him alive for nine more months. He died on June 24, 1931, at the age of 91 of a chronic heart condition and hardening of the arteries.

Two days after death, Mears' remains were cremated by Turner and Stevens Undertaking Parlor of Pasadena. In late July, Cora Pitcher, in accordance with her father's wishes, wrote Fred Ingley, bishop coadjutor of the Colorado Episcopal Diocese, about commemoration services. The bishop was asked to officiate at the services in Silverton. Ingley replied in the affirmative, but stated he would not be available until mid-August. The next round of correspondence settled on August 17, 1931, as the date of the funeral.[6]

In preparation for the funeral, Cora and James R. Pitcher, Jr., accompanied Mears' ashes to Silverton in early August. The funeral was conducted two weeks later, on a Monday. An official day of mourning had been declared, and all businesses in the town were closed. The townspeople attended the services at St. John's Episcopal Church on Snowden Street. Assisting Bishop Ingley were Rev. S.A. McPhetres of Durango and Rev. John Foster of Montrose.

The high point of the service was Bishop Ingley's moving tribute to Mears. The pioneer's career was compared to that of Charles Steinmetz, the famous electrical engineer. The bishop pointed out that both men were of foreign birth and had to overcome great obstacles to achieve success. The crowning work of both, according to the cleric, was an increase in the happiness and comfort of thousands of people through contributions to the development of communications and transportation.

After the funeral, Mears' ashes and those of his wife were taken to Eureka, the long-time terminus of the Silverton Northern Railroad, and scattered into the wind. The pioneer had directed that his and his wife's remains be disposed of in this manner because of his daughter Laura's similar request in 1915.

Bishop Ingley's eulogy was practically the only public recognition Mears received for the ensuing 12 years. In the decade following his death, the individual who made such a great contribution to Colorado development was nearly forgotten. His reputation was rescued from obscurity, however, by a singular tribute in 1943. In early September of that year, one of the 24 Liberty ships being built at the navy yard in Richmond, California, was named after him.

Soon after the launching of the ship, Mears' name again passed into obscurity. Today, nearly 40 years later, only the specialist in frontier history is likely to know anything about the pioneer's remarkable achievements. A striking 13,496-foot peak on the Ouray-San Miguel county line bears his name, but few are aware of its nomenclature. To the resident or tourist who travels the many state and federal highways constructed over Mears' old toll roads or who tours the state capitol building, his name is virtually unknown.

It is ironic that in spite of Mears' importance in Colorado history, his accomplishments have been virtually forgotten. The railroad builder would not have liked it that way. In one sense his whole life was a struggle to achieve importance and acceptance. Overcoming tremendous obstacles, he clawed his way up the social and economic ladder by doing what others had dismissed as impossible. His more than 400 miles of toll roads built over very rugged terrain, his construction of three Colorado railroads over mountainous country, and his iron-fisted control of the Republican Party served to give him the importance he craved. Mears' widespread fame, however, lasted only as long as he lived. It is unfortunate, in view of his tremendous struggle and magnificent accomplishments, that he is not better remembered.

Notes by Chapter

Chapter 1

1. The author has been able to identify two out of Mears' four paternal uncles. James Mears is listed in the San Francisco directories as a proprietor of a liquor store from 1859 to 1871 and an H. Mears, who according to the records of the State Library of Victoria, Melbourne, Australia, disembarked at Melbourne from the ship *Lucky Star* on April 23, 1857. The ship's register lists H. Mears as being Russian, 38, and having boarded the ship at San Francisco. Otto's uncles were said to have gone from San Francisco to Australia in the early 1850s to participate in the gold rush. According to the Melbourne directories and the Victorian electorial poll there were quite a number of Mearses in Australia between 1851 and 1875. Some or all of these were certainly related to Otto Mears.

2. Mears claimed in his memoirs to have been naturalized in San Francisco in 1861. Actually he was naturalized on November 15, 1877, in Saguache. (Certificate of Otto Mears Naturalization, Otto Mears Papers, Colorado Historical Society.) Consequently, he probably only applied for citizenship papers in San Francisco.

3. The spelling "Kampfshulte" is from Mary Mears' grandson, Robertson Mears Pitcher, who recalls it as the original German spelling. The only known document on the couple's wedding is a hand-written affidavit, certifying that Otto Mears and Mary "Campshettler"—both residents of Saguache County—were married by justice of the piece [*sic*] David Goff.

4. Anne Ellis, *The Life of an Ordinary Woman* (New York: Houghton Mifflin Co., 1929), 25-26.

5. Marshall Sprague (*Massacre: The Tragedy at White River*, New York: Ballantine Books, 1972, 87-88) implies that Mears let Packer escape from the Saguache jail because Otto believed his Saguache promotion plans would be damaged by the adverse publicity resulting from the trial of the alleged cannibal.

6. John C. Bell to S.N. Wheeler, January 10, 1913. *Gunnison News Champion* Scrapbook, Volume I. Department of Western History, Denver Public Library.

7. Lake City *Silver World*, September 11, 1875.

8. *San Juan Prospector* (Del Norte) as reprinted in the Lake City *Silver World*, July 10, 1875.

9. *Solid Muldoon* (Ouray), December 8, 1882.

10. Robert G. Athearn, *Rebel of the Rockies: A History of the Denver and Rio Grande Western Railroad* (New Haven and London: Yale University Press, 1962), 106. Mears claimed in 1926 to have received $40,000 for the road. See: Helen M. Searcy's essay "Otto Mears," *Pioneers of the San Juan Country, Volume I*, Sarah Platt Decker Chapter, D.A.R., Durango, Colorado (Colorado Springs: The Out West Printing and Stationery Co., 1942), 31.

11. Historians have supplied at least two explanations why Day named his newspaper the *Solid Muldoon*. Most likely was that Day named it after William Muldoon, a New York City boxing promoter whom he greatly admired. (Helen M. Searcy, "Col. Dave Day," *Pioneers of the San Juan Country, Volume I*, Sarah Platt Decker Chapter, D.A.R., Durango,

Colorado. Colorado Springs: The Out West Printing and Stationery Co., 1942, 78.) Muriel Sibell Wolle attributes the name of Day's newspaper to a song popularized by Ed Harrigan, a New York entertainer. One stanza of this song went "There goes Muldoon—he's a solid man!" (Muriel Sibell Wolle, *Stampede to Timberline: The Ghost Towns and Mining Camps of Colorado*, Denver: Artcraft Press, 1949, 372.)

12. *Solid Muldoon* (Ouray), June 15, 1883. Mears may well have flattered Day as well. The language of the latter's complimentary obituary in the *Silverton Standard* suggests Mears may have been its author. *Silverton Standard*, June 27, 1914.

13. Mears would never reveal even to Day everything he was doing. The following quotation exemplifies this: "Otto Mears was in the city this week looking after his interests. The *Muldoon* man had the cheek to propound some leading questions in regard to Mr. Mears' future intentions, but he didn't strike a very big streak of luck in worming out much news. Mr. Mears has a kind of a heathenish practice of attending to his own business and not entrusting it to the care of others. Hence his success." *Solid Muldoon* (Ouray), August 30, 1879.

Chapter 2
1. Letter from Second Lieutenant Calvin T. Speer to Governor Edward M. McCook, November 11, 1869. Bureau of Indian Affairs, General Services Administration, National Archives, Washington, D.C.
2. *Denver Daily Times*, October 9, 1873.
3. *Washington Evening Star*, October 24, 1873.
4. Examples of the outraged public opinion over the events of September 29, 1879, are to be found in almost any issue of any Colorado newspaper for the subsequent six months. Some comments from the *Solid Muldoon* are quoted below to show just how intense the feeling was against the Utes and what Mears had to contend with to be fair to the Indians. When Dave Day heard that Carl Schurz was trying to deal justly with the Utes, he printed the following in the January 23, 1880, edition of his paper: "If Captain Jack will return in our midst with the scalp of Schurz and Adams dangling from his belt, all his other sins will be forgotten." In another issue, Day summed up the point of view of most Coloradoans when he stated: "The Utes are highly pleased with Washington. Well, we are perfectly willing that they should stay there." *Solid Muldoon* (Ouray), January 30, 1880.
5. *Solid Muldoon* (Ouray), February 18, 1881.
6. Walker D. Wyman, "A Preface to the Settlement of Grand Junction, the Uncompahgre Utes 'Goes West,' " *Colorado Magazine*, X (January, 1933), 24.
7. *Denver Catholic Register*, February 27, 1941. Ida Uchill doubted the authenticity of this letter, asserting that "the language does not sound at all like Mears." See: Ida Uchill, *Pioneers, Peddlers and TSADIKIM* (Denver: Allan Swallow, 1957), 67. The author believes the letter is genuine. Not only does the internal evidence in the letter suggest that he wrote it, but it accurately represents his sentiments.
8. It is ironic that the Utes would try to kill Mears when he was excoriated by some newspapermen for appearing to be too protective of the Ute interest and for not removing them from the state faster than he did. See for example the *Ouray Times*, February 14, 1880. Dave Day, Mears' best friend, was one of his most severe critics, but came to his defense humorously in the May 20, 1881, issue of the *Solid Muldoon* when he

stated that "Otto Mears is really not a Ute. It is his complexion that makes him look that way."

9. *Denver Republican,* December 6, 1906. At first, Col. MacKenzie refused to pay the toll and was about to tear down the gates when Mears told him it would cost him his commission if he did so.

Chapter 3

1. Betty Wallace, *History with the Hide Off* (Denver: Sage Books, 1965), 23
2. *Solid Muldoon* (Ouray), March 30, 1883.
3. *Solid Muldoon* (Ouray), November 28, 1884.
4. There were numerous editorials in the *La Plata Miner* in the late summer and early fall against having Mears build the road. One published October 13, 1883, is typical. Dave Day suggested that Raymond was an opponent of Mears because Raymond wanted to go into the toll road business himself. See the Ouray *Solid Muldoon,* October 19, 1883.
5. *Silverton Democrat,* June 28, 1884.
6. *Silverton Democrat,* July 12, 1884.
7. Arthur Ridgway stated, for example, that except for the toll roads to Red Mountain, Mears' toll roads "were not even moderately remunerative." See: Arthur Ridgway, "The Mission of Colorado Toll Roads," *Colorado Magazine,* IX (September, 1932), 169.
8. Robert Weitbrec, 1888 Journal, 71. Colorado Historical Society. The stock ownership figures of Mears and Walsen were arrived at after $105,000 of Ouray and Lake Fork Toll Road stock was deducted. The subsequently discussed feasibility study on the Silverton Railroad is also from this source.
9. *Rocky Mountain News,* September 1, 1926.
10. *Solid Muldoon* (Ouray), July 29, 1887.
11. *Solid Muldoon* (Ouray), August 12, 1887.
12. *Solid Muldoon* (Ouray), August 31, 1888.
13. *Solid Muldoon* (Ouray), August 8, 1890.
14. *Solid Muldoon* (Durango), April 27, 1892.

Chapter 4

1. *Saguache Advance,* September 9, 1882.
2. *Solid Muldoon* (Ouray), November 9, 1882. See also the *Rocky Mountain News,* November 8, 1882.
3. *Denver Republican,* January 29, 1883. Montrose was named after a duchess in one of Sir Walter Scott's novels.
4. For accounts of this episode see: Carl Ubbelohde, Maxine Benson and Duane A. Smith, *A Colorado History,* 207; Duane A. Smith, *Horace Tabor, His Life and the Legend* (Boulder, Colorado: Associated University Press, 1973); *Rocky Mountain News,* May 1, 1884; and *Denver Republican,* January 27 and 29, 1883.
5. *Denver Republican,* January 27, 1883.
6. *Solid Muldoon* (Ouray), April 25, 1884. Mears was not always so non-committal about his opinions on current issues, as an observation from the previous week's *Muldoon* exemplifies: "To whisper free-trade in the presence of Otto Mears has about the same effect as stepping on the toes of a gouty man."
7. *Rocky Mountain News,* August 23, 1884.
8. *Rocky Mountain News,* September 15, 1884.
9. *Rocky Mountain News,* October 1, 1886.

10. *Rocky Mountain News*, November 7 and 8, 1886. Mears believed that Meyer lost because of his German heritage.
11. *Solid Muldoon* (Ouray), October 26, 1888. The *Muldoon* of October 19, 1888, stated the following about Dunbar's nomination: "Tom Bowen got it in the neck in Ouray County. The nomination of Dunbar was a pronounced and unanimous victory for Mears and Wolcott. It is a frigid day when Otto returns good for evil."
12. *Solid Muldoon* (Ouray), October 26, 1888.
13. *Solid Muldoon* (Ouray), October 26, 1888. This newspaper came to an untimely end in late November when its editor and type were thrown into a creek by an irate subscriber. Day commented on this incident: "The grand jury should roast Jack Carroll for pitching the type, press editor of the *Pacific Slope* in Red Mountain Creek. Admitting that the *Slope* was a fake and its editor a calamity, there is then no grounds for such harsh treatment. Pitching the editor in the creek was all right, but the press and type could easily have been traded for whiskey, and the gloom that was wafted in from New York and Indiana made less poignant." *Solid Muldoon* (Ouray), November 23, 1888. Mears is also credited by some researchers with founding the *Bonanza Enterprise* in Saguache County and a short-lived newspaper in Salida during his life.

Chapter 5

1. The feelings which Mears and the majority of Coloradoans had about the Utes is summarized by the following editorial by Dave Day: "To civilize an Indian is to put him into a wooden overcoat and lay him gently under the sod. His affairs and government should be taken out of the hands of church denominations and given over to the military. He understands what a gun means better than the teachings of a catechism." *Solid Muldoon* (Ouray), March 21, 1890.
2. *Western Slope* (Dallas), November 13, 1890. Dallas eventually became a ghost town. The *Western Slope* editor commented on this as early as September 11, 1890: "Dallas is slowly but just as surely moving up to Ridgway. Building after building is being torn down and carted off to that octopus-like town which will eventually draw us all into its folds. There seems to be a fatality about it which is amusing—the very men who swore they wouldn't never no never wouldn't go to Ridgway—these same men are now buying lots." The ironic peregrinations of the newspaper were not ended when it, too, moved to Ridgway. In late September, 1894, it moved to Ouray. See the *Ouray Herald*, September 27, 1894.
3. *Solid Muldoon* (Ouray), July 25, 1890. The editor of the *Western Slope* in the issue of September 11, 1890, responded to Day's comment of July 25 with the remark: "To those who think that Otto Mears never eats anything since he has become a railroad builder, we will say that he was seen drinking a cup of coffee one morning this week."
4. *Solid Muldoon* (Durango), June 18, 1892. For the liberal wage scale of the Rio Grande Southern, see the *Ridgway Herald*, January 7, 1892.
5. *Solid Muldoon* (Ouray), October 30, 1891. See the *Western Slope*, October 2, 1890, for a humorous account of another employee who failed to live up to expectations.
6. Day had been paid $5,000 for the *Muldoon* stock by the *Durango Daily Herald* management. See the *Durango Democrat*, July 6, 1907. But Day did not think very much of George N. Raymond, editor of the *Durango Daily Herald*. On one occasion he stated that Raymond ". . . has been

268

guilty of all that is mean, all that is dishonorable, all that is despicable in the realm of journalism. He has neither honor, conscience or the sense of shame." *Durango Democrat,* August 6, 1907.

7. *Ridgway Herald,* April 20, 1893. Rumors of a possible takeover of the Rio Grande Southern by the Denver & Rio Grande were circulating late in the month. See *Ridgway Herald,* April 27, 1893.

8. Otto Mears to Charles H. Graham, July 3, 1893. Otto Mears Personal Letterbook. Colorado Historical Society.

Chapter 6

1. *Rocky Mountain News,* February 27, 1891. See also the *Denver Republican,* February 27, 1891. Dave Day differed in his opinion about railroad rates as noted in the following editorial from the *Solid Muldoon* (Ouray) December 12, 1890: "The demand for an equitable and conservative railroad law seems to be very general throughout the state but we incline to the belief that it will be the old story when the Eighth Assembly shall have adjourned. The mere fact that Otto Mears is to have charge of the 'oil room' is rather discouraging to the victims of exorbitant rates." An "oil room" was a room in a hotel where cash payments were dispensed. The title of this chapter comes from a similarly straightforward article in the October 2, 1886, *Rocky Mountain News.*

2. Otto Mears to George Coppell, November 22, 1892. Otto Mears Personal Letterbook. Colorado Historical Society. In another letter, Mears added this intriguing comment about making overtures to legislators: "In dealing with members we meet, of course, some very peculiar people and they must be approached through different methods." Otto Mears to George Coppell, January 13, 1893.

3. *Rocky Mountain News,* April 14, 1891. See also the *Denver Republican,* April 13, 1891. Dave Day's views about these charges: "Christ is not alone in the work of performing miracles, as Justice Helm of the Supreme Court is credited with making a governor out of Routt, and Otto Mears accused of transforming Hanna into an alleged speaker. Next thing Colorado's senate will be visiting atrocities equally as nauseating and ridiculous. For a free government, we are too—beastly liberal." See *Solid Muldoon* (Ouray), January 23, 1891.

4. *Rocky Mountain News,* April 15, 1891.

5. *Denver Republican,* April 22, 1891. See also the *Silverton Standard,* April 25, 1891. To many reporters the episode had degenerated into a farce by the time the second grand jury was called. Mears was portrayed by them as being an innocent victim who was being tormented by villains or inept clowns. See, for example, the *Denver Republican,* April 16, 1891, the *Ridgway Herald,* April 23, 1891, and the *Solid Muldoon* (Ouray), April 17, 1891. What exactly happened at the hearings of the second grand jury is impossible to determine as the proceedings were kept secret from newspapermen and because no documents survive which give the results of its investigations.

6. This and the subsequent quotation from: Otto Mears to George Coppell, January 13, 1893. Otto Mears Personal Letterbook. Colorado Historical Society.

7. *Durango Herald,* October 27, 1894.

8. *Rocky Mountain News,* September 11, 1896.

9. *Rocky Mountain News,* September 13, 1896.

10. This incident was recalled in the *Montrose Daily Press,* June 27, 1931.

Chapter 7

1. For material on the Chesapeake Beach Railway, see: Hugh G. Boutell, "The Chesapeake Beach Railway," *The Railway and Locomotive Historical Society Bulletin*, No. 58 (May, 1942). Boutell believes that Mears interested Moffat in the project. In the author's opinion, the facts known about Mears' life do not support this position.

2. Otto Mears to David H. Moffat, June 23, 1899. Otto Mears Personal. Letterbook, Colorado Historical Society.

3. Otto Mears to Capitol Yacht Club, January 3, 1901. Otto Mears Personal Letterbook, Colorado Historical Society. Mears maintained his social position in Denver while in Washington. During this period he was a member in good standing of the Denver Athletic Club, the Denver Chamber of Commerce and of Lincoln Post No. 4 of the G.A.R.

4. *Montrose Daily Press*, June 27, 1931.

5. Otto Mears to David H. Moffat, June 7, 1902. Otto Mears Personal Letterbook, Colorado Historical Society.

6. *Durango Democrat*, June 27, 1907.

7. C.S. Thomas, "Otto, the Long Distance Politician," *Polly Pry*, II (April 2, 1904), 28.

8. *Durango Democrat*, June 2, 1908.

Chapter 8

1. *Denver Republican*, January 20, 1903. *Rocky Mountain News*, January 23, 1903.

2. *Denver Times*, October 24, 1899. See also the *Durango Democrat*, October 24, 1899.

3. This quotation appears in the dome of the capitol building. The author has been unable to find the newspaper source for it.

4. *Rocky Mountain News*, August 24, 1904. Mears had to make a special trip to Denver to force the capitol managers to hang the plate glass portrait. He revenged himself on Thatcher in February, 1906, when the latter was forced to resign from the Board of Capitol Managers. See *Rocky Mountain News*, February 8, 1906.

5. *Rocky Mountain News*, January 2, 1907.

6. *Durango Democrat*, February 9, 1906.

7. *Rocky Mountain News*, January 5, 1907.

8. *Durango Democrat*, July 30, 1907.

9. C.S. Thomas, "Otto, the Long Distance Politician," *Polly Pry*, II (April 2, 1904), 28. See also the *Rocky Mountain News*, September 27, 1910, for an analysis of Guggenheim's political expertise.

10. *Rocky Mountain News*, January 22, 1915. See also the *Denver Post*, February 10, 1915.

Chapter 9

1. Alexander Anderson to J.L. McNeil, September 16, 1897. Alexander Anderson Letterbook, Colorado Historical Society.

2. *Denver Times*, June 9, 1899.

3. George Vest Day, "The Animas Forks Railroad," *Pioneers of the San Juan Country, Volume I*, Sarah Platt Decker Chapter, D.A.R., Durango, Colorado (Colorado Springs: The Out West Printing and Stationery Co., 1942), 182.

4. *Silverton Standard*, June 2, 1906.

5. *Silverton Standard*, July 11, 1903. From the 1890s on, Mears was

apparently ready to build to any camp in southwestern Colorado if traffic warranted it and the money necessary for construction could be raised. The Colorado Railroad Museum at Golden has in its possession an undated map, presumably from the early 1890s, showing the proposed extension of the Silverton Railroad to the most important San Juan mining camps.

6. *Silverton Standard,* September 4, 1909. Mears had been quick to exploit the situation to make money. Not only had he signed a lucrative contract with the Denver & Rio Grande management but he was charging passengers $1.40 per round trip to observe the flood damage along the Silverton Northern route. So many people took advantage of this opportunity that throughout the late summer his trains were always crowded. See the *Durango Democrat,* August 15, 1909.

7. *Silverton Standard,* September 18, 1909.

8. *Silverton Weekly Miner,* October 1, 1909. *Silverton Standard,* October 2, 1909.

9. *Durango Democrat,* October 14, 1909.

10. *Silverton Weekly Miner,* October 29, 1909. In spite of Mears' assistance normal service was not restored on the Rio Grande Southern for a long time after the washout as the following quotation noted: "One iconoclastic drummer, in Telluride over Sunday, is seeking to rob Otto Mears of the honor of building the Rio Grande Southern Railroad, and cites the Bible in support of his contention, claiming that it says, 'God created all creeping things!' " *Durango Democrat,* January 20, 1910.

11. This and the following story from: Helen M. Searcy, "Otto Mears," *Pioneers of the San Juan Country, Volume I,* 42.

12. Otto Mears to J.B. Andrews, November 13, 1911. Otto Mears Personal Letterbook, Colorado Historical Society.

Chapter 10

1. Prosser, Warren C. "Silver Lake Basin, Colorado." *Engineering and Mining Journal,* XCVII (June 20, 1914), 1230. See also the *Silverton Standard,* July 11, 1914, March 14, 1914 and June 27, 1914.

2. Arthur Redmond Wilfley Papers, Western History Collection, Norlin Library, University of Colorado, Boulder. During the period the partners operated the mill, the return on investment was as high as 14 per cent annually and sometimes materially higher.

3. Ironically, the gold deposits were there, as production by Standard Metals Corporation in the late 1970s and early 1980s has documented. In the interim, dismantling of the Silverton Northern and the Durango-Chama segment of the Denver & Rio Grande has broken forever the rail route over which so much mineral production was exported.

4. Interview of Robertson Pitcher by Robert W. Richardson, Colorado Railroad Museum.

5. The date of the construction of the Ouray and San Juan Toll Road, however, was 1883, not 1881.

6. Why Mears chose an Episcopal bishop to officiate at his funeral is not known. That he was still considered a Jew in good standing at his death is indicated by the fact that his demise was reported to the *New York Times* by a Jewish Telegraphic Agency Denver employee. See the *New York Times,* June 26, 1931.

Table of Illustrations

272

107   Engine No. 461 gingerly carries a Rio Grande Southern tender over the Butterfly Trestle on Mears' Ophir Loop in this June 5, 1951, photograph by R.H. Kindig. The engineering achievement served its purpose for well over a half century.

116   Long-time Mears colleague Fred Walsen acquired 310 shares of stock in the Ouray and San Juan Wagon Road Company with this certificate in June, 1891—six months before the two helped incorporate the Ouray-Ironton Electric Railroad, Light and Power Co. with the idea of using the road bed for an electric railroad.

142   Simon Guggenheim was both financier and political protege of Otto Mears. The quotation is from a 1904 Mears interview (See: Note 9, Chapter 8).

152   Seashore fashion adorned the 1902 Chesapeake Beach Railway passes. No. A-1812 was issued to A.W. Helmboldt by Mears.

165   This 24-horsepower Mack Brothers creation captured the attention of both the public and investors early in the automotive age. It was priced at $5,500, and was advertised to get seven miles to the gallon. This advertisement appeared in the November 18, 1903, issue of *The Horseless Age*.

168   Silverton Northern Railbus No. 1 served some publicity purposes for the railroad, even it if never did come into widespread use. James R. Pitcher Jr. and his family pose with the *Mary M* in this view.

170   A leased D&RGW locomotive—No. 464— headed this train over the Rio Grande Southern's Dallas Divide on June 27, 1945. Noted railroad photographer Otto Perry took this picture, with 13,496-foot Mears Peak at the left in the background. The mountain is in the immediate vicinity of Mount Sneffles and Hayden Peak. The Rio Grande Southern was eventually abandoned in 1952, and the last of its rail taken up in the summer of 1953.

181   A *Rocky Mountain News* cartoonist named Taylor captured Mears' ire at a possible lobbying setback in this July 22, 1903, *News* political cartoon, but misnamed Otto's Chesapeake Beach Railway.

201   The Silverton Northern and Silverton, Gladstone & Northerly Railroads pursued different canyons north and northeast of Silverton.

207   Animas Forks, nearly 11,200 feet above sea level, was the farthest and highest point the Silverton Northern ever reached. This view of the mining camp was taken in 1888 looking southeast toward Burns Gulch and Crown Mountain.

221   Mears, second from the right, led an influential party to Gladstone to look over the Gold King Mill and the terminus of the Silverton, Gladstone & Northerly in this photograph, assumed to have been taken by Warren Prosser around 1910. Other members of the group, from the left, were W.Z. Kinney, Alfred Harrison, Ed Holman, B.B. Galvin and Fritz Hoffman.

226   This Croxton-Keaton was the first automobile into Silverton, posed in this August, 1910, view in front of the Grand Hotel. Mears, who well appreciated the significance of the event, is believed to be looking on directly under the "O" in the hotel's window sign, while the far-sighted motorists are Louis Wyman in the rear seat of the vehicle and David L. Mechling, whose hat obscures the "E" of the same window sign.

229   The mid-summer, 1911, Denver Chamber of Commerce promotional

trip arranged by Mears included this columbine picking foray at Animas Forks. The Gold Prince Mill, damaged the previous winter by an avalanche, stands in the background of this photograph.

233   The route of the Denver & Rio Grande Railroad past this water tank near Elk Park below Silverton is barely discernable in this portrayal of the 1911 flood damage which Mears and his crews faced on the north end of the line. Warren Prosser took the photograph.

242   The Wilfley Mill stood alongside the Silverton Northern tracks on the west bank of the Animas River, across from the old Silver Lake Mill. This 1914 Warren Prosser photograph shows the flume crossing the Animas at the lower right and entering the facility under the tracks. A Denver & Rio Grande boxcar is spotted on the tracks for loading.

255   This formal portrait of Otto and Mary Mears was taken around 1916, near the time of the couple's golden wedding anniversary.

258   The Bear Creek Falls crossing, by now shored up with concrete and adorned with metal railing, was the scene of the August 29, 1926, dedication of the Mears monument, pictured here.

261   Mears poses beside the monument at Bear Creek Falls during his last visit to Colorado in 1929. Both the plaque and the cliff were removed for a road widening project, but the slightly damaged tablet was finally returned to virtually the same location in 1970.

Index

Geographic references are to Colorado unless obvious or otherwise noted
Italicized numbers denote illustrations

276

277

278

Selected
Bibliography

BOOKS

Athearn, Robert G. *Rebel of the Rockies: A History of the Denver & Rio Grande Western Railroad.* New Haven and New London: Yale University Press, 1962.

Breck, Allen duPont. *The Centennial History of the Jews of Colorado 1859-1959.* Denver: The Hirschfeld Press, 1960.

Carter, Charles Frederick. *When Railroads Were New.* New York, 1909.

Cochran, Thomas C. *Railroad Leaders: 1845-1890; The Business Mind in Action.* Cambridge, Mass.: Harvard University Press, 1953.

Crum, Josie Moore. "Auxiliary Railroads in the San Juan Basin," in *Pioneers of the San Juan Country*, Sarah Platt Decker Chapter D.A.R.,

Durango, Colorado. Vol. I. Colorado Springs: Out West Printing and Stationery Company, 1942.

Crum, Josie Moore. *The Rio Grande Southern Story.* Durango, Colorado: Railroadiana, 1957.

Crum, Josie Moore. *Three Little Lines.* Durango, Colorado: Durango Herald News Printing, 1960.

Davis, Carlyle Channing. *Olden Times in Colorado.* Los Angeles, 1916.

Day, George Vest. "The Animas Forks Railroad," in *Pioneers of the San Juan Country,* Sarah Platt Decker Chapter D.A.R., Durango, Colorado, Vol. I. Colorado Springs: The Out West Printing and Stationery Co., 1942.

Day, George Vest. "The Pathfinder of the San Juan, Part II. As Crew Members Remember Him," in *Pioneers of the San Juan Country,* Sarah Platt Decker Chapter D.A.R., Durango, Colorado, Vol. III. Colorado Springs: The Out West Printing and Stationery Co., 1942.

Dill, Robert. *Political Campaigns in Colorado.* Denver, 1895.

Emmett, Robert. *The Last War Trail: The Utes and the Settlement of Colorado.* Norman, Oklahoma, 1954.

Ferrell, Mallory Hope. *The Silver San Juan: The Rio Grande Southern.* Boulder, Colorado: Pruett Press, 1973.

Fossett, Frank. *Colorado.* Denver: Daily Tribune Steam Printing Press, 1876

Gantt, Paul H. *The Case of Alfred Packer the Man Eater.* Denver, 1952.

Hafen, LeRoy H. *Colorado and Its People.* 4 volumes. New York: Lewis Historical Publishing Company, 1948.

Hall, Frank. *History of the State of Colorado.* 4 volumes. Chicago: Blakely Printing Company, 1889.

Hill, Alice Polk. *Tales of the Pioneers.* Denver: Pierson and Gardner, 1884.

Jocknick, Sidney. *Early Days on the Western Slope of Colorado and Campfire Chats with Otto Mears, the Pathfinder.* Glorieta, New Mexico: Rio Grande Press, 1968.

Kushner, Ervan F. *Otto Mears: His Life and Times.* Frederick, Colorado: Platte N Press, 1979.

LeMassena, R.A. *Colorado's Mountain Railroads.* Vol. II and III. Golden, Colorado: The Smoking Stack Press, 1964-65.

O'Connor, Harvey. *The Guggenheims.* New York: Covici-Friede, 1937.

Rankin, M. Wilson. *Reminiscences of Frontier Days.* Denver, 1935.

Representative Men of Colorado in the Nineteenth Century. Denver, 1902.

Rickard, T.A. *Across the San Juan Mountains.* New York and London: *The Engineering and Mining Journal,* 1903.

Rockwell, Wilson. "Portrait in the Gallery, Otto Mears, Pathfinder of the San Juans." *The 1967 Denver Westerners Brand Book.* Ed. by Richard A. Ronzio. Vol. XXIII. Denver: The Westerners, 1968.

Rockwell, Wilson. *The Utes, A Forgotten People.* Denver: Sage Books, 1956

Searcy, Helen M. "Col. Dave Day." *Pioneers of the San Juan Country,* Sarah Platt Decker Chapter D.A.R., Durango, Colorado. Vol. I. Colorado Springs: The Out West Printing and Stationery Co., 1942.

Searcy, Helen M. "Otto Mears." *Pioneers of the San Juan Country,* Sarah Platt Dekcer Chapter D.A.R., Durango, Colorado. Vol. I. Colorado Springs: The Out West Printing and Stationery Co., 1942.

Sloan, Robert E.; and Skowronski, Carl A. *The Rainbow Route, An Illustrated History.* Denver: Sundance Publications, Ltd., 1975.

Smiley, Jerome C. 'Otto Mears,'' in *History of Colorado.* Vol. II. Chicago: Lewis Publishing Company, 1913.

Sprague, Marshall. *Massacre: The Tragedy at White River*. Boston: Little, Brown and Company, 1964.

Ubbelohde, Carl; Benson, Maxine; and Smith, Duane A. *A Colorado History* Third Edition. Boulder, Colorado: Pruett Press, 1972.

Uchill, Ida Libert. *Pioneers, Peddlers and TSADIKIM*. Denver: Allan Swallow, 1957.

Williamson, Ruby G. *Otto Mears, Pathfinder of the San Juans: His Family and Friends*. Gunnison, Colorado: B & B Printers, 1981.

ARTICLES

Borland, Lois. "The Sale of the San Juan." *Colorado Magazine*, XXVIII (April, 1951), 107-126.

Boutell, Hugh G. "The Chesapeake Beach Railway." *The Railway and Locomotive Historical Society Bulletin*, No. 58 (May, 1942), 32-45.

"Colorado's Famous Silver San Juan Route." *Narrow Gauge News*, No. 29 (November, 1952), 1-6.

Crum, Josie Moore. "The Otto Mears Passes." *Railway and Locomotive Historical Society Bulletin*, No. 73 (May, 1948), 7-15.

Cummins, D.H. "Toll Roads in Southwestern Colorado." *Colorado Magazine*, XXIX (April, 1952), 98-103.

Dawson, Thomas F. "The Godfather of Marshall Pass." *Trail*, XLII (September, 1920), 5-12.

"Freighting in the San Luis Valley," as told by "Uncle" John Blades to C.E. Gibson, Jr., *Colorado Magazine*, XI (July, 1934), 133-136.

Hafen, LeRoy R. "Otto Mears, 'Pathfinder of the San Juan.' " *Colorado Magazine*, IX (March, 1932), 71-74.

Hafen, LeRoy R. "The Coming of the Automobile and Improved Roads to Colorado." *Colorado Magazine*, VII (January, 1931), 1-16.

Hochmuth, C. Arthur. "The Roadbuilder of the Rockies." *Tradition*, V (August, 1962), 13-18.

Hutchinson, Arthur. "Pioneer Days in the Upper Arkansas Valley." *Colorado Magazine*, IX (September, 1932), 184-192.

Mock, S.D. "The Financing of Early Colorado Railroads." *Colorado Magazine*, XVIII (November, 1941), 201-209.

Prosser, Warren C. "Silver Lake Basin, Colorado." *Engineering and Mining Journal*, XCVII (June 20, 1914), 1229-1231.

Ridgway, Arthur. "The Mission of Colorado Toll Roads." *Colorado Magazine*, IX (September, 1932), 161-169.

Thomas, Charles S. "Otto, the Long Distance Politician." *Polly Pry*, II (April 2, 1904), 28-29.

Thompson, Thomas Gray. "Early Development of Lake City." *Colorado Magazine*, XL (April, 1963), 92-105.

Wyman, Walker D. "A Preface to the Settlement of Grand Junction, the Uncompahgre Utes 'Goes West.' " *Colorado Magazine*, X (Jan, 1933), 22-27.